GOVERNMENT BY
ALL THE PEOPLE

Da Capo Press Reprints in

AMERICAN CONSTITUTIONAL AND LEGAL HISTORY

GENERAL EDITOR: LEONARD W. LEVY
Claremont Graduate School

GOVERNMENT BY ALL THE PEOPLE

*The Initiative, the Referendum, and the
Recall as Instruments of Democracy*

By Delos F. Wilcox

DA CAPO PRESS • NEW YORK • 1972

Library of Congress Cataloging in Publication Data

Wilcox, Delos Franklin, 1873-1928.
  Government by all the people.

  (Da Capo Press reprints in American constitutional
and legal history)
  1. Referendum—U.S. 2. Recall—U.S. I. Title.
JF493.U6W6   1972   328.73   72-1117
ISBN 0-306-70502-8

This Da Capo Press edition of *Government By All the People* is
an unabridged republication of the first edition published in New
York in 1912. It is reprinted with permission from a copy of the
original edition in the Library of the University of Virginia.

Published by Da Capo Press, Inc.
A Subsidiary of Plenum Publishing Corporation
227 West 17th Street, New York, New York 10011

Manufactured in the United States of America

GOVERNMENT BY ALL THE PEOPLE

THE MACMILLAN COMPANY
NEW YORK · BOSTON · CHICAGO
DALLAS · SAN FRANCISCO

MACMILLAN & CO., Limited
LONDON · BOMBAY · CALCUTTA
MELBOURNE

THE MACMILLAN CO. OF CANADA, Ltd.
TORONTO

GOVERNMENT BY ALL THE PEOPLE

OR

THE INITIATIVE, THE REFERENDUM AND THE RECALL AS INSTRUMENTS OF DEMOCRACY

BY

DELOS F. WILCOX, Ph.D.

AUTHOR OF "THE AMERICAN CITY," "MUNICIPAL FRANCHISES"
"GREAT CITIES IN AMERICA," ETC.

New York
THE MACMILLAN COMPANY
1912

All rights reserved

PREFACE

AN irrepressible conflict of political ideas is going on in the
United States to-day. The Republicans cannot compose
their differences. Neither can the Democrats theirs. The
split between plutocratic Democrats and democratic Democrats and between standpat Republicans and progressive Republicans yawns deeper and more unbridgeable than the ancient fissure between mere Democrats and mere Republicans.
The earth has been quaking of late and new cracks are appearing on its surface. A realignment of political parties is pres-
ently inevitable. The quarrel is about the nature of government. Is it a private industry, or a public enterprise? All
agree that government is *of* the people. Indeed, most of the
disputants assert that it is *for* the people, but a subtle difference in the uses of the word "for" is perceptible. Some use
"for" in the sense in which a skillful advertiser of merchan-
dise announces that he is in business to "please" his cus-
tomers, to work *for* them. Others use "for" in the sense that
government is, in good faith, designed primarily for the
benefit of all the people, made to order and sold at cost. But
in regard to the central member of Lincoln's triad, government *by* the people, there is a great crunching of mighty
words. Of course, all parties agree with Lincoln, but they
are unable to agree among themselves as to his meaning or
as to the attitude he would assume toward the divisive issues
of to-day if he were alive among us. What is government
by the people? The author of this book lays no claim to
impartiality in the great national conflict now going on.
The argument will have to speak for itself. It is based upon

v

the conception that government is a public coöperation, not
a private industry; that it is not an institution where a few
turn out goods which certain people want and others do not.
All men produce government; all men consume it.   There
may be too many lawyers, too many doctors, too many
priests, but not too many voters, for voters do not live off
the services they perform for other people.   There may be
an overproduction of apples or of shoes, but under a democracy there can be no overproduction of government; for when
the people have produced all they want, they stop.   The
people do not stand in front of government and receive and
criticize its services as shoppers examine and criticize goods
that are handed to them over the counter.   Rather, they
stand behind it and use it as a tool fashioned by their own
hands.   Their criticisms, if they make any, are directed at
themselves and stimulate them to new creative efforts.   Government represents not only the want, but the will of every
man.   Such is democracy.

In the revised edition of his work on "The Referendum in
America," Mr. Oberholtzer says that his book "has often
been quoted as favorable to a system of direct government
in America."   He expresses a "wish to correct any misappre-
hension which may have existed on this point hitherto," and
adds that he has probably "made himself clear" in the supplementary chapters which appear in the new edition.   He
certainly has.   Referring to "the people," he says: "What
they would do on one day they will often repent of the next,
for which reason a government of checks and balances, of
reversal and veto was devised, recommended and adopted.
It was not intended that the process should be simple.   Instead virtue was found in its very complexity."   And again,
he says, speaking of the effect of the Initiative, the Referendum, and the Recall upon the character of public officials:
"Only timid, shambling, ineffective men can come out of a
system which strips public office of character and authority

and makes it directly subservient to popular whim." He cites a number of great names—Lincoln is the latest of them —who "were not the products of any political system in which bodies of mediocre men with hobbies robbed the legislature of its dignity and authority, and subjected executive, legislative, and judicial officers to the fear of recall when they pursued a course distasteful to some fraction of the electorate." I have referred to Mr. Oberholtzer's book for the purpose of emphasizing the difference between his point of view and mine.   I am equally solicitous with him about being misinterpreted, and the reader is cautioned, before quoting this book on the strength of any of its chapter headings, to peruse the chapters themselves, where, it is hoped, my views have been made tolerably clear.

In this work I have not attempted generally to discuss the specific forms of the Initiative, the Referendum, and the Recall that have been adopted in various states and cities, or to cite in support of the argument the experience of these states and cities under the new forms.   I have felt that this experience is too recent and too incomplete to be a safe guide to the future, and have therefore rested my argument almost entirely upon a consideration of the failures of our old system of checks and balances and upon the *a priori* reasons for believing that the new political instruments will be more effective in establishing popular self-government.   Readers who are interested in the particular forms which these instruments are taking are referred to Professor Beard's excellent compilation of "Documents on the State-Wide Initiative, Referendum and Recall" issued a few months ago.   Because the Constitutional Convention of Ohio has just agreed upon an Initiative and Referendum amendment, not included in Professor Beard's book, and because this amendment represents on the whole an advanced and excellent form of these measures, I have reproduced the proposed Ohio amendment in the appendix.

For their unconscious help in the preparation of this book I am grateful to the nameless pioneers who have spent their strength and haply lost their lives struggling to roll away the stone from the sepulchre of democracy; to William S. U'Ren and John R. Haynes, annunciators and provers on the other edge of the continent of the resurrection of the body politic; to William J. Bryan, Robert M. LaFollette, Woodrow Wilson, and Theodore Roosevelt, the great apostles to the gentiles; and last but not least to Joseph G. Cannon, James R. Day, Joseph W. Bailey, William Barnes, Jr., and Nicholas Murray Butler, intrepid rearguards of retreating paganism.

DELOS F. WILCOX.

ELMHURST, N. Y.
April 19, 1912.

CONTENTS

PAGE

PART I: INTRODUCTORY I
   I. Conditions that Invite a Partial Revival of Pure
      Democracy in the Present Age 3

PART II: THE INITIATIVE 11
   II. The Initiative Explained 13
   III. First Objection to the Initiative—That it would
      Destroy Constitutional Stability 36
   IV. Second Objection to the Initiative—That it would
      Foster the Tyranny of the Majority . . . 51
   V. Third Objection to the Initiative—That it would
      Tend to the Subversion of Judicial Authority . 68
   VI. Fourth Objection to the Initiative—That it would
      Result in Unscientific Legislation . . . 77
   VII. Fifth Objection to the Initiative—That it would
      Lead to Radical Legislation 89
   VIII. Sixth Objection to the Initiative—That it would be
      Used by Special Interests to get the Better of the
      People 98
   IX. First Argument in Favor of the Initiative—That it
      would Utilize the Individual in Politics . . 104
   X. Second Argument in Favor of the Initiative—That
      it would result in the Drafting of New Laws by
      those who Wish them to Succeed . . . 112
   XI. Third Argument in Favor of the Initiative—That it
      would enable the Sovereign to Enforce its Will
      without the Consent of the Legislature. . . 115
   XII. Fourth Argument in Favor of the Initiative—That
      it would provide an Orderly Means of Extending
      or Restricting the Suffrage 120

PART III: THE REFERENDUM 129
   XIII. The Referendum Explained 131
   XIV. First Objection to the Referendum—That it would
      afford the Legislative Branch an Excuse for
      Shirking Responsibility 139

PAGE

XV. Second Objection to the Referendum—That it would Interfere with the Orderly Performance of Governmental Functions 146

XVI. First Argument in Favor of the Referendum—That it would Remove Temptation from the Legislative Branch by Withdrawing its Ultimate Power to Bestow Special Privileges 149

XVII. Second Argument in Favor of the Referendum— That it would Conduce to the Conservation of Public Resources 154

XVIII. Third Argument in Favor of the Referendum—That it would serve to Keep Legislation in Line with Public Sentiment 160

XIX. The Referendum on Judicial Decisions . . . 164

PART IV: THE RECALL 167

XX. The Recall Explained 169

XXI. First Objection to the Recall—That it would Tend to Weaken Official Courage and Independence . 177

XXII. Second Objection to the Recall—That it would make Public Office less Attractive to High-Class Men 185

XXIII. Third Objection to the Recall—That it Violates the Moral Right of the Official to hold Office during the Full Term for which he was Chosen . . 192

XXIV. First Argument in Favor of the Recall—That the People should have a Continuing Right to Correct Mistakes in the Selection of their Public Servants 196

XXV. Second Argument in Favor of the Recall—That it would Clear the Way for the Concentration of Responsibility and Longer Official Tenures . 200

XXVI. The Recall of Appointive Officers . . . 206

XXVII. The Recall of Judges 211

PART V: MAJORITY RULE—THE INITIATIVE, THE REFERENDUM, AND THE RECALL COMBINED 229

XXVIII. First General Objection to Majority Rule—That it is Destructive of the Republican Form of Government Guaranteed by the Federal Constitution . 231

XXIX. Second General Objection to Majority Rule—That in reality it is Rule by the Minority . . . 235

PAGE

XXX. Third General Objection to Majority Rule—That it Involves the Furore and Expense of Frequent Elections 242

XXXI. Fourth General Objection to Majority Rule—That it Lays too Heavy a Burden upon the Time and Intelligence of the Electorate 247

XXXII. Fifth General Objection to Majority Rule—That it is Based on the Idea of Equality, which is a Will o' the Wisp 256

XXXIII. Sixth General Objection to Majority Rule—That it would mean Government by Newspaper . . 260

XXXIV. First General Argument in Favor of Majority Rule— That it would Simplify Political Issues . . 266

XXXV. Second General Argument in Favor of Majority Rule—That it Educates Citizenship and Leads to General Participation in Public Affairs . . 272

XXXVI. Third General Argument in Favor of Majority Rule—That it would make Parties and Political Organizations more Adaptable to the Needs of the Time 280

XXXVII. Fourth General Argument in Favor of Majority Rule—That it would be a Means of Perfecting Representative Government 285

XXXVIII. Fifth General Argument in Favor of Majority Rule— That it would be a Bulwark of True Conservatism 290

XXXIX. Majority Rule in Great Cities 299

XL. The Initiative, the Referendum, and the Recall in Relation to the Federal Government . . . 305

Appendix 313

Index 321

PART I

INTRODUCTORY

GOVERNMENT BY ALL THE PEOPLE

CHAPTER I

CONDITIONS THAT INVITE A PARTIAL REVIVAL OF PURE DEMOCRACY IN THE PRESENT AGE

ATHENS in its golden epoch is the joy of history. All men are glad in her glory. Even after the flight of twenty-four centuries we are proud to live on the same planet where she flourished. In spite of her paganism, in spite of the primitive status of the physical sciences in her day, in spite of her narrow territory and comparatively small population, her primacy in art, letters, philosophy, and general culture remains undisputed. Even the proud Saxons of the present day, whose dominions encircle the earth, are constrained to admit that nowhere else in history has the average value of human life by reason of the intelligence and culture of the people reached so high a level as in ancient Athens under the democracy.

We speak of the form of government that prevailed in Athens and in certain other city-states of ancient and mediæval times as a "pure democracy." By this we mean that these city-states were governed by

3

popular assemblies. It was only their narrow area and their limited population that made this possible. Yet in the modern sense even these democracies were limited. Slavery existed everywhere and it is believed that the slaves were at least half of the entire population. Moreover, political rights were not easily acquired by aliens, who also formed a considerable proportion of the inhabitants. Women, also, were much more strictly excluded from participation in public affairs than they are in modern cities. The most important of these limitations upon democracy, as contrasted with modern conditions, was slavery, which insured to the ruling citizen-class freedom from menial occupations, and leisure to devote to culture and politics. Yet, even under these circumstances, democracy led a rather turbulent life. The Athenians manifested wonderful political intelligence and self-control. Yet they in common with all city-states governed by mass meeting were subject to quick fluctuations of public opinion and the influence of eloquent demagogues. In ancient and mediæval times democracies, oligarchies, and tyrannies followed each other in rapid succession in many of the free cities.

With the growth of national states pure democracy as a mode of government came to be discredited, partly because of its supposed instability, and partly because it was physically impracticable in wide territories with scattered populations. Even in cities it was rendered less and less practicable by the growth of population, by the admixture of aliens of many tongues, and by the widening of the basis of citizenship. It is noteworthy that when the American Republic was established pure democracy found its only practical refuge in the New England town-meeting, where a virile citizenship in small rural communities made it practicable as a mode of government in local affairs, and its only theoretical refuge in the brains of the Virginia aristocracy, which like the ancient Athenians dwelt upon a high plateau of privilege supported by the institution of slavery. In writing the constitution, the fathers did not give pure democracy a serious thought as a mode of government in the nation or in the separate states. The political areas involved were of an extent too vast and the population was too widely dispersed. Nevertheless, the success of the town-meeting soon attracted the attention and excited the admiration of statesmen and publicists. Indeed, the town-meeting has had a profound influence upon the political thought of America and as a practical institution has spread over a considerable portion of the country. But early in the nineteenth century its unsuitableness as a mode of government for large cities became apparent. It is distinctively a rural institution, and with the growing predominance of urban and national problems its relative importance has been much diminished, until now the town-meeting is a sort of national memory, a regret of days gone by and conditions that have passed. Even yet it occasionally happens that some ardent civic reformer, his soul burdened with the political failures of American city government, brings forward some complex and curious plan for reëstablishing town-meeting methods in a metropolis. But these schemes are so manifestly visionary and impracticable that they hardly attract a passing notice. The town-meeting belongs essentially to the past.

It is not to be wondered at that the writers and orators of the conservative or reactionary party, which attributes the failures of popular government in America to too much democracy in our institutions as they are, should deem "pure" democracy to be more and more hopelessly consigned to the limbo of discarded political theories as the years go by. Not discerning that the times have changed, they are filled with disgust when they find themselves confronted in the political twilight of the present day by this ancient ghost which they had thought to have been exorcised long since from the haunts of practical politics. To them democracy is a terrifying spectre of ignorance in power, of political vagaries applied, of public disorder, of confiscation of hoary privileges, of mob-rule, of social ruin. Pity the sad soul of a Tory who dreams of democracy as his country's fate!

But the old weapons of attack are impotent. Against them the new democracy is fully armored. Printing was invented some time since. The free school stands at every cross-roads. The newspaper flourishes wondrously. The telephone and the telegraph send the voices of debate to the ends of the continent. The railroad conveys books, magazines, and men a thousand miles in a single day. The voting-booth and the ballot-box enable millions of individuals simultaneously to pass judgment upon candidates and measures of the highest import to the state. There is no longer any territorial limit to the action of a democracy. There is no longer any population limit. There is no longer any need of a slave-class to give citizens leisure to frequent the public places and absorb political wisdom by the slow and crude methods of past times. There is no longer any danger of the popular assembly being broken up by a mob or carried off its feet by an impassioned demagogue; for the biggest crowd that gathers on election day consists of two or three policemen, half a dozen election officers, and a few citizens standing in line for a chance to vote one by one in the solitude of the voting-booth. Though electoral privileges be extended to the humblest laborer in the state, though the electorate be doubled by the extension of the suffrage to women, though more than half of the entire population of a great city be given the ballot, yet there is no congestion at the polls. In other words, the conditions that limited democracy in ancient times to the citizen-class of a little city-state and a century ago to the sparse population of a small New England town have been completely changed by the marvellous mechanical inventions of modern times, and especially by their intensive application in the last half century. Old things have passed away. All things have become new, except human nature, and even that has changed. Now it is the House of Representatives at Washington and the assemblies at the state capitals that are in danger of being swept off their feet by the rush of lobbyists and the noise of many people clamoring for favors from government. These representative assemblies have become so unwieldy as deliberative bodies that they have been driven to harness themselves with iron rules and submit themselves to guidance by tyrants whose powers

Pisistratus himself would have envied. Every safeguard is required to keep these assemblies from being
stampeded. There is much less danger of the people,
acting through the ballot-box, being hurried into
inconsiderate and ruinous action, for with the people
the issues have been framed for weeks or months
before the vote is cast. For weeks or months through
the medium of the newspaper, by means of political
meetings here and there and by conversation and argument, man with man, public opinion is crystallized
until on election day it is quietly and clearly recorded
in hundreds or thousands of precincts which together
constitute the city, the state, or the nation.

These new conditions, these new tools available
for political use, have reopened the question of the
practicability of a pure democracy. The unequalled
results of the old democracy in Athens and of the
newer democracy in the town-meeting invite us to try
democracy in our American national and state governments, if we can see a method of applying it. The
arguments that were conclusive against it under earlier
conditions have no force at all now. To be sure, it
is obvious that a "pure" democracy is not practicable
even now, if we understand that term to mean a government that acts through the ballot-box exclusively.
But such a democracy never was feasible under any
conditions and never existed in fact. Even Athens
had executive officials and the New England town has
its board of selectmen. Certain functions of government were always delegated to chosen men. The
extreme complexity of modern social and industrial
conditions makes necessary a multiplicity of laws and

ordinances. The delegation of the law-making power
in part to representative assemblies is unavoidable.
No modern advocate of democracy suggests anything
else. But it is proposed, by the popular nomination
and recall of public servants and by the enactment
or rejection by ballot of proposed laws in which the
people as a whole take a special interest, to supplement
representative government by a partial revival of the
spirit and methods of pure democracy. It is proposed
by means of the Initiative, the Referendum, the Recall
and the other modes of increasing the direct power
of the people, to guarantee so far as possible the end
which representative democracy has always pursued,
though with halting step, namely, that the will of
the people in political affairs, deliberately formulated
and unmistakably expressed, shall prevail in so far as
in the nature of things it can prevail. It must, of course,
comply with the laws of nature, which set a limit to all
governmental action.

"Democracy in Grecian antiquity," says Grote,
"possessed the privilege, not only of kindling an earnest and unanimous attachment to the constitution
in the bosoms of the citizens, but also of creating an
energy of public and private action, such as could
never be obtained under an oligarchy, where the utmost that could be hoped for was a passive acquiescence
and obedience."

"The Town meeting has been the most perfect school
of self-government in any modern country," says
James Bryce.

We may add that only with the advent of the most
modern tools of education and communication has it

become possible to extend the spirit of the Athenian democracy and the New England town-meeting to the government of great cities and wide-reaching commonwealths. But with the implements of democracy that now lie at our door, we have a right to expect a great forward movement toward stability, justice, and public spirit in American political institutions.

PART II

THE INITIATIVE

CHAPTER II

THE INITIATIVE EXPLAINED

In popular assemblies, mass meetings, and parliamentary bodies generally, the individual member has the right to propose resolutions and make motions. While the rules by which such bodies are governed are of infinite variety, the individual member usually has a right to bring his resolutions to a vote unless they are obnoxious to the overwhelming majority of his fellow members or are matters in which his fellow members take no interest. It sometimes happens as a result of the intricacies of parliamentary procedure that a minority is able to prevent a direct vote upon resolutions favored by a majority. This is quite frequently the case in representative assemblies tied down by rigid rules which provide for the committee system of considering and reporting upon all measures proposed. In fact, the fate of important legislation is often determined, not by the opinions of the majority of the legislators, but rather by the skill of the leaders of the assembly in manipulating the parliamentary procedure at critical times so as to prevent a decisive vote or so as to bring the question to a vote in a form that is contrary to the wishes of the majority. From the standpoint of those who favor political democracy, this manipulation of the rules of legislative bodies so as to defeat the will of the majority of the members is one of the most serious breakdowns of the representative system. But it may be said that every parliamentary body is governed by rules of its own adoption and that, therefore, revision of the rules to enable the majority to have its way is always in the majority's own hands. If we pass over these somewhat unusual and perhaps temporary perversions of parliamentary procedure, the general fact remains that every member of an assembly has the right of initiative. He can make a motion and in one form or another force the assembly either to take action or to refuse to take action on it. True, in many assemblies a motion is not considered unless it is seconded; and usually it requires a certain small minority of the members to call for a record vote upon any motion that is either adopted or defeated. Inasmuch as such a vote, taken by yeas and nays, is an open record, the members of a parliamentary body, especially if it be a representative assembly, are often anxious, for various reasons, to avoid the straight issue. The record may prove embarrassing to them when they go back to their constituents, some of whom very probably desire one thing and some another. If the vote were to be taken by secret ballot, there would often be less difficulty in securing decisive action, but the necessities of representation and responsibility to constituents make the secret ballot wholly unsuitable for use in such bodies.

The Initiative is the right to propose resolutions and force them to a vote, transferred from the ordinary assembly to the electorate as a whole. In other words, it is the right of the electors to start things and make them go. The exact rules governing a parliamentary body are obviously inapplicable to the procedure of popular political action through election machinery. A citizen cannot stand up and make a motion, for there is no presiding officer to be addressed and no body of citizens within hearing to vote upon it. The citizen desiring to initiate something must at least reduce his motion to writing and submit it in advance in order that it may be printed and distributed to the various polling places where the electors can see it and formally express their approval or disapproval of it. But inasmuch as under these conditions the motion cannot be disposed of by reference to a committee, or by being laid on the table, or by being indefinitely postponed, or by being consigned to the waste-basket, it is clear that the right of a single citizen to make a motion, force it upon the attention of the entire electorate of a great city or state and press it to a vote, would tend to confusion and disorder. The mere physical act of voting upon every motion that might be made by any one of the entire body of electors might well be actually impossible not only if there were but one election day in a year, but even if every day were to be made an election day and the electors were to be considered public officials and required to give their whole time to the job. So, in practice, the Initiative is limited. In order to present a matter to the suffrages of the people and secure a vote upon it, the citizen who proposes it must secure in advance the voluntary coöperation of a certain number or percentage of his fellow-citizens who are willing to join him in insisting

upon bringing the matter formally before the entire
body of voters. This requirement is analogous to the
parliamentary rule that a motion must be seconded
before it will be considered and that the yeas and nays
cannot be demanded by less than, say, one-fifth of the
members. The first signer of a popular petition, therefore, may be considered as the mover of the resolution
and all the other signers as seconders. The number
of seconders required is of the very essence of the
problem. In the nomination of a candidate for coun-
cillor in an English city, one elector proposes, another
seconds and eight others indorse. Obviously, popular
initiative in this case is easily workable. Under a
recent commission government act of one of our
American states, a petition for the recall of a public
officer had to be signed by 75 per cent of the electors. Under these conditions popular initiative would
be difficult and, except in very small political units,
practically impossible. These extreme illustrations
both lie outside the field of what is usually known
as the Initiative, as they relate to petitions for the
nomination or recall of public officers, rather than for
the enactment or repeal of legislative measures. The
advocates of the Initiative consider that if the signatures of, say, twenty-five per cent of the electors is
required to the petitions for the submission of a measure
to popular vote, this requirement is practically pro-
hibitive in state or national affairs and renders the
Initiative unworkable. The purpose of the Initiative,
the same as the parliamentary right of individual
members to offer resolutions in a popular body, is to
secure majority rule. If this plan were to secure

minority rule, it would defeat its own end. The problem of the number of signatures required on Initiative petitions is, therefore, a problem of political adjustment. The number must be fixed high enough to protect the majority from annoyance and, perhaps, domination by an importunate minority, while at the same time it must be low enough to make the Initiative practically available for bringing to an issue proposals which the majority desire to approve. When the friends of the Initiative have their way, they usually fix the number of signatures at from five to ten per cent of the electors. When the enemies of the Initiative dominate the situation, they fix the number at from twenty-five to thirty-five per cent in the hope of making the whole thing unworkable. It is reasonable that a higher percentage should be required in small political communities than in large and populous ones. It is also reasonable that a higher percentage should be required to cause the calling of a special election than is necessary where the measure is to be voted on at a regular election. It is usually considered reasonable also to require a higher percentage for constitutional or charter amendments than for ordinary laws or ordinances.

The basis upon which the percentage is figured is important. It may be the entire registered electorate, or it may be the total number of electors who voted at the last preceding election, which is likely to be a much smaller number.

In considering the number of voters required to start Initiative proceedings, it should not be forgotten that if a specified percentage is required, the extension of the suffrage to women will automatically increase, perhaps even double the size of the petitions. In some cases a fixed number, rather than a percentage, is required. Sometimes this number is a maximum or a minimum, to be used in those communities where the application of the general percentage rule would make the Initiative too difficult or too easy.

Another modification of the percentage rule is sometimes made in the requirement that the petitioners shall be widely distributed among the political subdivisions of the city or state. It may be required that not more than a certain proportion of the signers shall be residents of any one city or any one county, or that the signers shall include a certain percentage of the electors of at least a certain number of counties, or of a certain number of wards if the petition relates to a city matter. This requirement is in the nature of a concession to the political importance of territory. It is intended to save the people of an entire state or city from being compelled to vote on measures that are of interest to some one locality or subdivision only, no matter how populous such locality or subdivision may be. The nature and extent of this limitation are almost as vital to the Initiative as the determination of the total number of signatures required. Obviously, a requirement of five per cent of the electors in every county of a state might make the Initiative more hopelessly unworkable than a requirement of thirty or forty per cent of all the electors of the state without any limitation as to the local distribution of the petitioners. So the friends of the Initiative would usually omit any limitation whatever of this kind, while the enemies of the Initiative would insist on the widest possible distribution of the petitioners so as to make the scheme as hard to work as possible. If the aggregate number of signatures required is comparatively small, perhaps it is reasonable to insist that they shall not all be residents of one or two localities.

The Initiative is a delicate piece of political machinery. Whether or not it will work depends largely upon the skill and the motives of the persons who make the machinery and set it up. It is easy to fix the machine so that it will not go. As we have already seen in one particular, the details are practically all important. Now let us consider another phase of the matter. The filing of a petition by which the sovereign powers of the state are called into action is a matter of serious and almost solemn import. It is necessary that the form of the petition should be regular and the procedure carefully guarded. Who shall be permitted to sign the paper? How shall the signers identify themselves? How shall the genuineness of the signatures be verified? What public assistance, if any, shall be given in the circulation of the petitions? How shall the sufficiency of the petition be officially checked up? It is reasonable to require that all signers be registered electors, even though this might exclude a great many persons who otherwise would be qualified to sign. Where personal registration is the method by which the electoral lists are made up, failure to register ought to carry with it the usual disabilities of persons who are not qualified to vote. This rule might work injustice to some individuals, but that may reasonably be overlooked as being a mere personal inconvenience incident to orderly electoral procedure in a populous community. The signers may well be required to give their occupations and their business and residence addresses. All the signatures on any one paper constituting a part of the petition should be verified by some person in whose presence the signatures were given. Sometimes it is even required that all the signatures on any individual paper shall be residents of one precinct. This plan makes it easy to check up the petition after it is filed, but adds so much to the difficulty of securing the signatures that it should be rejected as unreasonable except in those cases where public aid is given in securing signatures in connection with the registration of voters or the holding of elections. Here again we come to a vital detail. It is sometimes required that the signatures shall be secured only on registration or election days and be verified by the regular registration or election officers. This plan may be admirable if it is made the duty of the registration and election officers to call the attention of all the electors to the petitions and make it easy for them to attach their signatures if they desire to do so. If, on the other hand, the registration and election officers are not given any function to perform except to certify that certain names attached to the petitions are the names of registered voters, the task of manning the polls or the registration places in enough precincts to insure success in getting the required number of signatures at a single election or registration is so great as to be practically impossible of accomplishment by any private individual or association, at least without the expenditure of great sums of money. It is a part of the theory of the Initiative that the securing of the signatures to the petitions is an enterprise for individuals interested in the measure for which the petitions are being circulated, but so it was at one time a part of our political theory that nominations to office and party procedure generally were private affairs. Now these party matters are being taken into the regularly constituted machinery of government, and it may well be that in the later development of the Initiative the securing of signatures to petitions will generally be taken under the wing of government. In that case it will be necessary to go one step further back to determine how the petitions which the government is to circulate may be originated. It might, perhaps, be feasible to permit a very small percentage of the voters to present a petition with enough printed copies to be distributed to all the precincts, leaving the matter to be carried further under strictly official auspices. In that way the presentation of the petitions to the voters would be a sort of preliminary or informal submission of the question which would later be submitted for a formal vote in case a sufficient number of electors to warrant it signed the petitions. Nevertheless, it must not be forgotten that the very essence of the Initiative is the right reserved to a certain number or percentage of the electors to compel the submission of a definite proposition to popular vote for formal enactment or rejection without depending at any point upon the discretionary act of any public official to carry the matter through. The theory of the Initiative permits a procedure that involves delay, consideration, discussion—but not the side-tracking or blocking of the measure before a vote is reached. In other words, the Initiative is willing to go slow, but insists on going.

Every petition after being filed with the city clerk, the county clerk, the secretary of state or other proper officer should be checked by him as to its formal compliance with the law and as to its sufficiency. The time within which this checking must be completed should be fixed by law, and the officer charged with this duty should be subject to mandamus or ouster from office if he neglects to perform it.

An Initiative petition should contain the full text of the measure to be submitted to vote. This is not necessary in cases where the Initiative is merely advisory, that is to say, where the petitioners have the right to start things but no right to keep them going. The advisory Initiative may be useful as a sort of straw vote on public questions, though a genuine straw vote is not taken for the purpose of being advisory to some body of representatives who may disregard it if they please, but rather for the purpose of being prophetic of what the electors are going to do at a subsequent election. If the power of private interests in government were thoroughly broken down and an effective public opinion built up, an advisory Initiative, where only the general purpose of a measure or its bare outline would be stated in the petition and placed on the ballot, with the work of elaborating the measure left to the representative assembly, might have all the force of the mandatory Initiative, with the further advantage of leaving the actual drafting of legislation to experienced hands. The contents of a petition under the advisory Initiative do not demand such close scrutiny as is the case where the full text of the measure is recited in the petition.

Complaint is often made by the opponents of direct legislation to the effect that the Initiative tends to confound all distinctions either in the form or in the content of law. In particular they assert that the difference between constitutional and statutory enactments is lost and the power of the courts to declare laws unconstitutional is nullified. It is true that the theory of the Initiative removes all absolute checks upon the action of the people. By means of it they can abolish constitutions and charters or expand them into comprehensive codes of laws and ordinances, if they wish to do so. But there is no reason to expect this result as a necessary consequence of the use of the Initiative. The people may impose limitations upon their own procedure, and any electorate capable of self-government almost certainly will do so. The people may retain the distinction between constitutional and statutory law and leave unimpaired the power of the courts to declare statutes null and void if they are in conflict with the constitution. They may subject themselves to the same limitations as to the form of laws and as to the mode of procedure that bind the legislature. In fact, it is especially important that they should do so in such matters as the discouragement of local and special legislation, where the people as a whole are manifestly even more incompetent to pass upon proposals intelligently than a legislative assembly is. A measure to be submitted to the people of an entire commonwealth should be one that affects the general interest. A measure submitted in a political subdivision should be one relating to the local interests of that unit. In order that correct forms may be preserved and regular procedure maintained under the Initiative, it might be well to provide that a petition either before or after the signatures have been secured should be submitted to the community's legal adviser, to a court or to a specially constituted body of legislation experts for examination as to its form and content. This expert examination would be similar to the inquiry into contracts and other city papers by the corporation counsel where that officer's " approval as to form " is required as a preliminary matter. Great care would be necessary, however, to prevent the expert authority from exercising discretion based upon its opinions as to the advisability of the proposed measure rather than upon the measure's legal fitness or unfitness.

In some cases the right of Initiative does not extend to constitutional amendments; in other cases, it is limited to them. It is urged against the Initiative on constitutional amendments that the constitution being the fundamental law of the state should not be subject to constant change; that its amendment should be made difficult rather than easy. In behalf of the opposite view it is urged that the constitutions themselves are enacted by the people and that constitutional amendments proposed by the legislature are submitted to popular vote, while statutory enactments seldom are so submitted. Moreover, it is urged that while statutes are often long and complex, constitutional provisions dealing with general principles are much simpler and better adapted for submission to popular vote. It is also pointed out that the legislature as the creature of the constitution should not be placed in a position where it can absolutely prevent the amendment of that instrument. Clearly, the Initiative on constitutional amendments is both more logical and more fundamental than the Initiative on ordinary legislation. The former is a means of exercising sovereignty and gives the electorate absolute mastery of the state, while the latter only makes them inferior partners of the legislature as governmental agents. I say "inferior" partners for the reason that the legislature almost always has the right to initiate constitutional changes as well as to enact ordinary legislation.

It may be urged that the people would be much less apt to put limitations upon their own modes of procedure than they would be to put them on the representative assembly, of whose powers they are characteristically jealous. While these limitations are important even in the enactment of laws that may easily be repealed at some future time if unsatisfactory, they are of much greater importance with reference to franchise grants, which establish contractual relations between the public and certain individuals. The granting of irrepealable privileges is a matter of such vital consequence, that the Initiative may reasonably be subjected to special limitations and compelled to follow a special procedure in dealing with franchises and the alienation of public property.

Sometimes, in the interest of conservatism and scientific legislation, no measure may be submitted to the electorate by petition until it has been introduced into the legislative assembly and failed of passage. This limitation upon the scope of the Initiative is, in strict logic, inconsistent with its fundamental concept. Yet, it is practically never impossible to find some member of the legislature who will consent at least to introduce a measure that has any considerable support among the electorate. The advantage claimed for this limitation of the Initiative is that it will give an opportunity in every case for the legislative assembly to pass the measure and thus avert the trouble and expense of submission to a popular vote, or at least to discuss and amend the proposition before it is crystallized into final form for submission.

In other cases the order of procedure is reversed, and every measure initiated by petition must be submitted to the legislative assembly after the signatures have been obtained but before a popular vote is taken. Under this procedure, the legislature has an opportunity to debate the proposition but not to amend it, unless provision is made for the submission of the amended measure as an alternative proposition along with the measure in the form originally proposed. This method is consonant with the theory of the Initiative, but care needs to be taken to prevent the introduction of the tricks of parliamentary procedure for the purpose of defeating the measure entirely. If an amended or alternative proposal is submitted at the same election, the vote in favor of the principle of the measure may be divided and both the original and the amended or substitute proposal be defeated even though a majority of the electors desire to ratify one of them. We may avoid this difficulty by first taking the total vote for and against the proposition as a whole, and then taking the preference of those who favor the measure as between the two forms submitted. If either gets a clear majority of all the votes cast, that form will be enacted. If there is a majority in favor of the proposition in some form, but the preferences are so divided as to give neither form a clear majority, then the form receiving the higher affirmative vote may be resubmitted alone for acceptance or rejection. This plan arrives at the will of the majority by giving those electors who favor the measure in the form not accepted at the first election, opportunity to vote against it entirely at the second election if they prefer its defeat to its enactment in a form they disapprove.

If the people are to vote on measures, some adequate means of publicity must be provided before the vote is taken. One of the essential elements of publicity is delay. It takes time for the understanding of a public measure to filter through the body of the electorate. It is a notorious fact in the advertising business that an advertisement inserted only once in a newspaper or magazine or posted for only one day on a billboard will seldom bring enough returns to justify its expense. A matter must be kept in the public eye for some time before the public will pay attention to it and understand it. This is partly due to the fact that people cannot lay everything else aside at the beck of an advertiser even if that advertiser be the city clerk or the secretary of state, and immediately give attention to a new proposal. It is necessary that Initiative petitions should be filed and published for several weeks in a small community or for several months in a big city or a commonwealth before a vote is taken. It is often urged against direct legislation that in many cases the people are indifferent to measures submitted to them and do not vote upon them except in small numbers. This lack of interest is due in part to the source from which the proposals submitted to vote emanate; partly to the inherently uninteresting character of many of the proposals themselves, and perhaps still more to defective means of publicity. The circulation of Initiative petitions gives a certain amount of publicity to the measures proposed and pretty well guarantees an inherent interest in them. But if the Initiative is to succeed in a large way, something more is needed. Newspaper discussions will generally be of great assistance in the popular consideration of measures submitted to vote. But the importance of reaching the entire electorate and enlisting widespread interest is so great as to make positive action by the governmental authorities necessary. In some places all proposed measures are printed in a sort of voter's handbook with arguments pro and con submitted by the friends and the opponents of each measure. Then copies of this handbook are placed in the hands of all the voters far in advance of the election. This plan is in accordance with the spirit of enlightened democracy and tends to lessen the power for evil and enhance the power for good of the newspapers. With the voter's handbook in his hand, the citizen can check up the discussions that appear in the press and form his own opinion on the merits of the measures he is to vote upon.

One of the most frequent objections to direct legislation is the expense of holding the elections which, it is alleged, will be many and frequent. The multiplication of elections is not a necessary result of the Initiative, and as a matter of fact the calling of special elections to vote on Initiative measures is usually discouraged by the requirement of a much larger number of petitioners than is required where measures are to be submitted at a general election. This handicap is a proper one, and yet it is undoubtedly desirable that the way should be left open for holding special elections where the demand is sufficient. Sometimes it is. particularly advisable to call a special election to pass upon some great question demanding nonpartisan consideration, at a time when the people are not engaged in an active political campaign. Sometimes, too, delay until the next general election would be disadvantageous. An important matter of detail comes into the problem when the vote required to carry a measure is a majority of all the votes cast, not for and against the measure itself, but at the election. Almost always more people vote on candidates than on measures. Accordingly, it may happen that a large affirmative majority of those voting on the particular question will still be ineffective because it is not a majority of the total vote cast at the election. Special elections, when no candidates are to be voted for, are sometimes called for the express purpose of making the ratification of proposed measures more likely.

Just how many votes should be required for the enactment of Initiative measures is a matter of lively dispute. Almost to a man the advocates of the Initiative would require only a bare majority of those voting on the particular proposition, while the ultra-conservatives would require a majority of the entire electorate, or even more than that. In some cases a four-sevenths, a three-fifths or a two-thirds affirmative vote is required. It would not seem theoretically unreasonable to require an affirmative majority of the entire electorate as shown by the registration lists, to enact constitutional and charter amendments, but practically this rule would operate very conservatively. Indeed, it might delay progress under some of our antiquated constitutions for a long time. While it would seem to be the best practical rule to permit the enactment of Initiative measures by a majority vote of those voting on them, subject to the requirement that the affirmative vote shall not fall below some fixed minimum, there are some matters in regard to which practical expediency may dictate a different rule. For example, the question of licensing saloons, which is submitted to vote every year in some localities, might perhaps very well be determined by somewhat more than a bare majority vote. The Ontario plan of requiring a three-fifths affirmative vote to banish the saloons from "wet" territory or to admit them again into "dry" territory tends to stability of local public policy, which is always much to be desired and especially so with reference to such problems as that of the liquor traffic. Sometimes Initiative questions are submitted not to the general body of the electorate, but to the taxpayers only. This distinction is not recognized as logical in a democracy, and has not proved particularly advantageous in practice, even where it is made only in cases involving bond issues, tax levies, and franchise grants. There seems to be no good reason for making the electorate to which Initiative proposals are submitted different from the electorate to which candidates for office are presented. It is often urged in favor of the Initiative that it leads to the self-disfranchisement of the unfit. It is notorious that a varying but generally considerable percentage of those who vote on candidates fail to express themselves on measures referred to the people. Certainly those who through ignorance, indifference, or carelessness fail to vote on propositions that are put in their hands at the polls make out a prima facie case of unfitness against themselves. Perhaps the decision of a smaller number consisting of those who voluntarily take an interest in the submitted measures may be a truer index of the intelligent will of the community than the decision of a larger number where many of the voters are dragged, coaxed or driven to the polls to cast their ballots for certain candidates in whom they personally take little or no interest.

It is customary to exempt Initiative measures from the veto power of the executive, and yet this is not theoretically necessary if the veto is merely suspensory. It would be rather inconsistent with the canons of democracy to require more than a majority vote of the people to overcome the executive veto, but there is nothing intolerable or oppressive in giving him authority to cause a measure to be reconsidered and voted on a second time. Care should be exercised, however, to facilitate the reconsideration, so that an executive would not be able to delay unreasonably a measure deliberately favored by a majority of the people.

A further question arises with reference to Initiative measures as to what power the courts shall have over them. It is sometimes alleged that the Initiative logically leads to the subversion of judicial authority, and especially to that particular authority characteristic of the American judiciary, namely, the right to declare legislative enactments null and void when, in the opinion of the court, they contravene the provisions of the constitution or charter. Indeed, there is at the present time a great outcry against the exercise of this power by the courts which, it is alleged, they have clearly usurped. It would seem that with the Initiative firmly established in the political practice of the country, there would be at hand an adequate means for checking judicial usurpation and correcting judicial errors in law-making. There may be said to be even more necessity under the Initiative than under the representative system pure and simple for an expert body of interpreters to harmonize law and maintain fundamental distinctions of procedure. At any rate, there is no conclusive reason inherent in the Initiative for stripping the courts of this power. It is said that the power would be useless for the reason that the people could turn around and change the constitution at the next election, thus overcoming the obstacles interposed by the courts. But it is likewise true that under our present system the legislature one of whose acts is voided by judicial decree may repass the measure in another form or submit to the people a constitutional amendment to subvert the foundation of the court's reasoning.

Another matter of great interest and importance

is the question of resubmission, repeal or amendment of measures which have been enacted by vote of the people. In order that unnecessary turmoil may be avoided, a limit may well be placed on the frequency with which the same proposition may be submitted. This is especially desirable where a measure has been approved and enacted into law, or where it has been rejected by an overwhelming majority. In the first case the act should be given a fair trial before it is resubmitted, while in the other case the people should not be bothered to keep voting down a measure that is desired by only a small minority. These limitations, if carefully worked out, will not handicap the Initiative. In regard to the amendment or repeal of Initiative measures by the legislative assembly, it is readily seen that if the legislature and the electorate are named in the constitution as coördinate authorities for the enactment of laws, a measure adopted by the people may be immediately repealed by the other legislative authority. This would certainly bring about an anomalous situation. Yet it is much to be desired that the revision or amendment of legislation in the light of experience should be reasonably easy. The legislative assembly is the body to which we should naturally look for the drafting of such amendatory measures. It may well be that amendments to Initiative laws, even if not proposed by petition, should always be submitted to popular vote. It would certainly be unseemly and undemocratic to leave the way open for a conflict between the people and their own representatives in the legislative assembly. In other words, democracy insists that the representative body should

act as the helper and guide of the people, not as the
people's ruler. The office of leader and adviser of the
people in a democracy is highly honorable and calculated to bring out the best that is in men. It is not
admissible in a democracy that the electors should be
reduced to the position of merely nominal sovereignty
occupied by the British king, who is compelled to take
the advice of his own ministers because they are in
fact responsible to Demos, whose personality and interests are quite distinct from those of the monarch.
In a democracy, the representative assembly would
occupy a position with reference to the electorate
more nearly like that occupied by the Cabinet towards
the President of the United States. Practically, their
powers would be more considerable because the people
would not be present in person to preside over and guide
their deliberations, but nevertheless if the machinery
for expressing the people's will were in good working
order at all times, there would be in the speaker's chair
an invisible presence constantly controlling the procedure of the assembly and causing its members never
to forget that they are transacting public, not private
business. Under the Initiative the speaker would
be no mere colorless parliamentarian like the presiding officer of the House of Commons and no reactionary leader of a minority clique such as sometimes
occupies the chair in our House of Representatives,
but none other than Demos himself.

In this chapter I have tried to explain the significance
of the Initiative in its main outlines without overmuch
argument about its merits. It is desirable that this
instrument of democracy should be understood before

we go into the detailed discussion of its advantages and its drawbacks. The details in some respects are all-important. I have tried to define the Initiative not as those who wish it to fail would have it, but according to the ideals of those who desire it to succeed, who see in it a promising instrument which they and all men may use to stimulate and direct social progress, and make politics worth while.

CHAPTER III

FIRST OBJECTION TO THE INITIATIVE—THAT IT WOULD DESTROY CONSTITUTIONAL STABILITY

It was asserted by the opponents of the Liberal Party in Great Britain during its recent struggle to tame the Lords that its "desperate abuse of power" had thrown the British constitution "into the melting pot." Indeed, this idea of the melting pot, into which progressive democracy is constantly throwing constitutions, written and unwritten, and all the hoary institutions with which long-established ideas are identified, is a favorite figure of the conservative imagination, a frequently used "scare head" of reactionary eloquence, both spoken and written. It is an extreme and excited manifestation of the chronic opposition to change exhibited at all times and in all places by the human party that is, on the whole, well satisfied with things as they are and long have been. It is a sort of shibboleth of the standpatters the world over and time without end—lo, the melting pot, the melting pot!

Yet the mere statement that a particular objection to a specific change springs from habits of conservatism is not a sufficient answer to it. For the debate between reaction and progress is never ended. It is part of the process of life. It goes on not only in every nation and in every time, but in every individual in every period of his life. To be sure, the debate waxes and wanes, and waxes and wanes again, with victory frequently adjudged to one side or the other, but every victory proves to be merely a truce. Sooner or later the debate, the war of the spirit, breaks out again. In this conflict every point at issue must be settled on its own merits. Merely to dub it as an issue raised by the conservative party is not enough even in an age of progress, and in an age of reaction to stigmatize it as a proposal of the radicals will not suffice. Epithets have only a temporary effect upon the fortunes of the debate. We must consider soberly the charge against the Initiative that it is designed to serve as the melting pot for our most cherished political idols.

It is urged that hitherto in the history of the world democratic institutions have failed chiefly because of the instability of the government furnished by them. It is urged that the peculiar virtue of the American Republic is the stability given to its government primarily by the Federal constitution, which stands like a rock of refuge, unmoved by the storms of passion and prejudice beating upon it, and secondarily by the state constitutions, which serve as smaller rocks of refuge, sufficient for ordinary occasions but from which escape to the central rock is easy in especially troublous times. It is urged that material prosperity, industrial progress, the national accumulation of wealth are dependent upon the constitutional guaranties which protect property rights from felonious assault by madcap legislatures serving a discontented and greedy

populace. It is urged that liberty itself, the most
precious possession of the Saxon race, must depend
in America, where the stock is corrupted by the in-
fusion of countless alien strains, upon the stability
of the constitutions, which stand between the individual
and the possible oppressions of majorities prejudiced
by racial antipathy, religious differences, or social
intolerance. It is urged that the constitutions are the
foundation of our political dwelling and that to disturb
them, to change them, to replace them, except in the
most laborious and careful manner by the hands of
the most skilled and trustworthy builders, is to bring
the walls down about our ears and, if we escape at all,
to leave us shelterless and in sore distress. It is urged,
in particular, that the Initiative, of all radical propositions, is most peculiarly adapted to this fatal work.
With it in operation, the carefully wrought tools of
political experience may be broken in a moment in
some childish play of the baby giant. With it in operation, the very bulwarks of property under whose
protection American enterprise has ribboned a continent with steel, built cities that are the wonder of the
world and established as a single economic unit a widespreading nation of ninety million people, may be
wrecked any day by a stick of political dynamite
thrown by an angry mob temporarily in control.

Sad thoughts are these! Yet we must not assume
too hastily that conservatism is in its cups when it
gives utterance to them. They apply not so much to
the milder forms of the Initiative which are actually
being put to the test in numerous states and cities,
but to the radical Initiative which would strike at the

Federal constitution itself and throw it open to un-limited amendment by popular vote invoked by peti-tion. Accepting this definition of the Initiative, as a mode of ultimate sovereignty, we must face the apparitions and see whether they are in reality the warning spirits of the great masters of the world appealing to us, or mere bogie men conjured up by the resourceful sentries of the House of Have.

A constitution may be regarded in two aspects. It is a frame of government, a letter of instructions from the sovereign to the agents of sovereignty. It is also a rule of life voluntarily adopted by the sovereign itself. In the latter aspect it may be regarded as in a certain sense a working agreement between the in-dividual units which together constitute the sovereign. When a constitution is first framed by a constituent convention and ratified by vote of the people, it bears considerable resemblance to a contract worked out as a compromise among many conflicting interests and executed as a settlement binding upon all parties. But as it is only the majority for the time being that approve the agreement, obviously the agreement is subject to change from time to time as the will of the majority changes or as new majorities arise. It is true that sometimes a constitutional compact is loaded with solemn vows that there shall be no change or that no change shall be made unless it is agreed to by more than a majority of the units of sovereignty. But such vows can only be regarded as the sovereign's New Year's resolutions not to depart from the estab-lished ways until they are overwhelmingly discredited. After all, the self-imposed vows of sovereignty cannot be enforced by any outside tribunal, and for the sovereign to enforce against itself a vow of constancy even after it is fully convinced that change would be advantageous is not consistent with freedom and life. Viewed, then, in the aspect of a working agreement among the constituent units of the sovereign, a constitution cannot properly be regarded as a fixed contract. A promise not to amend it is binding neither in law nor in morals. A wise sovereign will make no unenforceable vows against change, but will merely adopt rules of procedure to insure that changes shall not be made hastily and without due consideration. The sovereign acts only in the establishment and amendment of the constitution. An absolute fixity in the constitution would mean the death of sovereignty. A man who lived by vows alone would become an automaton. There is every reason why a sovereign should live and why a constitution should grow, adapting itself continually to the changing conditions of social progress. It is unthinkable that in a democracy the sovereign should abdicate, or shut itself in a safety deposit vault with the key left on the outside, or commit suicide outright.

Viewed in its aspect as a letter of instructions to the agents of sovereignty, which is after all its most important aspect, a constitution should be subject to change without the consent of those to whom it is addressed. Life is fundamentally a private interest. Every conscious being must in the nature of the case be self-centered. Not to be self-circumferenced is the proof of ethical development. Man is a social being, a political animal, and the state, politics, government

are his modes of ethical expression. These represent
his secondary, or public interests. The people have to
be engaged about their private affairs. They constitute
government as the means of attending to their public
interests. To governmental agencies,—the legislature,
the executive, the permanent civil service, the judiciary,
—they delegate certain powers and give certain duties.
To prevent these agents from taking advantage of
their agencies to subvert the public interests and arro-
gate to themselves special privileges for private gain,
the sovereign establishes in the constitution certain
checks and limitations upon these agents. Certainly
it is sound theory that these checks and limitations,
as they prove ineffectual or insufficient, may be changed
or multiplied from time to time by the sovereign without the wishes of the agents themselves being consulted.
Likewise the powers and duties of the agents may be
enlarged as the public interest of the people demands.

Now, the difference between constitutional and
statutory law is simply this: the constitution is the
general law formulated by the sovereign, while the
statutes are the more detailed and flexible law formulated by the agents of the sovereign acting under
delegated authority. Whether a constitution should
be stable or not depends on two things: first, whether
or not it is right to start with, and second, whether or
not the governmental agencies do their work well.
Complaint is often made against the newer state
constitutions and constitutional amendments on the
score that they contain many details which would
properly be left to the statutes. This is wholly a
matter of practical expediency. There is nothing in the

domain of law that may not properly be incorporated
in the constitution, if the sovereign finds it expedient
to do so. Obviously, however, it is foolish for the
sovereign to make the letter of instructions to its
agents voluminous and replete with details unless
it keeps a close watch upon the conduct of its public
business and holds itself ready to amend the instructions
from time to time as the need arises. It seems clear
that the constitutional stability needed is not fixity,
but the stability of life, of growth, of healthful work.
In the old domain of private interests, gigantic social
and economic changes are being made almost overnight.
And, indeed, it often happens that the very men who
proclaim most loudly the advantages of social and economic progress are also most clamorous for stability in
the constitution. The secret of this apparent inconsis-
tency is this: in the last century the resources of nature
have been unlocked for human exploitation by certain
marvellous inventions and discoveries, and this has
given a tremendous stimulus to the private interests
of strong men, with the result that they resent and resist
the growth of the public interests and the enlargement
of the letter of instructions from the sovereign to its
governmental agents. In order to fulfill its purpose,
a constitution should have flexibility, and this means
that it should be easily amendable.

"The Constitution provides a simple, easy, and
peaceful method of modifying its own provisions,
in order that needed reforms may be accepted and
violent changes forestalled," said Judge Cooley, writing in 1880.[1] But this optimistic view is not borne

[1] Thomas M. Cooley, "Principles of Constitutional Law," p. 207.

out by the facts. Only ten years later Professor Burgess pointed out that it was possible under the existing process for less than 3,000,000 of the people successfully to resist more than 45,000,000 in any attempt to amend the constitution of the United States.[1] No amendment can be made except on the initiative of a two-thirds majority of both branches of Congress or on the initiative of a constitutional convention called in response to the demand of the legislatures of two-thirds of the states, and every amendment requires ratification by the representative assemblies of three-fourths of the states. By the census of 1910 there were twelve states, constituting more than one-fourth of the entire number, which together had only five per cent of the entire population of the country. It is now generally recognized that the amendment of the Federal constitution is extremely difficult. Professor Goodnow says on this account that "Americans are in many respects living under a political system which has been framed upon the theory that society is static rather than dynamic." [2]

If we turn now to the state constitutions we find somewhat more flexibility and greater ease of amendment. In most of the states amendments and revisions are ratified by popular vote, and in a few they may even now be proposed by the Initiative. But in one state [3] constitutional changes can only be made by a two-

[1] John W. Burgess, "Political Science and Comparative Constitutional Law," p. 151.

[2] Frank J. Goodnow, "Social Reform and the Constitution," p. 4. See also Professor J. Allen Smith's "The Spirit of American Government," Chap. iv.

[3] New Hampshire.

thirds vote of the people and in another [1] by a three-fifths vote. In many of the states constitutional amendments may be initiated only by a two-thirds or a three-fifths majority of both houses of the legislature, and in only a few states is a simple majority vote at a single legislative session sufficient to cause submission. Although in the aggregate many amendments are being submitted to the people of various states from year to year, the ease or difficulty of securing constitutional changes is not accurately measured by either the number or the bulk of these amendments. For, notoriously, many of the amendments submitted by state legislatures are so trivial in their nature or so local in their application as to be of no particular interest to the state at large, while great issues upon which the people are clamoring for an opportunity to vote are sometimes stubbornly withheld by the representative assemblies. The difficulty of securing important constitutional changes is accentuated in a few of the commonwealths by existing "rotten borough" systems of representation, in one or both of the houses of the legislature. It is apparent, however, that with a few possible exceptions the state constitutions are much less inflexible to amendment than the United States constitution. On the other hand, it is the Federal constitution that most frequently proves to be the obstacle in the way of important political and social reforms.

In urging the necessity of a radical change in the method of amending the Federal constitution, Professor Burgess says: "When, in a democratic political

[1] Rhode Island.

society, the well-matured, long and deliberately formed will of the undoubted majority can be persistently and successfully thwarted, in the amendment of its organic law, by the will of the minority, there is just as much danger to the state from revolution and violence as there is from the caprice of the majority where the sovereignty of the bare majority is acknowledged. The safeguard against too radical change must not be exaggerated to the point of dethroning the real sovereign." [1] The specific change suggested by Professor Burgess is not the Initiative and does not even include the ratification of amendments by popular vote. He sticks close to the representative system and yet his proposal is so radical as to spell the overthrow of the enforced stability now characteristic of the Federal constitution. Referring to the existing requirement of "artificially excessive majorities" as a safeguard against "too radical change," he says:

"There is another way, a better way and a natural way of securing deliberation, maturity and clear consciousness of purpose without antagonizing the actual source of power in the democratic state, *viz.:* by repetition of vote. If, for example, the Congress should, in joint session and by simple majority, resolve upon a proposition of amendment, and give notice of the same to the people in time for the voters to take the matter into consideration in the election of the members of the House of Representatives for the next succeeding Congress; and if the succeeding Congress should then repass the proposition in joint session and by like majority; and if then it should be sent to the legisla-

[1] Work cited, p. 152.

tures of the commonwealths for ratification by the houses thereof, acting in joint assembly and resolving by simple majority vote; and if then the vote of each legislature should have the same weight in the count as that of the respective commonwealth in the election of the President of the United States, and an absolute majority of all the votes to which all of the common-wealths were entitled should be made necessary and sufficient for ratification,—why would not this be an organization of the sovereign, of the state within the constitution, which would be truthful to the conditions of our national democratic society and our federal system of government; which would secure all needful deliberation in procedure and maturity in resolution; which would permit changes when the natural condi-tions and relations of our state and society demanded them; and which would give us an organization of the state convenient in practice and, at the same time, sufficiently distinct from the organization of the gov-ernment to prevent confusion of thought in reference to the spheres and powers of the two organizations?"

This change, radical as it is, assumes that representa-tive assemblies both in nation and in commonwealth will faithfully represent the deliberate will of the majority of the people. It would remove the present theoretical obstacles to well-considered amendments and put the Federal constitution relatively on a par with the constitutions of those states, such as New York and Pennsylvania, which may be changed from time to time, by amendments passed by majority vote of two successive legislatures and then ratified by the people. Indeed, Professor Burgess' plan is even more democratic in that it provides for action in all cases, both in Congress and in the state legislatures, by joint assembly of the two houses, where the particular interests and prejudices of the upper branch might be overcome by the superior numbers of the lower. Yet even thus, what warrant does experience give us for the assumption that the people's will would prevail? Is it not in joint session of the two houses that the state legislatures elect United States senators? And have not many states, driven by despair of securing proper representation in the United States Senate by that method, been forced to adopt direct nominations or preferential popular voting in order to reduce the constitutional method of electing senators to an empty form? Experience with state legislation, with the amendment of state constitutions and with the selection of United States senators, does not warrant the faith that even a bare majority vote in joint assembly would surely give us adequate relief from the present fixity of the constitutions. That a conservative thinker like Professor Burgess should make such a radical proposal as he has, is proof enough of our need to overcome the artificial constitutional stability from which we have long suffered. Whether some remedy such as he proposes would be adequate without resorting to the Initiative, and whether the Initiative if applied unflinchingly to all constitutions, including the grand palladium of privilege first erected in 1789 and then greatly enlarged in 1868, would go too far in the direction of removing the obstacles to change, are the questions we have to answer.

The old methods of amending American constitu-

tions have failed, not so much because the majority
of the people desiring to make changes was less than
the required majorities in the legislative bodies, as
because the action of the legislative bodies has been
paralyzed by special interests. Sometimes these interests are sectional, sometimes they are industrial or
commercial, and sometimes they are political. It is unnecessary to review in detail the history of sectionalism
in Congress and in the state legislatures. The abuses
of sectionalism have been perpetuated by every concession made to them in an inflexible constitution,
and sectionalism tends to be more marked in its representatives than in its people; for where it is indigenous
or can be cultivated by political leaders, they organize
it and fatten on it and represent it in its extreme
manifestations. Who can doubt that the sectionalism of the South both in the slavery days and in the
present era of negro disfranchisement has been stimulated and bolstered up by the representatives who
profit by it? Who can doubt that in the decaying
rural towns of Rhode Island and Connecticut the local
jealousy of any constitutional revision looking to the
equalization of representation in the legislature on the
basis of population has been diligently fanned into
a flame by the diminutive statesmen whose influence
in government and political intrigue is dependent
upon the continuation of the grotesque injustice of
the ancient order? That tariff beneficiaries, special
franchise-holders, railroads and exploiters of the public domain have often had a preponderating influence
in legislative bodies, from Congress down to the village
councils, is a fact too well known to need elaboration

or proof, in this place. "Big Business" has often mixed in politics for private ends and has warped to its will the legislatures elected nominally as representatives of the people. Finally, the wholly illogical plan by which the consent of the legislature is required to a change in the constitution even where the change affects the powers, the duties and the mode of election of the legislators themselves, has borne its legitimate fruit in the blocking of constitutional reform. The theory that legislators represent the people who elected them and continue to maintain a single eye to the public welfare, knowing no favored class among their constituents and wholly unmindful of their own private interests in the midst of subtle temptation, is a beautiful theory, but one that is especially unworthy of utterance by the class of men who profess to despise theory and to be intensely practical. It is the facts of misrepresentation where the sovereign has disarmed itself in favor of its agents that make inadequate the proposal of Professor Burgess and all similar schemes which depend wholly upon the representative bodies to propose constitutional amendments. Constitutional stability secured by the abdication of the sovereign people leaves government to be exploited by organized private interests and this condition, if long-continued, threatens the very stability from which it springs.

Would the Initiative destroy the real stability that results from the healthy development and constant adjustment of political means to social ends? I think not. On the contrary, it would tend to give our institutions greater stability. Men generally are anxious to maintain orderly relations in which they can work with some assurance that they will enjoy the fruits of their own labor. The mass of mankind is conservative. The strength and usefulness of constitutions depend not upon their artificial fixity but upon their adaptation to the needs of society and upon the resulting reverence of the people for them. Public opinion is stronger than mere written constitutions and statutes. The Initiative may not favor stability of vested wrongs. It may not be solicitous for the continuance of conditions where a few men reap the mighty rewards of socialized industry and clutch in their fingers the threads of a nation's complex life. It may not be favorable to the continued ownership of the highways by private corporations organized for profit. It may not guarantee the perpetuity of franchises and the integrity of family fortunes based upon landed privileges. We can make no promises on behalf of the Initiative to that class of men who consider it a legitimate and praiseworthy purpose in life to amass a fortune by various devices for getting other people's money. But to honest toil and honest thrift we can promise that the Initiative will furnish the constitutional stability necessary for their protection—unless, indeed, the riot of misrepresentation is continued too long, until democracy has become not only actually but even potentially impossible. If that happens we can look only for cataclysm and disaster, and the fixity of the Federal constitution will not save us. But we still have reason to hope that it is not too late to entrust our lives, our liberties, and our property to the educated political responsibility of the sovereign people.

CHAPTER IV

SECOND OBJECTION TO THE INITIATIVE—THAT IT WOULD FOSTER THE TYRANNY OF THE MAJORITY

THE objection most gravely urged against the Initiative is that it would subject the individual to the danger of losing his liberties by reason of the temporary whims or the sustained prejudices of the numerical majority. "The notion, that the people have no need to limit their power over themselves, might seem axiomatic," says John Stuart Mill,[1] "when popular government was a thing only dreamed about, or read of as having existed at some distant period of the past. . . . In time, however, a democratic republic came to occupy a large portion of the earth's surface, and made itself felt as one of the most powerful members of the community of nations; and elective and responsible government became subject to the observation and criticisms which wait upon a great existing fact. It was now perceived that such phrases as 'self-government,' and 'the power of the people over themselves,' do not express the true state of the case. The 'people' who exercise the power are not always the same people with those over whom it is exercised; and the 'self-government' spoken of is not the government of each by himself, but of each by all the rest. The will

---

[1] "Essay on Liberty."

of the people, moreover, practically means the will of the most numerous or the most active part of the people; the majority, or those who succeed in making themselves accepted as the majority; the people, consequently, *may* desire to oppress a part of their number; and precautions are as much needed against this as against any other abuse of power. The limitation, therefore, of the power of government over individuals loses none of its importance when the holders of power are regularly accountable to the community, that is, to the strongest party therein." This warning against the "tyranny of the majority" was uttered with reference to American political institutions even before the Initiative was thought of in this country. Indeed, still earlier, in Andrew Jackson's time, De Tocqueville had said: [1] "If ever the free institutions of America are destroyed, that event may be attributed to the unlimited power of the majority, which may at some future time urge the minorities to desperation, and oblige them to have recourse to physical violence." The keen-eyed Frenchman found "the power of the majority in America not only preponderant but irresistible." He saw trouble on the horizon. "A proceeding which will in the end set all the guaranties of representative government at naught is becoming more and more general in the United States," said he: "it frequently happens that the electors, who choose a delegate, point out a certain line of conduct to him, and impose upon him a certain number of positive obligations which he is pledged to fulfill. With the exception of the tumult, this comes to the same thing as if the majority

[1] "Democracy in America," Vol. I, Chap. 15.

of the populace held its deliberations in the market-place." The cloud as large as a man's hand which De Tocqueville saw did not overspread the sky until recent times when the agitation for the Initiative, the Referendum, and the Recall became crystallized into a definite nation-wide program. In a society like ours in the United States minorities change rapidly. At the present time the minority whose rights are most frequently alleged to be endangered by the Initiative is the group of men of great wealth against whom the people have cried out. The *New York Times* is an able exponent of private interests. As a newspaper, it sets itself in strenuous opposition to all the political "fads and fancies" that come out of the West. It decries any attack upon the rich or any curtailment of their privileges, outside of the tariff. It loves to dwell upon the benefits that trickle down to the common people when the bowl of prosperity is full for great corporations controlling transportation and other public services. The *Times* has taken notice of the radical program enunciated in Oregon, California, Wisconsin and other far-off States, and even proclaimed by a voice in New Jersey, just across the North River,— New Jersey, the very citadel of the minority for which the *Times* is most solicitous. "Now, that the definite will of the majority of the voters, deliberately formed, consistently adhered to, and fairly expressed, should determine the treatment of public affairs in all branches, even the judiciary, is the fundamental principle of democracy," says the *Times*.[1] "But that the hastily formed, rashly expressed wish of a majority should at

[1] Editorial article, "In the Enemy's Country," January 24, 1912.

any moment be able to make radical changes is not a principle of democracy at all. It is really not government, but the negation of government and the introduction of chaos; nor is it the exercise of real freedom, but rather the installment of the despotism of a fleeting majority, the oppression of the minority for the time being."

Although it may seem a strange doctrine that the minority should have its way against the majority, even for a time, in matters affecting the public interests, we must admit the necessity of giving careful consideration to anything upon which De Tocqueville, John Stuart Mill, and the *New York Times* seem to agree. There undoubtedly is a bad thing that is known as "the tyranny of the majority." The question for us is this: Will the Initiative foster this tyranny? and if so, will it deliver us from worse tyrannies, and thus establish a claim to our adherence by substituting a lesser for a greater evil?

John Stuart Mill defines his object in writing his Essay on Liberty as being the assertion of one simple principle "as entitled to govern absolutely the dealings of society with the individual in the way of compulsion and control." This principle is "that the only purpose for which power can be rightfully exercised over any member of a civilized community, against his will, is to prevent harm to others." The danger of tyranny on the part of the majority is frequently alleged in connection with what has generally been called in America "sumptuary legislation." This includes particularly the laws prohibiting irregular sexual relations, the laws against gambling, the laws prohibiting

or restraining the traffic in intoxicating liquors, the
sale of cigarettes, and the sale or use of opium and other
harmful drugs, the Sunday "blue laws" and generally
all laws that attempt to regulate personal conduct in
matters not involving recognized criminal acts. The
futility of this so-called tyranny of the majority is often
asserted in the statement that "you cannot make men
good by statute." The inexpediency and even the fundamental obliquity of such legislation are alleged by the
extreme advocates of personal liberty. Mill regarded
the legal prohibition of the liquor traffic as unquestionably a tyrannous exercise of the power of the majority.
It is obvious, however, that the mere statement of his
principle setting forth the true limits of governmental
interference with individual liberty does not settle any
specific question. It is easy to find arguments specious
or otherwise in favor of any sort of sumptuary legislation on the ground that the restriction of the individual is designed "to prevent harm to others." For-
tunately, we are not required in this chapter to pass
upon the ultimate desirability of all the various forms
of restrictive legislation, but only to discuss in a general
way the probable effect of the Initiative upon the government's relation to minorities. We should not fail
to note, however, that the strength and permanency
of democracy are peculiarly dependent upon the general intelligence and self-restraint of the people.
Democracy cannot long thrive on personal debauchery.
So far as legislation can be effective as an educational
instrument to induce morality and orderly personal
habits, its use for this purpose is not at all contrary
to the genius of democracy. Social freedom and what

is called "personal liberty" may often be in the highest
degree inconsistent. In so far, therefore, as the Initiative
is calculated to bring about a more perfect democracy,
we may expect that it will lend itself to such legislation
as shall prove to be effective in raising the general
moral standards of the community, in suppressing organized educational wickedness and in creating an
environment favorable to decency and self-restraint.
How far the Initiative will push the social theory of
self-protection against the desire of the individual
to choose for himself between good and evil and to
do as he pleases, we cannot now foresee. This much is
clear: the brewers are generally opposed to the Initiative
in "wet" territory and the ultra-prohibitionists are
against it in "dry." In our continual groping for an
effective means of closing the yawning hiatus between
law and its enforcement in our great cities, it has
sometimes been suggested that the question of suspending the law requiring saloons to be closed over Sunday
should be submitted to popular vote in particular
communities where public sentiment does not support
a steady enforcement of the existing state law. When
this particular brand of municipal home rule is offered,
the radical sabbatarians can ordinarily be depended
upon to oppose it. It may be said in general that those
who have a financial interest in the liquor traffic or in
any other organized exploitation of human passions
and human frailties are hotly opposed to the Initiative
when they fear the curtailment of their business by
this means, while social puritans warmly favor the
Initiative as long as they believe the majority to be of
their own mind. A great deal of popular voting is done

in the United States upon questions relating to the
saloon. This voting is not confined to the occasions,
quite numerous in the aggregate, when the question
of state-wide prohibition is submitted to the people
of this or that commonwealth, nor even to the much
more frequent occasions when the question of prohibition comes up on petition in individual cities,
counties, towns or other subdivisions, under local option laws, but it extends in some localities to an an-
nual redetermination, under a fixed statutory requirement, of the question of "license" or "no license."
It cannot be denied that frequent balloting on the
saloon question is attended, in some communities, by
social disorder, factional recrimination and a general
dislocation of the machinery of political thought.
Where the people are almost evenly divided on the
issue and the balloting takes place once a year, as regularly as the arrival of Christmas Day, or the Fourth
of July, it may be said, that the times are, indeed, out of
joint. I do not wish to minimize the fundamental
political and social importance of the saloon question,
but I am inclined to think that the habit of voting
on it annually, throwing the saloons out one year,
and readmitting them the next, or *vice versa*, is not
conducive to the orderly development of general
political intelligence and its sane application to the
problems of government.

Would the general introduction of the Initiative
into the political machinery of the United States tend
to over-emphasize the practical importance of particular controversial issues such as the prohibition of the
liquor traffic? It is well known that the liquor interests

have almost universally exerted a concentrated and
powerful influence over American legislative bodies
in nation, state, and municipality. The participation
of these interests in practical politics has extended
continuously over a long period of time and has reached
the utmost corners of the country. On the other hand,
no other organized moral sentiment has brought such
powerful and recurrent pressure upon legislative bodies
as the temperance or anti-saloon movement. Still,
the convivial habits usually developed by politicians
and office-holders and the substantial nature of the
inducements offered by the liquor men have ordinarily
overbalanced this moral pressure, and kept legislatures and boards of aldermen in large measure subservient to the brewers. It may reasonably be expected,
therefore, that the general introduction of the Initiative would bring the question of prohibition and
other questions affecting the liquor traffic much more
generally to the arbitrament of the polls than is now
the case where the people cannot vote upon any
question until it is submitted to them by the legislature. There is reason, however, to expect a diminution, in some respects, of the ardor of the struggle,
because the terms of the issue will be more flexible,
under the Initiative. At the present time, usually the
only question referred to popular vote is a choice
between two fixed policies—absolute prohibition on
the one hand and the general system of regulation
worked out by the legislature on the other. There is
no leeway for the initiative of the people themselves
in working out a rational solution of this complex and
vexing problem. With the free play of political ideas

which the Initiative is designed to foster, there would
seem to be more likelihood of the development of
an effective policy, consistent with the public welfare
as determined by enlightened public sentiment, than
there is under the present mode of procedure, where
the methods of regulation and even the form of the
issues occasionally submitted to popular vote are fixed
from time to time by a representative body subjected
to tremendous pressure from a sleepless property
interest of vast proportions and at the same time
being intermittently bombarded from the opposite
side by an insistent body of moralists claiming to bring
a mandate from the Almighty. We certainly have
little to boast of thus far in our handling of the liquor
problem in America, and the political aggravations
that have resulted practically in connection with the
people's voting upon the saloon question may be
attributed not to the inherent unfitness of the majority
to legislate in such matters but rather to the stereotyped forms in which the issue has been submitted
by the legislative body.

It seems highly improbable that under the Initiative,
American governmental policies with reference to
drunkenness, gambling, prostitution, and other vices,
would be any less effective than they are at present.
As it is now, commercialized vice flaunts itself defiantly
full half of the time and pushes itself insidiously at all
times into our social environment, until the tyranny
of this minority has become intolerable. Democracy
cannot stand it. The composite nature of the American
people and its complex training in tolerance toward
the manners and customs of various nationalities are

a pretty sure guaranty against the general adoption in this country of measures destructive of any legitimate privileges of individuals and minorities in all matters of personal conduct.   While it may be true that in some respects our formal enactments are too rigid and too intolerant of individual liberty in matters of morals, our practical standards of actual interference with various forms of vice are altogether too low for a democracy.   For virtue is life, self-restraint is power, cleanliness is wisdom, and upon these things democracy depends.

"When an individual or a party is wronged in the United States, to whom can he apply for redress?" cried De Tocqueville.   "If to public opinion, public opinion constitutes the majority; if to the legislature, it represents the majority, and implicitly obeys its injunctions; if to the executive power, it is appointed by the majority, and remains a passive tool in its hands; the public troops consist of the majority under arms; the jury is the majority invested with the right of hearing judicial cases; and in certain states even the judges are elected by the majority.   However iniquitous or absurd the evil of which you complain may be, you must submit to it as well as you can."   He cites two specific illustrations of the despotism of the majority.   One was the case of a Baltimore newspaper that opposed the war with Britain in 1812.   Its offices were mobbed and its editors attacked.   The militia was called out, but no one came.   Then the newspaper men were thrown into jail to save their lives.   But even that was ineffectual.   The mob reassembled, broke into the prison, killed one of the editors, and left the rest for dead. The guilty men were tried and acquitted by the jury. The other illustration was the treatment of negro freedmen in Pennsylvania where they enjoyed the legal right of suffrage but were kept from the polls by fear of mal-treatment. "In this country the law is sometimes unable to maintain its authority without the support of the majority," was the explanation he received. "In this case the majority entertains very strong prejudices against the blacks, and the magistrates are unable to protect them in the exercise of their legal privileges." "What!" exclaimed De Tocqueville, "then the majority claims the right not only of making the laws, but of breaking the laws it has made!"

De Tocqueville found the majority supreme in America in 1830. Now we are crying out that this supremacy has been lost and proposing the Initiative as a means to restore it. Does it appear that the despotism of the majority observed by him was a product of the town-meeting method? He certainly put his finger on a sore spot in our body politic, a spot that is still quick to the touch. True, we have not lately murdered any editors for pro-British sympathies. The contributing editor of *The Outlook* has not slaughtered the managing editor of *The Independent* for his devotion to the cause of international peace. But in Tennessee not long since a Prohibition editor was murdered in the streets of the capital and the murderer was pardoned. Lynchings and race riots prove that in many parts of the country certain majorities are not only tyrannous but murderous. But are these expressions of unrestrained power confined

to those parts of the country where the people have
the use of the Initiative? Is the record of Oregon worse
than that of Pennsylvania or Georgia? The fact is
that the cases cited by De Tocqueville and the cases
of violence characteristic of the present time are not
the acts of the untrammeled majorities clothed with
power to initiate and repeal laws on their own motion
and to hold their public servants strictly accountable
during their terms of office as well as at the end of them.
In some cases lynch law has been excused on account
of the delays of justice through the regular channels.
But in the violation of the Fifteenth Amendment,
either under forms of law devised for the purpose or by
intimidation such as De Tocqueville found in Pennsylvania eighty years ago, the Southern states ex-
emplify the most serious danger of the oppression of
minorities by majorities that exists in the United
States to-day. Has the Fifteenth Amendment been
violated by the Initiative? Would fewer Negroes be
allowed to exercise the right of suffrage if the Initiative
was now a part of the political machinery of every
state? Would lynchings and Kentucky feuds be more
common or more deadly, if the people had the right
to propose constitutional amendments and statutes
by petition and enact them by direct vote? It is more
likely that the contrary would be true, for with the
Initiative, local, state, and national, in free play, the
protection of the minority in any given political subdivision could be assumed by a larger political unit
uncontrolled by the passions and prejudices of the
local majority. In our representative bodies the
courtesies of log-rolling and other practical arts of

government make the majority at large supine to protect local minorities, unrepresented in the assembly and voiceless at the polls, against oppression. The Initiative could lend itself ultimately to the tyranny of race prejudice only in case of a prejudice extending over the widest political unit in which the Initiative could be used, and even in such a case there is reason to believe that in the long run the majority, voting at the polls after the enlightenment of public discussion, would be more tolerant than the representative assembly, whose members feed upon and capitalize the prejudices of the prevailing party unless, indeed, the minority has other means than numbers to enlist the sympathy of legislators. Certain it is that the people's fearsome habit of instructing their representatives how to act, which De Tocqueville noticed in its beginnings with such profound foreboding, was not responsible for the specific instances of tyranny which he pointed out, and has not been responsible for the oppressions of the minority that stain the pages of our more recent history.

We now come to the tyrannies feared by the *New York Times* and the minority it represents. There is a saying that "one, with God, is a majority." This epigram contains a profound and solemn truth. In it are consolation, strength, and courage for the men who dare to be right when the numerical count goes heavily against them. But who is God in this country? We have heard that the American people worship the God of wealth. If one, with the Almighty Dollar, is a majority, here is the secret of our discontent. It is from the oppressions of this majority that we seek

deliverance. Go to, *New York Times*, we the majority in numbers, demand our constitutional rights to be
free from the tyranny of one, or a few, with this God,
money, on their side. We have reverence for property.
Money is our God as well as theirs. We demand
our share in the possession of him and in the favor
he bestows. I do not speak flippantly and irreverently.
Money is, in a true sense, the God of Life. Money is
the token of human effort. It represents the power of
industry and foresight. It is the symbol of freedom
from the raw, material domination of physical need.
It stands for opportunity to cultivate the soul. It
is the hard-earned savings of human progress crystallized into serviceable forms. It is not strange that men
worship this God, though he is their own creature.
But we deny that he can rightfully be captured and
possessed, like the ark of the covenant, by a small band
of Philistines. We deny that he should be worshiped
as a malignant spirit. He is our creature. He must
serve us. He must not be permitted by his favoritism
to transform an infinitesimal numerical minority into
a tyrannizing majority of power. The *New York Times*
and its ilk have sequestered our God. They fear the
attack of the numerical majority to recover possession
of him. They are opposed to "radical changes" on
the impulse of the moment. They are pretty well
satisfied with the present status of affairs. They are
for parleying and delay. They shudder at the possibility of sudden action by the people en masse. To
them the Initiative is anathema, for it means the
breaking down of the stockade they have built around
our sequestered divinity. It means the removal of the

obstructions that keep the people as a whole from enjoying the benefits of social wealth, except as they are doled out by the courtesy of the garrisons that occupy the strongholds of privilege.

It is almost universally asserted, or admitted as the case may be, that the American people are now suffering from the tyranny of the numerical minority made powerful by the possession or control of wealth. It is natural that the minority which participates in the benefits of this tyranny should vigorously resist its overthrow. But from the standpoint of the public welfare, what effect may the Initiative be expected to have in this matter? Will it lead to the spoliation of the rich by the poor? Will it lead to the waste of wealth? Will it lead to paralysis of the individual and the fatal curtailment of enterprise? No one will have the hardihood, in the light of history, to deny that a wide diffusion of wealth among the people is essential to the strength and permanency of democratic institutions, or that the concentration of the ownership or control of a nation's material resources in the hands of a few men is a menace to the freedom of the people. If it is true that this menace confronts us in America to-day, then the sooner we take steps to remove it, very radical steps if necessary, the better it will be. If the Initiative will help us to success in our endeavor, that is a point in its favor. If, on the other hand, it be untrue that the ownership or control of wealth is unduly concentrated in America, then the Initiative becomes a balance-wheel of conservatism; for the majority, having its own share in the wealth of the country, will naturally protect itself at the polls. There can be little doubt that the Initiative would be invoked, whether successfully or not remains to be seen, as an instrument for limiting the concentration of wealth and for encouraging its diffusion. Thus the purpose of the majority using the Initiative would be good. Would the manner of its use be bad? This question cannot be answered in advance to the satisfaction of all parties. Indeed, the most ardent advocate of the Initiative will admit that mistakes are likely to be made in its application in some places under some conditions, but we hold that the sooner it is made available everywhere as a political tool, the less likely it is to be rashly used. There is still a wide diffusion of material interests in this country. The people still have great respect for private property. They are still in most communities at most times conservative. Unquestionably the Initiative will be used, if necessary, to enforce trusteeship in the control of capital. Such measures as employers' liability, the regulation of public utilities, conservation of natural resources, taxation of large incomes, the inheritance tax, the land tax, the protection of women and children against exploitation in the fields of industry and the enlargement of the functions of government, would doubtless be put upon the statute books more quickly and in more radical form under the Initiative than would be the case if dependence for progressive legislation had to be upon representative bodies alone. Those who favor such measures will generally welcome the Initiative. Those who oppose them will naturally be against it, unless they have more hope of convincing the people at large than of holding the legislature in check. I shall not attempt to impeach the intelligence of the *New York Times* in opposing the Initiative. It knows what it wants, and it does not want many of the things which the Initiative will bring, if it proves to be of any use. At the same time, when radical remedies promptly applied are essential to ultimate conservatism, as I believe they now are in the matter of the distribution and control of wealth in the United States, the Initiative may easily prove to be the safety-valve of our political institutions and, in the long run, serve the interests of the wealthy and powerful minority better than an exclusively representative form of government that might become a mere shell, ready to go to pieces at the first onset of revolution.

Finally, in all those fields of action where it is feared by some that the Initiative would promote the tyranny of the majority, we have ultimately to rely upon the character of the American people to prevent abuses of power. Americans well know that the right of the individual to life, liberty, property and the pursuit of happiness, is precious beyond comparison. Every man is in the minority at some time and in some matters. Religious intolerance and educational snobbery have largely disappeared. Ultimately race hatred will also disappear, and society will attain a better distribution of wealth and more steady standards of moral life so that the greatest present dangers of majority despotism will become less threatening. America, with the blood of all nations mingled in its veins, cannot ultimately be intolerant of anything that does not endanger the public welfare. It seems likely that the Initiative, opening the way to free public debate and effective public action, will tend to sober the majority by the very gift of responsible power.

CHAPTER V

THIRD OBJECTION TO THE INITIATIVE—THAT IT WOULD TEND TO THE SUBVERSION OF JUDICIAL AUTHORITY

WE must refer to De Tocqueville again. "In visiting the Americans and in studying their laws we perceive that the authority they have entrusted to members of the legal profession, and the influence which these individuals exercise in the government, is the most powerful existing security against the excesses of democracy," says he, in one of his most illuminating chapters.[1] He finds it necessary to explain the tendencies of the legal profession at some length, for he notes that in different countries and at different times the lawyers have taken exactly opposite positions with reference to constitutional politics. "In the Middle Ages they afforded a powerful support to the crown, and since that period they have exerted themselves to the utmost to limit the royal prerogative. In England they have contracted a close alliance with the aristocracy; in France they have proved to be the most dangerous enemies of that class." These seeming inconsistencies in reality result from unusual consistency in the pursuit of happiness, which, in the case of the lawyers, is meas-

[1] Chap. XVI, "Causes Which Mitigate the Tyranny of the Majority in the United States."

68

ured in terms of distinction and practical influence. "In a state of society in which the members of the legal profession are prevented from holding that rank in the political world which they enjoy in private life, we may rest assured that they will be the foremost agents of revolution," says the candid Frenchman. "In a community in which lawyers are allowed to occupy, without opposition, that high station which naturally belongs to them, their general spirit will be eminently conservative and anti-democratic. When an aristocracy excludes the leaders of that profession from its ranks, it excites enemies which are the more formidable to its security as they are independent of the nobility by their industrious pursuits, and they feel themselves to be its equal in point of intelligence, although they enjoy less opulence and less power. But whenever an aristocracy consents to impart some of its privileges to these same individuals, the two classes coalesce very readily, and assume, as it were, the consistency of a single order of family interests." This may explain the subtle influence that $100,000 fees have upon the attitude of lawyers towards large vested interests. "The object of lawyers is not, indeed, to overthrow the institutions of democracy," says De Tocqueville, "but they constantly endeavor to give it an impulse which diverts it from its real tendency, by means which are foreign to its nature. Lawyers belong to the people by birth and interest, to the aristocracy by habit and taste. . . . I am not un-acquainted with the defects which are inherent in the character of that body of men; but without this ad-mixture of lawyer-like sobriety with the democratic principle, I question whether democratic institutions could long be maintained, and I cannot believe that a republic could subsist at the present time if the influence of lawyers in public business did not increase in proportion to the power of the people." Here is the balance-wheel of democracy which explained to De Tocqueville the unusual stability of the American republic! "If I were asked where I place the American aristocracy," says he, "I should reply without hesitation that it is not composed of the rich, who are united together by no common tie, but that it occupies the judicial bench and the bar.

"The more we reflect upon all that occurs in the United States the more shall we be persuaded that the lawyers as a body form the most powerful, if not the only counterpoise to the democratic element. In that country we see how eminently the legal profession is qualified by its powers, and even by its defects, to neutralize the vices which are inherent in popular government. When the American people is intoxicated by passion, or carried away by the impetuosity of its ideas, it is checked and stopped by the almost invisible influence of its legal counsellors, who secretly oppose their aristocratic propensities to its democratic instincts, their superstitious attachment to what is antique to its love of novelty, their narrow views to its immense designs, and their habitual procrastination to its ardent impatience.

"The courts of justice are the most visible organs by which the legal profession is enabled to control the democracy. The judge is a lawyer, who, independently of the taste for regularity and order which he has contracted in the study of legislation, derives an additional love of stability from his own inalienable functions. His legal attainments have already raised him to a distinguished rank among his fellow-citizens; his political power completes the distinction of his station, and gives him the inclinations natural to privileged classes.

"Armed with the power of declaring the laws to be unconstitutional, the American magistrate perpetually interferes in political affairs. He cannot force the people to make laws, but at least he can oblige it not to disobey its own enactments, or to act inconsistently with its own principles. I am aware that a secret tendency to diminish the judicial power exists in the United States, and by most of the constitutions of the several states, the government can, upon the demand of the two houses of the legislature, remove the judges from their station. By some other constitutions the members of the tribunal are elected, and they are even subjected to frequent reëlections. I venture to predict that these innovations will sooner or later be attended with fatal consequences, and that it will be found out at some future period that the attack which is made upon the judicial power has affected the democratic republic itself."

I must crave pardon of De Tocqueville's shade for these copious quotations. It may be thought that I am trying to borrow lustre for my own humble work from the luminous pages of an old masterpiece. But I have been drawn to quote De Tocqueville's words by several "moving considerations" that I could not resist. In the first place there is the historical interest

in seeing how the problems of democracy that are now
pressing for solution appeared to the great political
analyst in their beginnings. De Tocqueville was a seer.
His pages written more than three-quarters of a century
ago read almost as if they had been written yester-
day. To be sure, there is lacking the recognition
of the power of concentrated wealth and corporate
organization which is characteristic of later American
history, but his delineation of the character and influence of the legal profession has not depreciated in
the least by obsolescence. In the second place, his
frankness and felicity of expression are not surpassed
even in the mighty editorials of the twentieth-century
metropolitan dailies, the speeches of a peripatetic
President or the spirited outpourings of the heads of
endowed universities. Finally, I desire to give to the
opponents of the Initiative all the advantage that
could come from a lucid statement of the function
of judicial authority in American politics as seen by
a master critic far removed from the passions and
prejudices of our time. There are certain important
elements in De Tocqueville's analysis of the problem
that seldom appear even in the most able statements
of the conservative position in current discussions.
Strengthened by historical perspective, dignified by
the prestige of a great name, made pleasant by happy
phraseology, shorn of its subtleties by masterful candor
and completeness of statement, the great claim of the
conservative party that judicial authority must be
preserved at all costs stands forth to be examined.
What would be effected by the Recall of judges will be
considered in another chapter. Here we are concerned

with the effect of the Initiative. Would it tend to the subversion of judicial authority? If so, would the results be good or evil?

The authority of the judiciary as the ultimate guardian of the established order rests upon its power to declare legislative acts unconstitutional and void, or to interpret laws in such a way as to divert them from their original purpose or to lessen their effectiveness in accomplishing that purpose. Under the Initiative, when the courts refuse to give effect to a law on the ground that it is unconstitutional, or read into the law their own peculiar political philosophy, it will be possible for the people on their own motion to change the constitution or to pass a new law declaring their intent in unmistakable terms. If the courts persist in flouting the will of the people, the Initiative can be invoked to curtail the constitutional powers of the judiciary and deprive them of all authority to pass upon the constitutionality of legislation. But these possibilities of attack upon specific judicial doctrines or upon general judicial powers are no greater than now rest with the legislative body in coöperation with the people, except that under the Initiative, constitutional amendments could be more easily proposed than under the old system. Legislatures do, as a matter of fact, frequently repass statutes, once declared unconstitutional, in forms designed to steer clear of the technical objections of the courts. And legislatures do, in some cases, submit constitutional amendments for the purpose of subverting judicial decisions. All that the Initiative would do would be to make such action easier where the judges run counter to the deliberate will of the majority of the people. Practically, however, this small theoretical change might have momentous consequences. Legislative measures, designed to meet new conditions, and embodying constructive forward policies, are often forced through the legislature only by means of an overwhelming public sentiment persistently applied through a series of years. When such a measure has been voided by the courts, it may be more difficult than ever to secure its repassage by the legislature in amended form and perhaps it will be wholly impossible for its friends to get the necessary majorities in the legislative bodies to submit a constitutional amendment. Uncertainty, delay, and long-continued failure are likely to attend any effort to overcome the mandate of the judges. Under the Initiative, the way to do it would be simple and direct, if the people favored such action.

In recent years the courts in America are being severely criticized for their exercise of the power to set aside legislation as being in conflict with the constitution. Much of this criticism is more vigorous than illuminating. It is a matter of common knowledge that the people resort to the courts for protection against the tyranny or folly of the legislative body quite as often as the reactionary interests resort to them for protection against the demands of political and social progress. When a fleeting majority in the legislature attempts to intrench itself in power by obnoxious legislation or to barter away the people's inheritance or to misapply public funds, there is great satisfaction to the public in being able to apply to the courts for protection against the violation of constitutional guaranties. The manner in which legislatures often make use of the emergency clause to get around constitutional restrictions and the popular veto, and the way in which they often violate the well-understood spirit of the constitution in other respects to obtain their own selfish ends, make it clear that legislative bodies as at present constituted in America are unsafe repositories of the ultimate authority to interpret the constitution. If the trusteeship of the legislature is made responsible directly to the people by means of the Referendum and the Recall, the present necessity for maintaining the authority of the courts to review legislation will, in some measure, disappear. Even by the Initiative, legislative indiscretions, unless they were of a contractual nature, could be cured by amendatory or repealing legislation enacted by direct vote of the people. Nevertheless, the Referendum, the Recall, and the Initiative are all much more cumbersome and difficult means of defense than the direct appeal to the courts. It is not likely, therefore, that the people themselves through the Initiative would deprive the judiciary of authority to declare the acts of the legislature unconstitutional. They might, however, forbid the courts to void any act adopted by popular vote, although it is more likely that the existing distinctions between constitutional and statutory law, even when the people had supreme ultimate authority in both, would be maintained, at least for a considerable time. The Initiative would tend to subvert judicial authority in so far as that authority is now regarded as privileged and irresponsible. The courts would soon find themselves placed on a par with the legislature and the executive in their obligation to enforce the will of the majority. The atmosphere of a privileged class would no longer surround the judges in the performance of their functions. They could no longer play the rôle of "the American aristocracy" assigned to them in connection with the lawyers as a class by De Tocqueville. The secret instinct that now makes the judges lean toward the Powers-that-Be would have to yield somewhat. For while the courts would doubtless continue to be vested with authority to protect the people against the usurpations of the legislature, they would be shorn of the power to perpetuate their own usurpations and misinterpretations of the public will. In other words, the courts would be reduced from their present privileged supremacy to the position of a coördinate branch of government, responsible, like the other branches, to the democratic sovereign.

This change in the position of the courts, we submit, is theoretically necessary and practically desirable. It is too late in the history of the world for the American people to give allegiance to the doctrine of the divine right of the judiciary. The courts are a necessary and useful instrument of democratic government, but they should be nothing more. So far as the Initiative would make them feel like the servants rather than the masters of the people, the results would be good from the standpoint of enlightened democracy. In the performance of their legitimate function of the guardians of the public interest against legislative and executive usurpations they would be sustained. In any attempts to shackle progress by outgrown precedents they would be sharply overruled.

CHAPTER VI

In a modern community, with all its interwoven interests, the formulation of governmental policies is a complex and delicate process. The very highest type of ability, coupled with the widest and deepest knowledge of social conditions, is necessary for the proper exercise of the legislative function. It is often alleged that the Initiative, in its ordinary form, would throw the process of legislation into the hands of the mob, subject to the use of designing miscreants and of hare-brained reformers alike. Such a proceeding, it is said, would be like leaving the most complex modern machinery, which can be operated only by intelligent mechanics after long and careful training, to be manipulated by any blundering hod-carrier or ditch-digger or even by any tramp that comes along. Concocted in the brains of agitators, not subjected to the impact of criticism during the process of its formulation, drafted in secrecy in profound disregard of expert knowledge, filled with iridescent promises which even the Almighty could not fulfill, measures proposed by the Initiative, it is alleged, would reduce government to chaos and in time overthrow democracy itself. Great stress is laid upon the advantages of the ex-

77

perience of practiced law-makers, of discussion in legislative committees, of public hearings, of debate in the newspapers, of the compromises made necessary by conflict of opinion and of other factors in the ordinary process of legislative enactment by representative assemblies.   It is alleged not only that Initiative measures will be unscientifically drafted, but that the people will be unable to understand them and thus will be wholly disqualified for discriminating between wise proposals and foolish ones.

This criticism, it seems to me, is guilty of a triple error.   It overvalues the results obtained and the methods used in present practice.   It undervalues the intelligence of the people and the probability of care and wisdom in bill-drafting under the Initiative.   It ignores the fact that the Initiative is not designed to supplant the representative assembly entirely, but rather to supplement and correct the ordinary legislative process in exceptional cases.

That legislation produced by representative assemblies in America is often woefully deficient in scientific design as well as in accuracy of expression is a fact too well known to require proof.   It only requires explanation.

Congress, the state legislatures, and city councils generally, except where the commission form of government has been adopted, are composed of men elected by and from districts.   In the constitution of these bodies the aim has been, not to secure skillful law-makers or men with the widest knowledge of public affairs, but rather to get local representatives of the dominant public sentiment of every political subdivision.   In

cities, where population is largely segregated according
to occupation and social standing, the ward containing
a large proportion of the men of experience, education
and proven ability, has only the same representation
in the city council as the slum ward occupied princi-
pally, so far as residence is concerned, by the un-
thrifty, the ignorant, the unassimilated foreigners and
the transients who live in lodging houses. Though the
slum ward may contain the business district with its
skyscrapers, its unthinkable land values and its teem-
ing day population, including the strongest and best-
educated men in the city, no one who does not sleep
in the ward is permitted to vote there or to be elected
to represent the ward in the city council. Moreover,
the constant movement of a growing city's population
toward the outlying districts usually results in giving
the down-town wards, with their least-fit citizenship,
a disproportionate influence in the council. Almost
always it is many years after the outlying wards, with
their more enterprising citizenship, have outstripped
the down-town wards, with their grog shops, their vice
districts, and their lodging-house dwellers, before
the ward boundaries are readjusted so as to equalize
population. These faults are not inherent in the representative system, but they are characteristic of that
system as established in American cities. No doubt
the English plan of allowing men to vote where their
business is and of permitting the selection of non-
residents to represent the local subdivisions, would
greatly improve the character of our city councils
and, by the same token, improve the quality of the
legislation produced by them.

Another reason for the inferior results obtained from the law-making bodies of American cities may be found in the nominating methods in vogue. With few exceptions, candidates for aldermen or councilmen are nominated by the local branches of the national political parties and without due reference to their fitness for the duties of their offices or for the representative character of their opinions on civic issues. There is a legitimate connection between municipal government and state and national government in so far as they are concerned with the same general problems from different viewpoints and in so far as the successful operation of the one is dependent upon the coöperation of the others. But the evil known as the prostitution of civic affairs to the interests of national and state politics has long been a real one, though it has been somewhat diminished in recent years by the growing pressure of local issues to be heard on their merits and by the increasing recognition in state and national politics of those issues that are closely related to municipal problems. In so far as municipal patronage is regarded as a pawn in the game of national politics, city councils cannot be expected to produce legislation of a high grade.

Still another cause of unscientific local legislation is the interference of special interests in the nomination, election and conduct of aldermen. The use of the city streets as locations for conducting private business, or for conducting public business for private profit, leads inevitably to organized efforts to control the city councils on behalf of interests inimical to the public welfare. The same thing results from the control of saloon licenses by the local legislature and from its control of contracts for public improvements. Whenever a special interest seeks to dictate the nomination or election of an alderman, or to constrain him to act in a particular way after he is elected, it strikes a treasonable blow at the intelligence and efficiency as well as the honesty of the representative body. Special interests are found supporting the men whose actions they can control in the particular matters that affect themselves. Wherever a special interest dominates, the general interest is neglected even when it is not positively opposed. Scientific legislation can be had only as a result of single-mindedness in the public service. Any influence that tends to befog or corrupt the morals of a representative body also tends to confound its intelligence.

If we turn from the city councils to the state legislatures, we find similar causes at work on a larger scale. True, the population of a state is better distributed than the population of a city. There is less segregation of the more intelligent and less intelligent classes. But the influence of national politics is just as baneful, and often more so, especially in the years when United States senators are to be elected. Then the personal fitness of the candidates for the legislature and even their views on state issues are likely to be subordinated to their attitude toward various aspirants for the senatorship. Often the money contributed by a senatorial aspirant or his friends pays the election expenses of legislative candidates. Under these circumstances, what hope is there of getting honest and intelligent legislation from a pseudo-representative body? In-

deed, the case with the state legislature is even worse
than that with the city council, for the sessions of the
former are held at the state capital far removed from
the immediate observation of the members' constituents, and there are usually only one or two sessions of
the legislature during a term of office, while in most
cities the council meets weekly throughout the year.
Thus the municipal legislature has the double advantage of continuous contact with the people and continuous application to the problems of legislation. State
legislators are generally ill-paid though they are required to be away from their homes and private business for long periods. The result is that the assemblies
are filled up largely with young lawyers seeking to
make acquaintances and get their names before the
public for professional purposes. It seems that almost
everything conspires to inefficiency in state legislatures.
When the corrupting influence of the railroads, the
insurance companies, the mine owners, the power interests, the transmission lines, and other concentrated
forces of capital investment or monopoly service, is
added to the other things, it is a matter of some surprise that the people get anything at all out of the
legislatures. As it is, the results are lamentable in the
extreme. The law governing any particular class of
corporations is often a crazy patchwork, the original
ill-fitting garment having been rendered less fit by
holes punched in it here and there for the benefit of
particular unruly members and later overlaid with
burlap or stuffed up with rags until the very sight of
it compels uproarious laughter or maddened disgust
except in the lawyers who made it or who profit by its

intricate defects. Even the limitations imposed upon
the legislature by the constitution as an expression of
the distrust of the people sometimes make the confusion
worse, for in its attempt to evade these limitations the
legislature resorts to the most ludicrous expedients of
language.

In Congress conditions are little better, though the
longer terms of senators and the despotic organization
of experience in the House tend to give to national
legislation the benefit of established practices. Moreover, there is no higher category of politics to which
national interests are subordinated in national elections.
But the Senate is still well sprinkled with millionaires
who have bought their way in by the expenditure of
enormous sums in the election and control of state
legislatures and with the legal minions of vast corporate
interests which have expended similar sums in similar
ways. Congress is farther removed from the immediate
surveillance of its constituents than even the state legislatures are, and to the vast special interests which seek
to control those bodies, other and powerful interests
are added in the form of gigantic trusts, tariff beneficiaries, and great financial institutions. Things have
come to such a pass that no matter how careful the
constituencies are in selecting representatives, the
intelligence and the conscience of the average high-
grade man are pretty sure to fail before the subtle
machinations, the specious arguments, and the manifold tyrannies of the power of concentrated wealth
seeking to protect or further to enlarge itself.

These reasons for the failure of the present methods
of legislation in city, state, and nation do not directly

impeach the representative system. The opponents of the Initiative may urge with considerable force that a remedy can be had by reconstituting the legislative branch of our government and removing the causes which have made representation a failure. Even if this were granted, it would be no argument in support of the objection that we are considering in this chapter. It would be no proof that the Initiative would lend itself to the enactment of unscientific legislation. On the other hand, as we shall see in a subsequent chapter, there is reason to believe that the necessary reconstitution of the legislative branch to make it efficient cannot be secured directly from the legislature itself. Abuses are perpetuated by their beneficiaries. If they are to be eradicated, it must be by outside agencies or at least by the overwhelming pressure of outside influences.

But it may be said that, of course, legislation is not actually drafted by legislators, but only passed upon by them. It may be said that the bills are usually drawn outside of the legislature by the people specially interested in them and then submitted to a vote, much as referendum measures are submitted to the people. It may be urged that the representative assembly being a compact body with a limited membership and yet containing duly accredited delegates from every locality of the state is even better qualified to discriminate between good and bad measures than the people themselves would be. But in practice the legislature does not confine itself to enacting or rejecting proposed legislation submitted to it, and the blundering processes of amendment which it pursues are one of the causes of inadequate and incoherent legislation. A measure drafted by administrative experts for the improvement of the public service or by special students of public policy for the purpose of crystallizing into law the progressive sentiment of the community with reference to a particular matter, often falls into hands, ignorant, or hostile, or both, when it is referred to the legislative committee appointed to consider measures relating to the same subject-matter. How appropriate it would be to submit the perfected plans for a suspension bridge to a tunnel contractor, who expected and hoped that all bridges would ultimately tumble into the river anyhow, for final amendment! What splendid results we could expect if a school curriculum, after being fashioned by the most skilled educators, were to be submitted to the teamsters' union, not for suggestions and criticism, but for final revision before it was installed in the public schools! Legislation may be improved by criticism while it is in the formative stage. It may even profit by the suggestions of its enemies. But it would be an imposition upon credulity to assert that proposed legislation is benefited by being amended and enacted by those who are indifferent or hostile to its success, or who do not understand what it is about. The very process of amendment in the hurry and confusion of an ordinary legislative session, in the midst of the complex play of political, factional, and personal forces, is particularly conducive to blundering. In this environment the gentle art of joking has been so seriously cultivated that the first impulse of the inquisitive citizen when he gets hold of a new law is to look for the "jokers."

When the terrors of unscientific legislation move the conservative soul to oppose the Initiative, we should hardly expect to hear pæans in praise of the legislature or the board of aldermen.

As a matter of fact the process of legislating by the Initiative is much less disorderly and unintelligent than the objectors would have us think. While there are undoubted advantages in the consideration of legislative measures in committee with provision for public hearings and amendment, the Initiative method also has its advantages. If a measure as drafted by its proponents should happen to be hopelessly unscientific and ill-constructed, this fact would inevitably come out in the newspapers, on the stump and in the corner groceries. If the people enacted the measure, in spite of this knowledge, experience would soon teach them their error, and it would not be long before Initiative measures would be subjected to a much more relentless and searching criticism than is now applied to measures in the legislature. There would be no hope for an ill-drawn bungling attempt at law-making when the people got accustomed to the fact that a measure drafted by the best experts in the community could be brought to a vote simply by the filing of a petition. The natural result would be that any group of citizens desiring to invoke the Initiative would take the utmost care in drafting their measure, employing the best available skill in all complex cases. This course would be necessary if they hoped to avoid the waste of time, money, and effort incident upon a futile use of the Initiative. If once the lesson is learned that Initiative measures must be carefully drafted, the opportunity for scientific legislation along certain lines will be much greater under the Initiative than through the legislature. Certainly an act can be more carefully drafted in the freedom of voluntary councils in the house of its friends with such public discussion or private inquiry as may be necessary to check it up against the possible arguments of its opponents, than in legislative committees and secret partisan gatherings where every big bill is likely to be a reluctant concession to outside pressure or a compromise between conflicting views, and in either case, unsatisfactory to everybody. Initiative measures will naturally relate to issues that have been much discussed and in which there is already a considerable public interest. Under these circumstances, it is fortunate rather than the contrary that the measure as originally drafted by those who offer it for enactment cannot be emasculated or confused by hostile or variant amendments. This makes the issue simple and clear; it avoids the quagmire of parliamentary sharp practice; it keeps the question the same at the end that it was at the beginning of debate.

If the Initiative provides for submission of the proposed measure to an expert counselor or commission to pass upon its form before the circulation of the petitions, and if the measure is referred to the legislature for criticism and report with the right to submit an alternative or amended measure along with the one petitioned for, it would seem that the qualms of our scientific friends should be satisfied. When we add that no one proposes the Initiative as a general substitute for the action of legislative bodies, but only as a supplementary and exceptional means of securing fundamental reforms not easily secured through the defective legislative machinery now available, the objection that the Initiative would result in unscientific legislation is left without any support in reason. Indeed, one of the most likely uses of the Initiative would be to reconstruct the legislative machinery in such a way as to restore the truly representative character of Congress, the state legislatures, and the municipal councils, to the end that the legislative mill may produce something for human consumption more digestible than shredded straw.

CHAPTER VII

FIFTH OBJECTION TO THE INITIATIVE—THAT IT WOULD LEAD TO RADICAL LEGISLATION

Is the untrammeled majority radical or conservative? We all know that the trammeled majority, hedged in by the Federal constitution, rebuked by the judiciary, exploited by the trusts and the public service corporations, outwitted by the political bosses, flattered by the demagogic press and ridiculed by the organs of plutocracy, often shows signs of impatience, which, under cumulative provocation, might blossom out into radicalism. Indeed, there are not wanting signs that the American people, in the course of a century or so, unable to learn the lesson of servility, might flame up into revolution if their constitutional collar were not kept properly lubricated. Yet the radicals allege that the majority is normally conservative, while the conservatives allege that it has certain unmistakable tendencies toward radicalism, and in any case is not to be trusted. Strange to say, the radicals urge the conservatism of the majority as the best of reasons for unleashing it and seeing what it will do. It certainly is a curious thing that there should be such an atmosphere of uncertainty about the characteristic tendencies of this leviathan which De Tocqueville found in supreme control of American governmental agencies eighty years ago.

It would seem that the lawyers must have been too smart for it. They must have been quite successful in giving democracy "an impulse which diverts it from its real tendency." The American people must have been repeatedly "checked and stopped by the almost invisible influence of its legal counselors." The American advocates of the Initiative even now, in the twentieth century, feel themselves compelled to appeal to Switzerland to prove how the majority acts where it has a free hand. To be sure, they also cite Oregon's experience since 1902, but the Declaration of Independence was signed in 1776. How does it come that we have to skip a period of 125 years and jump across a continent of free states to the extreme western coast to find a majority openly at work in an American commonwealth? How elusive are the habits of this mysterious monster, the Majority!

The objection to the Initiative that it would lead to radical legislation is closely allied in certain respects to the objection that it would lead to the tyranny of the majority. This alliance applies particularly to the alleged danger of radical legislation affecting injuriously the rights of vested property. Will the poor majority oppress and rob the rich minority, undermining the sacred foundations of the state by radical measures clothed in the forms of law? If we have the Initiative, will confiscation run riot in the land? Will the citadels of capital be sacked and its temples despoiled? We cannot say for certain. It appears that the people as a whole, when educated, are a good deal like the lawyers as a class. If prevented from having a goodly share in the accumulations of social wealth, they are likely to become "the foremost agents of revolution." In other words, in a country where human beings are pretty generally educated, the concentration of the ownership or control of wealth in a few hands gives rise to a dangerous social condition. The majority, if both intelligent and hungry, might make a new definition of conservatism to suit its own case. It might become interested in conservation and read the meaning of that word into the word conservatism. It might in time allege that the conservation of the natural resources of the earth for the common benefit of all the people in this and succeeding generations is a conservative policy. It might allege that the conservation of the health and opportunities for happiness of all human beings is a conservative policy. It might even go so far as to assert that a conservative financial policy would require cities to conserve the reservoir of wealth created by their own growth for public use and devote the income from the unearned increment of land values to pay the outgo caused by the undeserved decrement of natural resources in cities. If the majority should get to playing on the words conservatism and conservation, there is no telling into what unfathomable heresies it might fall. We cannot vouch for it. Still, nothing is certain in this life but death and taxes, so they say, and it seems there would be nothing to do under the Initiative but for us all to take our chances together.

The fact is that contented men are conservative. Discontented ones are either radicals or reactionaries according to their point of view and according to the point of view of those who classify them. A certain

amount of healthful discontent is generally considered
to be a good thing as a stimulus to progress, but when
discontent becomes sullen or vicious and at the same
time widespread it is indicative of social disorders
that demand attention. The ideal condition of a
people is one of general happiness tempered by ambition to explore the possibilities of life as yet unknown
or not fully known. If at any particular time or in
any particular place this condition does not prevail,
whatever measures may be necessary to bring it about
must be taken, whether they be radical or reactionary.

The potential radicalism of the people that is
feared by the opponents of the Initiative is not
very clearly outlined. Yet there are fluid in American political society certain thoughts which continually try to crystallize themselves into law and, not
succeeding very well under the present legislative
system, look with hope to the unfettered rule of the
majority promised by the Initiative. Among the most
persistent of these are single tax, socialism, government
ownership of public utilities, control of corporations,
regulation of rates and prices, expansion of the social
functions of municipal government, enlargement of
the people's direct participation in government, the
democratization of the monetary system, and regulation of the conditions of labor. All such thoughts
tend to disturb the peace of mind of those who distrust
democracy. And yet Germany and England, without
the Initiative, and even without the republican form
of government, have progressed much further along
most of these lines than the United States has. It does

not even appear that Switzerland, the home of the Initiative, is more radical than Germany and Britain. Indeed, it is said that the Swiss people, exercising the full prerogatives of sovereignty, have proven themselves less progressive than their own representatives. It is not clear that the Saxon race, even as modified in the United States, loves novelty. The mass of the people is a great conservative force. It is difficult to move it with a new idea. But many of the radical thoughts mentioned above are not new. The people have pondered on them. Doubtless, in regard to some of them the people are ready to take action. How the socialist program or the single-tax program will fare in the long run at the hands of the Initiative it is impossible to foretell with certainty. There may even be some doubt as to what the people will do concerning the ownership and operation of public utilities, urban and national. Yet unquestionably the movement for municipal ownership will get a forward impulse from the general introduction of the Initiative. It may also be safely predicted that the movement for the expansion of municipal activities to include a more ambitious program of recreation, housing reform, industrial education, health protection, and so forth, will be stimulated by the Initiative. The regulation of the conditions of labor, with special reference to dangerous occupations and to the employment of women and children, will doubtless be carried further and faster under the Initiative, at least for a time, than it is now being carried by the legislative assemblies within the limitations imposed upon them by the courts. The people are also inclined to go far enough in the regulation of corporations to establish once for all the supremacy of the state over its own creatures. The people are inclined to think that a corporation's only right is the right to be of service, and if the service it renders is only to private interests and especially if in rendering this service it runs counter to the general welfare of the people, it has no claim upon the state for protection or even for the continued privilege of existence. In the regulation of rates and prices the people might temporarily go to extremes in their eagerness to get services and commodities cheap and to cut off the nourishment of the parasitic classes. Yet the unsoundness of the policy of lowering rates to the point where public utilities cannot maintain themselves in good condition for service is a lesson that will be quickly learned as soon as the people have full responsibility in the matter and have made provision limiting the profits of franchise monopolies to a fair return upon legitimate investment and a sufficient reward for operating efficiency.

In regard to the movement for more general direct participation of the voters in the affairs of government, of which the Initiative itself is one manifestation, this instrument will undoubtedly be used to accelerate the change. With the Initiative the people will get direct nominations, the Recall, the commission form of government, the short ballot, and any other reform that for the time being seems to further the opportunities of democracy. With the Initiative the people are likely to keep tinkering with the governmental machine until they get it to go to suit them. Some persons expect them to get the machine so that it will not go at all. But democracy means government by the people. Surely government affects all the people and is therefore of universal interest to them. It is not a mysterious category of activity far beyond the ken of the average man. Its purposes are simple and patent to every citizen. Suffrage is a part of its processes. If the masses of the people are now qualified to select men to conduct the government, they certainly can become qualified by practice to participate in other ways in the service of the state. The country surely will suffer no harm from the increasing intelligence of its people. They cannot find anything better to do than to busy themselves during their leisure hours with the affairs of state. Some folks who fear the radicalism of the majority proclaim the ignorance and incompetence of the people as if it were a fine national asset, something to be cherished in perpetuity at any cost. Their point of view is wrong. Society is pledged to popular enlightenment. Any class that desires to monopolize knowledge and wisdom deserves no consideration and will not receive any.

Unquestionably, the Initiative will open the door to radical legislation. That is what it is for, if the word radical is defined etymologically. Legislation that goes to the root of the matter is what the people want and what the conditions of the age demand. Yet there is no reason to suppose that freak measures will, in the long run, have any chance at the polls. The people simply want to get things to moving by clearing away the artificial obstacles put in the way of legislative progress by the predatory or self-complacent interests that have captured the machinery of representative government. In the issuance of state or municipal bonds, the people even now act as a check upon the recklessness and extravagance of their representatives. It is fairly certain that some of the radical groups now favoring the Initiative will suffer many setbacks and disappointments in its use. It may be that they will sometimes long to bring back the era of final authority vested in the legislature. They may conclude that it would be easier to persuade a small body of representatives than the entire body of the citizenship. At any rate, whatever the event may be, we may have considerable confidence in the elemental soundness of the decisions of the majority, reached after free discussion in the habitual course of an experienced democracy. If the minds of the people will not respond to reason, we may suspect that something is the matter with the reason, for what is reason but the law of mind? and what is the law of mind except the manner in which the intelligence of the great body of mankind manifests itself?

The conservatives might as well throw down the gauntlet to the radicals. Socialism demands an answer. Single tax demands an answer. Municipal ownership demands an answer. Conservation of natural resources demands an answer. Unless the answer is forthcoming and unless it is such an answer as will convince the minds of the majority, these policies are bound to prevail. The Initiative offers a convenient means of formulating the issues in the great debate. There will be no appeal from the ultimate decision. We shall all have to abide by it. Then why should conservatism, armed with its prestige, with its accumulated wisdom and its immense resources, with its imposing array of cunning counsel and valiant editors, shrink from the contest of wits? Does it insist that there is "nothing to arbitrate"? Is it satisfied stolidly to hold to things-as-they-are? If so, the debate will be quite one-sided, and the victory will be adjudged to the radicals by default.

The Initiative is an orderly and peaceful way of making complaint. The jury is large and patient. The burden of proof is on the plaintiff. Why should we expect the defendant, if his cause is just, to refuse to come into court?

CHAPTER VIII

SIXTH OBJECTION TO THE INITIATIVE—THAT IT WOULD BE USED BY SPECIAL INTERESTS TO GET THE BETTER OF THE PEOPLE

THUS far we have been considering objections to the Initiative that have their origin in conservatism. We now come to one that arises out of radicalism. It is by the friends of the people that we are warned against the wiles of the privilege-seekers. It is said that public contracts and franchise grants are different from ordinary legislation. They create vested rights which cannot be disturbed even by subsequent vote of the electors while the constitutional guaranties of the sacredness of contracts and the inviolability of property remain. It is pointed out that at certain stages of a city's development, when the ambition to grow and get rich quick is strong upon it, the people will vote almost any kind of a franchise in order to secure public utilities without delay. It is a notorious fact that real estate developers and, indeed, any group of citizens in dire distress for artificial lighting, telephone communication or street car transportation, will bring tremendous pressure upon the public authorities to induce them to grant the necessary franchises to companies willing to provide the service. At such times the insistent citizens take offense at aldermen who inquire too curiously into the terms and conditions of proposed franchises. To stand in the way of public improvements is considered almost sufficient cause for the revival of the ancient Greek institution of ostracism. Because of this attitude of the people toward public utilities, which is likely to manifest itself on a large scale at some critical time in the history of every city and is always characteristic of certain groups of citizens, it is said that public service corporations would be able to secure privileges by the use of the Initiative which they could never get through the more tortuous channels of aldermanic procedure.

It cannot be denied that the Initiative affords a company the opportunity to draft a franchise to suit its own desires and secure the submission of the proposed grant unamended to popular vote. A company already rendering a public utility service has the organization, the money in hand and the widespread influence required for a successful canvass for signatures to an Initiative petition. Its advantages in this respect over a voluntary organization of citizens having no large financial interest at stake are ten-fold. With the opportunity to draft a franchise for itself and with the ability easily to secure the necessary petition, what is to prevent a company from securing a renewal or an enlargement of its rights upon its own terms? The answer is, nothing but the ill-will or the canniness of the electorate. Although popular ill-will towards public service corporations seems to be generally chronic, there are some indications that the people's good will could easily be secured for the companies by friendly and direct treatment.

Public resentment is only partly due to indifferent service and excessive rates. It is sometimes due in even greater measure to the suspicion of corrupt dealings with public officials and of exorbitant profits hidden in secret accounts. If a company changes its tack and "takes the people into its confidence," eschewing all negotiations with the aldermen, who are no longer the final arbiters of the matter anyhow, there may be a sudden reversal of the characteristic popular ill-will and instead of it an easy-going good nature may manifest itself, with the result that the company only has to ask favors to receive them. While friendly co-operation between the people and the corporations is a good thing for peace and progress, they should not be too convivial together, for if the people should "get under the table" the companies might go through their pockets.

It is also urged that the people are not qualified to give a franchise the careful scrutiny it deserves. Franchises are notorious for what they are not. They may read very well, indeed, to the casual glance, when in fact they are nothing but resolutions of confidence. It takes a practiced eye with the help of an X-ray to see their hidden significance. Moreover, if the people once breathe the breath of life into them, they become the most persistent of living creatures. A cat is nothing to a franchise. And so, the companies have every incentive to take advantage of the people's necessity to force unwise concessions from them, or of their good will to impose upon their credulity. When extensions are sorely needed, it may be the promise of them that catches the people's favor. When the city treasury is low, it may be a good-looking lump sum. When the old system is reduced to a bag of bones, it may be immediate rehabilitation. When public ownership is a popular cry, it may be a high-sounding purchase clause. When service is poor or rates exorbitant, it may be the promise of competition or low fares.

All this sounds quite reasonable, but in a number of cities the people have already actually proven themselves to be keen critics of franchise propositions. There is certainly no reason to believe that worse franchises, on the whole, would be granted by popular vote than are now granted by city councils and state legislatures. As a matter of fact, most franchises heretofore granted have been originally drafted by the applicants for them, though they have often been amended considerably by the public bodies granting them. It may be urged that the Referendum on franchises will be a sufficient check upon corporate desires, without the Initiative, while at the same time avoiding the dangers set forth in this chapter. But there is no policy more vital to the future welfare of a city and the freedom of its citizens than its franchise policy. There is no interest more likely to dominate a legislative body and choke its expression of the people's will than a public service corporation. In order to get a rational franchise policy established, the people may need the Initiative. If the people of any given locality are prevented by the terms of the general law from bartering away the public rights of future generations, the dangers of the Initiative in franchise-granting are not sufficient to overbalance its advantages. Yet, perhaps, the process of establishing contractual relations between the cities and the public

service corporations should be somewhat more carefully guarded than the general Initiative. Besides the
general limitations contained in the constitution and
laws of the state, special procedure might well be required in the granting of franchises. More copious
advertising, longer delay before the election, reference
to a skilled board or officer for report upon the merits
of the measure, and other precautionary steps, may be
taken to guarantee full consideration of the project
on its merits and to prevent snap judgment. The
greatest danger under such circumstances would be
the subsidizing of the newspapers to favor the franchise
and to suppress the news of adverse discussion of the
question. In most large cities, however, there remains
a rivalry between newspapers keen enough to furnish
an organ for any important franchise criticism. If the
newspapers fail, a virile. opposition can have recourse
to bill-boards and public meetings, and the very fact
of newspaper unanimity under subsidy or the suspicion
of subsidy will strengthen the opposition.

The main precautions to be taken with regard to the
use of the Initiative in granting special privileges are,
first, the limitation of the power of the municipality
to alienate the rights of future generations; second, the
reservation in the general laws of the state of the right
to regulate public utilities in excess of their specific
franchise conditions, and third, to surround the Initiative procedure with all the safeguards necessary to
insure public deliberation and understanding before
the vote is taken.

It is to be expected that, in learning to use the
Initiative as an instrument of democratic government,

the people will pass through a stage of experiment, in which they will have to rebuke not only public service corporations seeking to get favors from them, but also many other kinds of special interests having a pecuniary stake in legislation proposed by themselves. It may be the school-teachers, or the letter-carriers, or the policemen, proposing legislation for the increase of their own pay. It may be the brewers trying to knock holes through the liquor law. It may be the labor unions trying to outlaw the open shop. It may be any compact body or class of men, even though constituting a small minority of the people, offering some legislation for their own benefit or for the advancement of their pet ideas. But the expense involved in securing petitions and the experience of standing up to be counted and incidentally to show how few in numbers they really are, will soon have a deterrent effect upon their use of the Initiative where it is certain to fail. A special private interest is always in the minority in a large community and can be beaten every time it calls for a count of noses. Of course, there is some danger of the people's being wearied by much importunity, and letting a minority have its way in a moment of apathy. But even that is not necessarily fatal. The aroused majority will still have the power of repeal, except in the case of contracts, and for them special safeguards have already been recommended. Certainly, we have less reason to fear the tyranny of the minority under the Initiative than we now have under the unchecked caprices of representative bodies.

CHAPTER IX

FIRST ARGUMENT IN FAVOR OF THE INITIATIVE—THAT IT WOULD UTILIZE THE INDIVIDUAL IN POLITICS

IT is a matter of grave wonder to the student of politics who divests himself for a moment of the habitual attitude of toleration toward familiar things to see how tragically stupid and short-sighted in many directions American government is. The average American city is a monument of lost and neglected governmental opportunities. The cities go lumbering on guided by policies that are known to be futile or even criminal in their tendencies. Political inertia perpetuates abuses. Perpetual or improvident franchise-grants; deadly congestion of population; the encouragement of mere size, with its hideous smoke, and dust, and noise; the taxation of personalty on assessments that are mere guesses and can be sworn off entirely by those who regard an oath merely in a Pickwickian sense; the pouring of sewage into the water supply; the cultivation of debt as if it were the city's best friend; the maintenance of a police force for the protection of vice and crime that will divide the spoils; the pumping of vast quantities of water into a distribution system that is full of leaks; the city's conspiracy against the virtue of women, the joy of children, and the reward of labor—

all these and more meet the astonished gaze of the student who looks out upon American city life as it is. If we turn to the states, we have the spectacle of expensive, loose-jointed, blundering machines that fuss about what they ought not and that ignore what they ought to concern themselves with. Great commonwealths allow their forests to be destroyed by fire; their soils to be washed away by the unchecked flow of the waters; their agricultural lands to be "mined" by ruthless adventurers who call themselves farmers; their water powers, their minerals, their oils and their gases to be clutched in the fingers of monopoly; their courts and their lawyers to consume the substance of the poor and tire out justice by unconscionable delays and technical quibbles; their corporate creatures to tangle themselves up beyond the power of control in order to lend themselves more effectively to the service of genteel thieves; their departments of government to remain disorganized and impotent. The nation as a whole does little better. It sleeps while the liberties of its people are being destroyed through local prejudice. It makes the people pay several dollars in taxes to the trusts for every dollar paid into the United States treasury. It makes princely gifts to the railroads and then allows the companies to charge rates that will pay dividends on the appreciated value of these gifts. It is useless to attempt to give a complete list of our governmental follies. Some of them are controversial, not so much because the facts are disputed as because we like some kinds of folly and some of us like all kinds.

I do not speak of these shortcomings of American

political institutions primarily as evidences of wickedness and corruption, but rather as proofs of the backwardness and unfitness of the governmental methods heretofore followed for coping with the situation. In every line of useful work, there is a demand for men with initiative. Now, it seems to me that America's greatest governmental failure is its neglect to take full advantage of individual initiative in politics. I do not make odious comparisons. I do not know but that, on the whole, our government is as efficient in promoting human freedom as any other. We may, indeed, surpass all others. But the facts of positive failure remain. Democracy is necessarily progressive. We ought to do better than the rest of the world in order to justify ourselves. We ought, of all things, to be able to adopt reforms where the recognition of their need is universal. But in practice we find that hoary evils are sheltered in the alcoves of the constitution or in the lean-tos built on to it by the courts. When attacked they retreat to this temple and cast themselves upon the altar. If a hand is raised against them it is stricken with palsy for the sacrilege. Under this hard and fast system, the priesthood of privilege has established itself. Great party organizations, in close alliance with protected interests, stand guard over the sacred relics of old governmental futility. While science and art and commerce and industry rush on to new and wondrous conquests, politics is in stripes, chained to the iron ball. Progress in all those wide fields that represent private interest is welcomed, but in government, alas, is not that which was good enough for our grandfathers good enough for us? Having established a government with instructions never to interfere with the free play of private interests except to subsidize them, what else can we expect but that it will be out-run?

The curse of our politics is apathy. The people work themselves up into a state of considerable excitement over the personal drama of office-seeking. But office-seeking is not politics. When it comes to real issues of state, they are generally so befogged at election time as to render the people well-nigh helpless in regard to them. Men elected on different tickets turn out to be servants of the same system. Men who were supposed to be honest as private citizens, fall under a mysterious spell when they get into office. Time after time the people elect men who betray them. The result is discouragement and indifference. At one time a few citizens, aroused to keen interest in public affairs, set forth to secure reform. They find it necessary to exert themselves tremendously in order to make any headway at all, and straightway when discouraged by experience of the difficulties in the way or driven by economic necessity, they lay down their arms and go back to business, all their effort comes to naught and the ancient order stands out triumphant with nothing changed except for the addition of a few more battle scars to swell the pride of the old guard. A new attack is made at another time by another group of enthusiasts who have awaked to the hope of political progress. The same fortress is assaulted, though perhaps from a little different angle, and the same result is obtained. The party organization is the standing army. The political reformers are the unorganized insurrectionists armed

only with clubs and brickbats. Mutiny inside the army
is followed by a court-martial and summary execution.
The legislator who refuses to be transformed upon his
induction into office is a marked man among his colleagues. He is regarded as a traitor to his class. He
finds his efforts blocked in every direction. Beaten
and discouraged, he retires to private life, destined to
a harder struggle than he had before, while his more
complaisant colleagues are promoted to higher office
or rewarded with remunerative employment in private
life. The executive who stands out for the reorganization of governmental departments and the installation
of efficient methods, finds himself opposed at every
point by the great conservative force of the old order.
Whatever he accomplishes, it will be at the cost of
great sacrifices, and when his term of office expires
he is likely to be repudiated with all his reforms by the
organization that controls his party. The institution
of any real reform, cutting to the roots of time-honored
abuses, requires a tremendous expenditure of personal
energy that saps the very life of the strongest man.
And so the dead hand of the past is laid upon us to
bind us and torture us with its invisible terrors till we
consent to acquiesce. American government is organized with an elaborate system of checks and balances
devised to hold things steady. Under this system
politics has become a privileged occupation, controlled
by the rules of caste. Individual initiative is penalized.
Lock-step is the mode of locomotion prescribed for
public servants.

Government is the most complex of all the functions
of society. In politics, if anywhere, there is need of all

the ability available for use. Nowhere else is it so imperative that individual initiative be rewarded, not penalized. New ideas, new methods of adaptation, new reservoirs of personal energy are always potentially in demand. The state is hungry for them. It is of the very essence of democracy that the whole people should freely participate in government. Only thus can leadership spring forth from the ranks, and without leadership democracy has neither eyes to see, nor feet to walk, nor hands to build.

The Initiative, as its very name implies, is designed to unlock for the uses of the state all the potential political capacity of the people. With this tool at hand, political ideas go to a premium. Willingness to "take orders" ceases to be the prime qualification of an assemblyman, a mayor, or a magistrate. If a boss-ridden city council, or state legislature, or Congress refuses to give ear to the ideas of a member, even though he stand alone, he has an instrument at hand by which he can appeal from his colleagues to the people. If he is fighting the people's battles, he cannot be driven from the representative assembly at the end of a single term with the odium of practical failure upon him. If it is a mayor, a governor or a president who is hampered at every point in his program of reform by a reactionary legislative branch, he need not submit to bartering offices with the legislative leaders or to defeat as the result of his refusal to barter. He can appeal to the people and by an orderly and sure procedure carry his purposes through, if the people approve of them, in spite of the hostility of legislative and party leaders. If it is the case of a private citizen, who under the old system would have been compelled to spend himself without stint with no assurance whatever of accomplishing any practical result, he can now formulate his ideas and invoke the Initiative to force them to an issue before the people. Indeed, with this instrument available for use, a private citizen or a group of private citizens may hold a more advantageous position for constructive statesmanship even than an elected legislator or executive, for the private citizens will not be hampered by limited terms of office or by a multiplicity of other public duties. Their work in formulating and carrying into law a definite body of policies calculated to cure some of the deep-seated evils in our present government can be carried on indefinitely. They are not compelled to give up their private business entirely for a time and then return to it exclusively, but they can work along as time and means permit, without great waste of energy and with reasonable hope of success if their efforts are intelligent and directed toward a proper end. The advantage of the Initiative may be seen especially in the case of men who have already had practical experience as legislators, executives, or magistrates, and who in the leisure time of their subsequent private life can devote themselves to working out the legislative reforms of which they saw the need while they were in office. The Initiative thus gives fluidity to politics, opens the door to the free application of ideas, constantly invites new leadership into the field of government, disarms the reactionary forces in the legislative body and conserves for the public weal the experience of public servants who have retired from office.

Government is badly behind in its task. It needs all the help it can get from citizens. The Initiative would tend to free for the uses of the state the potential political wisdom and energy of all the people.

CHAPTER X

SECOND ARGUMENT IN FAVOR OF THE INITIATIVE—THAT
IT WOULD RESULT IN THE DRAFTING OF NEW LAWS
BY THOSE WHO WISH THEM TO SUCCEED

BILLS introduced in the legislature are frequently the handiwork of outside parties, either persons having a pecuniary interest in the proposed legislation, or persons engaged in other branches of the government service or persons or organizations taking special interest in public affairs from patriotic motives. Whatever may be the actual origin of legislative bills, they are subject to amendment in committee either by the legislators on their own motion or at the solicitation of outside parties. This power of amendment sometimes makes a bad bill good, and sometimes makes a good bill better, but often it makes a good bill weak and ineffective. When special interests seek legislation for their own benefit, it is a fine thing to have their bills scrutinized with a sharp eye and worked over for the protection of the public interests. When legislation is proposed in awkward and incoherent forms, it is well to have legislative committees whip the measures into shape before enacting them. But when progressive legislation in the general interest is sought, the opportunity for amendment in the course of legislative procedure is often abused by hostile members who dare

not openly oppose the measure. It is the despair of
reform to see its measures fall into the hands of the
legislative surgeons who proceed to emasculate them,
pull their teeth, or reduce them to ineptitude in some
other way. Reform measures are often amended by
hostile legislatures for the very purpose of causing
them to fail, until sometimes reformers are driven to
oppose their own schemes after they have been wrought
over by the subtle alchemy of treacherous friendship.
Although this process of killing off progressive legislation has become classic in American capitals and is
well known to the public, there are not wanting those
who are misled by the fallacy that compromises in
legislation bring good results. They fail to see that
legislative measures are tools, instruments, machines
for accomplishing certain things. There may properly
be compromises in the aims of legislation, but not in
the instrumentalities adopted for the fulfillment of
those aims. Legislation should always be designed to
be as effective as possible. Once its aim is settled, the
machinery should be adapted solely to the accomplishment of that aim with the least possible friction and
the greatest possible thoroughness.

One of the great advantages claimed for the Initiative
is that it would provide a method by which new legislation could be drafted by its friends and submitted to
a vote without amendment. Direct primary measures
intended as a cure for machine politics would not then
be worked over in the process of enactment until they
become instruments for the perpetuation of bossism.
Indeterminate franchises meant to perpetuate the public control of the streets would not then be per-

verted into perpetual privileges for unregulated spoliation. Grants of authority to municipalities to engage
in public services would not be made ineffectual by
the imposition of impossible financial conditions. The
men who want a measure to succeed could have the
framing of it. Those who want it to fail would be
restricted to voting against it at the polls. In this way,
issues would be simplified and reforms could be secured
promptly. The political struggle to secure them would
more often be clear-cut and brief. The intolerable
nuisance of having to fight year after year to secure a
particular reform inch by inch only to find when it is
finally secured in full measure that other abuses have
been growing up unheeded, would no longer be so common an experience. Instead of having to devote our
energies to a persistent, almost superhuman effort to
accomplish one little thing, we could deal with each
problem effectively as it presents itself and keep the
docket clear instead of having it perpetually cluttered
up with things needing attention but not getting it.

Work, to be most effective, must always be done with
the heart as well as the hand. The Initiative would
make it possible for the heart and the hand to work
together.

CHAPTER XI

THIRD ARGUMENT IN FAVOR OF THE INITIATIVE—THAT
IT WOULD ENABLE THE SOVEREIGN TO ENFORCE
ITS WILL WITHOUT THE CONSENT OF THE LEGIS-
LATURE

THE legislative branch is a mere agent of sovereignty.
It is theoretically unsound and practically disastrous
to allow of no changes in the constitution without the
legislature's consent. One of the principal concerns
of a constitution is the organization of the legislature
and the delimitation of its powers and duties. If we
have a system under which this organization cannot be
changed, nor these powers and duties either curtailed
or enlarged, except with the approval, perhaps even
on the initiative, of the department composed of men
having a personal interest in the matter, the logical
relation of master and servant is reversed. It is a case
of the tail wagging the dog.

The fathers did not altogether fail to perceive this
flaw in the theory of a government under which constitutional amendments could be initiated only by the
legislative branch. In framing the Federal constitution, they treated the separate states as the units of
sovereignty, and lest Congress should some time fail
to submit constitutional amendments required by the
will of the sovereign, an alternative method was estab-

lished by which two-thirds of the states acting together could take the initiative and compel the calling of a convention to submit amendments independent of Congress. But even here a considerable power of control was left in Congress, because of the fact that the details as to the number and qualifications of members of the convention, the method of their selection, the time and place of their first meeting and all other preliminary matters remained within congressional jurisdiction. Moreover, Congress was specifically authorized to determine whether the ratification of amendments should be by the state legislatures or by state conventions. It is readily seen that while a constitutional convention, once it is assembled, may become an independent body and throw off any shackles with which the legislature has tried to bind it, nevertheless the power of determining all the preliminary arrangements might easily be abused by Congress in order to influence the character of the convention. If, for example, Congress desired a convention that would be conservative and friendly to corporate interests, it could go a long way toward insuring this result by the method chosen for the selection of the delegates, by their distribution among the states and by their qualifications prescribed.

In some of the states the convention method of constitutional revision is put beyond the control of the legislature by a provision requiring the submission of the question of calling a constitutional convention to a vote of the people at stated intervals, and specifying how such a convention shall be constituted. Even in these cases the legislature has considerable leeway in

determining procedure, especially the nominating procedure. By an arrangement practically compelling the
use of the established machinery of political parties
in the selection of delegates the legislature may make
it very difficult for the people to elect delegates free
from narrow prejudices and partisan control. But in
most of the states even the question of calling a constitutional convention cannot be raised except by the
legislature.

This obstructive power of the legislative branch
in questions of constitutional revision is wholly illogical. But the trouble is not confined to constitutional
questions. It extends to the entire field of legislation
having to do with political procedure in which the
legislators personally or the parties they represent
have a special interest in maintaining the established
order or in changing it in some particular way. True,
there must be some place in which ultimate responsibility shall rest, but logically this can only be the electorate organized as the sovereign power of the state.
There can be no appeal beyond that except the final
appeal to the laws of nature enforced by the Judge of
the universe. On fundamental questions there is no
safety in the lodgment of the ultimate power of decision in any mere agent of sovereignty such as a
representative assembly.

The Initiative affords an available method for the
exercise of sovereignty without the consent of the
ordinary governmental agencies. It opens the way for
dealing with constitutional and political questions
directly and effectively, without the necessity of re-
versing the laws of human nature in order to compel

the legislature to act unselfishly in matters peculiarly
affecting its members. By what right of reason must
we first induce the United States Senate by a two-
thirds vote to consent to a change in the method of
election of its members before we can put the change
into effect? Indeed, when we are able to persuade
the Senate to consent, the very need for the change has
largely disappeared. It is because of the refractory
nature of the upper house of Congress that we have
long since desired to overhaul it by a new method of
selection. By what right of reason can we expect a
partisan legislature to consent to the establishment
of a non-partisan legislative ballot? Upon what
ground can we ask a municipal council elected by
wards to let us vote upon a plan to abolish ward representation and substitute a commission form of government? How can we appeal to a state legislature to
divest itself of the powers of interference in municipal
affairs? How can legislators and aldermen be expected
to forbid themselves to use railroad passes? Why should
they be allowed to fix their own salaries? It is a marvel
that under our existing system we have so often been
able to induce men vested with authority and profiting
by established conditions to commit political suicide.
It is as if we gave every felon a rope and told him to go
hang himself. Nothing but a vigilance committee
can issue such orders with any hope of their being
obeyed. It seems incredibly stupid that a democracy
should so tie itself up that it cannot take a step forward except by using moral suasion to induce unwilling
persons to lead the way. The American people must
dearly love the glory of doing difficult things. We must

regard government as a sort of national game, else we would not put hurdles in the path of political progress just to see how high we can jump. If we really regarded government as serious business, we would not make a road through the woods by felling the big trees forward and then trying to drive over them.

The Initiative would afford relief from a huge practical joke that we played on ourselves long ago. It has passed the humorous stage. Like the bride that hid herself in a trunk to provide a diversion for the wedding guests, we are getting short of breath. Under the Initiative we would be freed from the domination of our own representatives and it would be possible by direct action to solve the problems of the election law, of nominations for office, of municipal home rule, of party organization, of the qualifications and emoluments of legislators, of the restriction or expansion of legislative powers. These are the big questions in the development of practical democracy. We must have a free hand to deal with them, or democracy will not exist.

CHAPTER XII

FOURTH ARGUMENT IN FAVOR OF THE INITIATIVE—THAT
IT WOULD PROVIDE AN ORDERLY MEANS OF EXTEND-
ING OR RESTRICTING THE SUFFRAGE

PERSONS who have no vote are dependent for their
liberties upon force, moral suasion, or the sense of
justice of those who do have a vote. They have no
share in sovereignty. American political institutions
are founded on the principle that sovereignty abides
with the people, that from them all governments
spring. It would seem to be a general corollary of this
principle, that the right of suffrage should be enjoyed
by every human being. But practical considerations
have led at various times to the exclusion of certain
classes of individuals from the electorate.

The first great limitation on the principle of universal
suffrage relates to children. Obviously, a share in the
authoritative control of society cannot be exercised
by persons so physically and mentally immature that
they are unable to care for themselves in the ordinary
affairs of life. While there is a tendency in a democratic society to relax the harsh discipline of children
that is elsewhere practiced, there is no thought of the
possibility of permitting them to assume complete independence. During the period of immaturity, the
process of reproduction is still incomplete. Individuals

not yet grown and educated are and ought to be subject
to the control of others. This rule does not permanently
exclude anyone from participation in sovereignty, but
merely postpones such participation until the individual
has become an adult. The only practical difficulty here
is in determining when a person is really grown up.
Shall the test be an arbitrary one, such as the arrival
at a certain age, or shall it be an individual one requiring special proofs of physical and mental maturity?
All arbitrary rules, all rules that deal with men as if
they were all alike, necessarily involve some injustice.
One person reaches physical maturity before another.
One becomes capable of self-direction before another.
Indeed, a few people never get over being children
so far as their mental development is concerned. Nevertheless, a rough sort of justice is secured by the
adoption of an arbitrary age limit at which individuals
shall be admitted to the suffrage. In America it is
twenty-one years; in Germany it is twenty-five. In
ancient Sparta it was thirty, while in Athens it was
only sixteen. The temporary hardship to the individual
and the loss to the state resulting from the continued
disfranchisement of those extraordinary young persons
who have attained wisdom a few years in advance of
the average have not been considered of sufficient
importance to warrant a departure from the arbitrary
age rule. Yet there is no reason why democracy should
be permanently satisfied with such a rough and easy
measure of maturity as a qualification for voting. It
may at some future time see fit to modify the standard
so that persons who are specially qualified will be admitted to the suffrage before they are twenty-one,

while others who are exceptionally deficient will not
be admitted until they have reached a more mature
age.   A civil service examination for all applicants
for the suffrage is not an unthinkable proposition.

The second great limitation on the principle of universal suffrage has to do with women, who still are
excluded in most parts of the country from general
participation in sovereignty.   This limitation, which at
one stroke reduces the adult electorate by half, is based
on a mixture of a number of theories and historical facts.
Women were at one time considered property, subject
to arbitrary control by their fathers, brothers, and hus-
bands.   Men, being physically stronger and holding
the weapons of war in their hands, established domin-
ion over women by virtue of physical force.   With the
gradual progress of the human race in civilization and
enlightenment, other theories have been invented to
support the continued lordship of the male, which for
personal reasons he was loath to give up.   It has been
to man's economic advantage to have power to make
woman work for him, but he has also been especially
solicitous about maintaining his superiority over her
in order that he might control her for sexual purposes.
He has, therefore, developed the theory of the natural
intellectual inferiority of the female sex.   He has attempted to prove that women always remain children
in the sense that they never attain to the full intellectual standard of adult, god-like manhood.   It is
natural, therefore, to keep them disfranchised along
with other immature creatures.   When this theory
proves to be unsatisfying, he turns naïvely to another.
He says that the work of the world is necessarily per-

formed by means of division of labor, and that in this division government falls to the lot of the men and house-keeping to that of the women. Voting is not woman's business. The family is a coöperative unit and the man represents it when he exercises the right of suffrage. He is designated to do for the group, consisting of man, woman, and children, this particular service. He votes, not arbitrarily, in his individual capacity, but as the organic representative of himself, his children, and his women folks. Even this theory experiences difficulty in the face of the fact that many adult females in modern society are nobody's "women folks" and so are unrepresented, and the corresponding fact that a large proportion of the males enjoying the suffrage are unattached men with nobody but themselves to represent. But the wish, if it is strong, can beget many thoughts. And so, a third theory is presented for our acceptance. We are told that women are vastly superior to men, especially in moral character, and that accordingly the use of the ballot is already controlled by them. "They are the power behind the throne." "The hand that rocks the cradle rules the world." It is urged that women do not need to soil their hands with politics. They would be stooping to a menial task. Men, after all, are merely their agents, doing the rough and dirty work for them. As a last resort, the men say that the women do not wish to vote. Mr. Roosevelt suggests that the question of the extension of the suffrage be left to a vote of the women themselves. This suggestion has the merit of recognizing in advance their right to the ballot, but it offers no explanation of why 5000 women who desire to vote should be prevented from doing so by 6000 other women who do not wish them to vote. If the men are prepared to offer the suffrage to women, sex thereby ceases to be recognized as a legitimate basis of political classification, and there is no reason whatever for permitting one woman who wants to vote to be deprived of the right to do so by other women. The very exercise of the privilege of voting on the question would be an admission of the appropriateness of woman suffrage and a negative vote would be a logical self-contradiction.

Another serious limitation on the principle of universal suffrage is based on the alleged inferiority of certain races as compared with the Caucasians. African slavery trained the white people of the Southern states through more than two centuries to regard the blacks as an inferior race, useful for service but intolerable for political and social coöperation. This view was bred in the bone until it became an instinct of the Southern nature. Democracy attempts to break down the barriers between races. Already Englishmen and Irishmen, Germans and French, Italians and Jews, Greeks and Hungarians, freely mingle with the native population to form the composite electorate of every large American city. There are many social and religious prejudices among them, but there is no longer any serious question of the advisability of permitting their equal participation in American sovereignty without regard to race. But Negroes are regarded as intrinsically and permanently inferior, as born to serve. Like children, "they should be seen, not heard." There is a similar prejudice in the far west against Orientals.

The American people have taken a positive constitutional stand to the effect that political rights shall not be withheld from any man "on account of race, color, or previous condition of servitude." In theory, therefore, the suffrage question is settled so far as the so-called inferiority of race is concerned. But practice in a large section of the country has resettled this question contrary to the decree of the constitution. Logically, the only reason for withholding the suffrage from a black or a yellow person, is that he never gets to be an adult human being. Yet it is well known that some black people and some yellow people do get to be stronger and more efficient men than the vast majority of whites. Race and color are mere arbitrary rough tests. To the proud southern Saxon these tests are nice enough, and yet it cannot be doubted that democracy will practically as well as constitutionally discard them, and determine the right of men to vote by other and better tests.

Besides these three great limitations of suffrage on account of immaturity, femininity, and race inferiority, there are numerous minor ones, such as non-residence, illiteracy, poverty, mental incompetence, and crime. In America, democracy has been very lenient in these matters. A residence of six months or a year within the particular state and of a much shorter time within the municipality and the voting precinct is required. Immigrants may become citizens in five years, and are often permitted to vote after they have taken the first steps towards naturalization. Educational qualifications, except where they are aimed at the color of the skin, are practically non-existent. There are a few scattering property or tax-paying qualifications left, but they are comparatively unimportant. Usually even the inmates of the poorhouse are allowed to vote. Only confined lunatics, imbeciles, and criminals are disfranchised. When not in confinement these groups even furnish recruits from time to time to the office-holding class.

When we urge that the Initiative would provide an orderly means for the restriction or the extension of the suffrage in accordance with the will of the majority and free from the interference of elected persons whose representative function makes it particularly inappropriate for them to tamper with the suffrage, we have to go by faith, not by sight. For here we have the ultimate trusteeship of sovereignty, the electorate, which, guided by its solemn responsibility as the fundamental organ of the state, is a self-perpetuating body. Conceivably, the electorate as it now exists might forever refuse to extend its privileges to any other person in the state. Conceivably, the electorate as it now exists might gradually reduce itself by a series of majority votes till it became a mere oligarchy. There is nothing to prevent this result except self-interest, sympathy, the sense of justice, the power of argument, and force.

Many conservative men believe that the suffrage is already too widely extended in this country. They believe in some tax-paying or educational qualification, or at least some permanent residential qualification that will disqualify the "floaters" with whose assistance city elections are sometimes carried by the powers of darkness. When the success of municipal ownership in Great Britain and Germany, or of the Referendum in Switzerland is mentioned as an argument for the general introduction of those policies in America, these conservative citizens deny the validity of the argument, saying that the conditions here are entirely different from the conditions abroad. Especially they point to our manhood suffrage as an insuperable barrier to the success of governmental undertakings in business. There can be no doubt that the suffrage is often abused in this country by venal, ignorant, and irresponsible voters, but they do not abuse it on their own initiative so much as on the initiative of powerful and intelligent men who hope to secure control of the government for their own purposes with the help of this abuse.

How much the suffrage would be extended or restricted under the Initiative we cannot tell. It seems reasonably certain that the majority of the present electorate in most American communities would vote for such moderate restrictions as would exclude from the suffrage the obviously undeserving and unfit. Probably, the majority would not hesitate to disfranchise the lodging-house population and those persons who cannot read and write. It is not likely that a property qualification could be established by vote of the electors. The spirit of democracy is strong in America, and few citizens are inclined to take away the fundamental rights of any of their fellows except on extreme provocation. On the other hand, under the Initiative it would be much easier to get the woman suffrage question submitted to a vote of the electors than it now is. Whether woman suffrage would fare better at the polls than in the legislatures is somewhat doubtful, except that every time the question is submitted it stirs up a state-wide discussion, and this alone is certain to help the woman suffragist cause as it does all causes identified with the further development of democracy.

After all, the extension or restriction of the suffrage is one of the most fundamental constitutional questions, and is not even now regarded generally as lying within the scope of the legislature. It is only in its power to maintain existing conditions by refusing to permit the amendment of the constitution that the legislature now has control of the suffrage except in certain minor matters. A vote of the people is necessary to make changes in the qualifications of the electorate. The Initiative would clear the way for a general discussion of the functions and responsibilities of the voters, with the inevitable result that, even if the basis of suffrage were not restricted, its significance would be better understood and the abuses of it lessened. The purely arbitrary qualifications such as sex and color could not long withstand the shock of reason, and democracy would at least have a chance to organize itself rationally for the performance of its political functions.

PART III
THE REFERENDUM

CHAPTER XIII

THE REFERENDUM EXPLAINED

THOUGH the Initiative usually involves the submission of a question to a vote of the people, or what is commonly known as a referendum, we should not fail to distinguish the Initiative from the Referendum as an instrument of democracy. The Initiative is the power of the people to do things without the consent of the legislature. It is a tool for use in carrying out a constructive program. It contains in itself alone the germ of complete democracy. The Referendum on the other hand is merely a popular veto on the acts of the legislative body. By means of it, the people have power to stop things, but not to make them go. It is an instrument of negation. It is conservative, while the Initiative is radical. It constitutes the electorate as a sort of fourth department of government, an additional check, another balance, but not as the supreme organ of sovereignty.

The Referendum has been widely used in America for a long time. It may be considered a well-established, though partially undeveloped American institution. Heretofore, it has been used mainly in connection with constitutional revisions and amendments, state and municipal bond issues, the adoption of city charters, the granting of franchises, the selection of county seats, and various minor municipal matters. As an integral and important part of the recent program of democracy, the Referendum is generalized and made applicable to the entire field of legislation.

There are several forms and variations of this institution, which may be classified under three main heads, as the Obligatory, the Optional, and the Advisory Referendum. Under the Obligatory Referendum, all acts of the legislative body, or all acts of a certain kind or dealing with certain subjects must be referred to the people for ratification, even though there be no opposition to them. This form of the Referendum applies almost universally to constitutional amendments, in many localities to bond issues and in a few to all franchise grants. It nowhere applies to the entire field of legislation and no one proposes that it should. When we consider the vast number of bills passed by the state legislatures and of ordinances and resolutions passed by municipal councils, it immediately becomes evident that no one but a lunatic would propose the submission of all these measures to the people for formal approval, unless he considered most of this legislation to be unnecessary or vicious and advocated the Referendum on all of it in order to induce a revolution. The Obligatory Referendum need not be extended very far beyond its present use. It may serve a useful purpose if applied to all local franchise grants where the service of each separate utility is to be rendered by a single company in each municipality. Under such conditions, franchise questions would come up at considerable intervals and each grant would be one of great importance to the entire community. There can be no harm in taking a vote on the question, even when the city is pretty well agreed that the franchise is a good one. But where a city is filled with competing utilities, and every separate extension has to be covered by a new franchise, the Obligatory Referendum on all franchises would often become a public nuisance. On constitutional questions, charter revisions and amendments, the purchase or construction of municipal utilities, the annexation of territory to cities, the issuance of public bonds under certain circumstances, and a few other important questions of policy, the Referendum may properly be obligatory.

The Optional Referendum may be in one of three forms or in a form that admits of three different processes. It may be so framed as to leave its use optional with the legislative body. The constitution or the city charter may simply authorize the legislature or the common council to refer measures to a vote of the people or not, in its discretion. We might naturally suppose that the legislative body would have this option anyway, whether the constitution or the charter said anything about it or not. But the courts have held otherwise. They say that legislative bodies are created for the purpose of legislating, not for the purpose of referring legislative questions to the people. But this form of the Optional Referendum is not fundamentally important from the standpoint of the popular control of government. It is convenient for the legislative body, but of comparatively little use to the people except as it removes an artificial barrier that prevents the legislature from throwing the onus of reform back upon the people and washing its own hands of the matter. Of greater value is the Optional Referendum where the option rests with a defeated minority in the legislative body or with the executive. It often happens that the minority in the legislature really represents the desires of the majority of the people upon a particular measure, and everybody knows it; or it may even be that a governor or mayor acting in opposition to a unanimous legislative body represents the prevailing sentiment of the community. Such an Optional Referendum would make legislative majorities cautious about defying the obvious mandates of public opinion, for it would put a minority representing the popular view in a dominant position. But the Optional Referendum that, theoretically at least, is most effective in establishing popular control, reserves to the people themselves the right, by petition, to require the submission of any act of the legislature to a vote of the electorate. In the usual form of this Referendum, the acts of the legislative body do not go into effect for a certain time, say thirty, or sixty, or ninety days after the legislature adjourns or after the ordinance is passed by the city council, and if within that time the petition is filed it has the effect of suspending the act until after it has been submitted to the people at the next regular election and ratified by them. It is generally deemed necessary to exempt emergency measures from the Referendum, but if the legislative body is left free to determine what are emergency measures, this privilege is pretty sure to be abused. One of the most difficult tasks in the drafting of the Referendum section of a constitution or charter is the task of so limiting the

emergency clause as to prevent its abuse by the legislative body without actually making it impossible for
the legislature to take effective action in a real emergency. Sometimes it is provided that a Referendum
petition may be filed against emergency measures.
In that case the measures are not suspended by reason
of the petition, but they are repealed if the popular
vote goes against them. Indeed, this plan might be
used generally under the Referendum, but it is deemed
more confusing and less effective than the usual plan
by which measures are suspended until approved at the
polls. Sometimes the executive is given an indirect
discretion on the question of emergency by a provision
authorizing him, if he so wishes, to call a special election
for the vote on measures suspended by the Referendum,
without waiting for the next regular election. Sometimes specific classes of acts are exempted from the
Referendum on the theory either that they are emergency measures or that they are not proper measures to
be passed upon by the electorate anyway. Sometimes
the constitution relieves the situation by permitting
Referendum petitions to be filed against particular items
or sections of an act, with the result that only such
parts of the act are suspended until the people have
voted. The California Referendum plan adopted in
1911 permits "acts calling elections, acts providing
for tax levies or appropriations for the usual current
expenses of the state, and urgency measures for the
immediate preservation of the public peace, health
or safety, passed by a two-thirds vote of all the members
of each house," to go into immediate effect. It is
provided, however, that whenever an act is given im-

mediate effect on account of alleged public necessity
"a statement of the facts constituting such necessity
shall be set forth in one section of the act, which section
shall be passed only upon a yea and nay vote, upon a
separate roll call thereon." Furthermore, it is provided
that "no measure creating or abolishing any office
or changing the salary, term or duties of any officer, or
granting any franchise or special privilege, or creating
any vested right or interest, shall be construed to be an
urgency measure." The Arizona constitution provides
that emergency measures exempt from the Referendum,
if vetoed by the governor, may be re-passed over his
objections only by a three-fourths vote of all the members elected to each house of the legislature.

The number of signers required to a Referendum
petition is of great importance, for upon this depends
the question as to whether or not the Referendum is
to be a usable instrument of democracy. The conditions
under which Referendum signatures must be secured
are quite different from the conditions under which the
Initiative may be invoked. In the first place, Referendum petitions must be signed and filed within a short
specified period, while ordinarily an Initiative petition
may be signed and filed at the leisure of the petitioners.
Even when an effort is made to handicap the Initiative
by the provision that all signatures must be secured
on registration or election days, the proponents of the
measure at least enjoy the advantage of having the
voters brought together where their signatures can be
solicited. But in the case of the Referendum, there is
usually no such opportunity, for the period within
which the petitions must be made up is determined

by the date of the adjournment of the legislature or the date of the passage of the measure involved in the petitions, without any reference to registration or election dates. Moreover, the function of the Referendum being conservative and obstructive rather than radical and constructive, its use is generally permitted upon the petition of a smaller number of citizens than is required in the case of the Initiative. This number may be fixed as an absolute number or may be reckoned as a percentage of the total number on the basis of the registration or of the most recent balloting. The friends of the Referendum usually think that five per cent of the votes cast at the last election is a large enough proportion of the electorate to be required on Referendum petitions on state issues. On municipal questions a larger percentage is sometimes approved, though there is the same reason for keeping the required percentage down in a big city as in a state, except that the people are nearer together and can be more easily reached in a city than in a state.

The proofs of the signatures and the official verification of the petitions present substantially the same problems in connection with the Referendum as with the Initiative, except that the election and registration officers cannot ordinarily be used in the securing and verification of Referendum signatures.

Before closing this chapter, I should refer briefly to the Advisory Referendum, which is the Referendum in its mildest form. This term is used to describe the process by which the legislative body sometimes takes the sense of the people on a particular measure or project and then does as it pleases about following the advice given. This process should be distinguished from the Advisory Initiative under which the people are allowed to give advice without being specifically asked for it. The Advisory Referendum may be useful where a conscientious legislature desires, before formulating a measure in detail, to find out how the people stand in regard to the principle involved.

In discussing the advantages and the disadvantages of the Referendum in the succeeding chapters, I shall assume, except as otherwise stated, that this institution is to take the form of the Optional Referendum applicable generally to legislative acts other than emergency measures, either at the will of the legislative body or upon petitions filed by electors to a number specified in the constitution or charter. Many persons who oppose the Initiative and the Recall are either favorable or indifferent to the Referendum. Such opposition as is directed against the Referendum in particular is mainly based upon two points: first, that the Referendum offers to the legislative body a temptation to shirk its responsibilities, and second, that the Referendum may be used by a minority of the people to interfere with and delay the orderly performance of governmental functions by the regularly constituted authorities. The chief arguments in favor of the Referendum as distinguished from its companion tools of democracy are three: first, that it provides a check upon legislative corruption; second, that it enables the people to prevent legislative improvidence; and third, that it provides a means of keeping legislation in line with public sentiment. These objections and favorable arguments will be considered in the next five chapters.

CHAPTER XIV

FIRST OBJECTION TO THE REFERENDUM—THAT IT
WOULD AFFORD THE LEGISLATIVE BRANCH AN
EXCUSE FOR SHIRKING RESPONSIBILITY

LEGISLATIVE bodies are admittedly subject to powerful temptations. Individual legislators often have
palpitation of the heart when circumstances compel
them to go on record. They are like other people who
are the prey of conflicting interests and desires. Capital is proverbially timid. Bankers and merchants are
known to be cowards on public questions. Politicians
are afraid of the cars. Everybody is scared about
something. A characteristic weakness of legislators
is their unwillingness to take sides openly between the
people whose votes are necessary for their reëlection
and the corporations whose support is necessary for
their renomination and their business prosperity.
Such a dilemma spells fear and indecision. Accordingly,
it is said, the legislator will take refuge in the Referendum to temporize with his two masters. Or it may
be that he is torn asunder by the desire not to offend
either of two strong factions among the people themselves. Or it may be that he is simply weak or inexperienced and is unable to make up his own mind about
the merits of a measure upon which the people want him
to use his own judgment, assuming that a legislator,

whose business it is to study legislative needs, will be more familiar with the demands of justice and public policy in this particular case than they themselves are.

Here we see three separate states of mind of the legislators which may lead them to welcome the Referendum as a means of avoiding embarrassment and shirking responsibility. Now, when the legislators are really trying to serve two masters,—the Interests and the People,—by the use of the Referendum they tend to diverge somewhat from a strictly neutral attitude and to squirm out of their secret obligations. The normal result of a nice balance between two conflicting interests is political paralysis, a condition that is very gratifying to those who sigh for governmental "stability" and "to be let alone." Usually, in these days of political unrest and attempted readjustment, it is the special interests and their sympathizers that hold legislative paralysis to be a normal and healthy condition. It is the people at large who clamor for action. Under such circumstances, one can easily see how disgusted the friends of inaction are with legislators who were supposed to have been carefully selected to serve as a bulwark against the assaults of the radicals upon existing institutions, when these same legislators, instead of standing up like men and advising their constituents firmly that no attacks on property or the established order will be permitted, lose their nerve and throw the responsibility for action upon the people. Verily, such legislators are unworthy of the rewards intended for them. What is the use of spending vast sums of good stand-pat money in maintaining the

political organizations to nominate and elect safe men
to the legislature, if in spite of everything they become
weak-kneed at last and yield the fortress to the foe?
Alas, weakness does not excuse ingratitude, that most
dangerous of all qualities in the beneficiaries of political
influence. Yet, from the standpoint of the people there
is something to be said for an institution that under-
mines the courage of legislators, when it is their courage
to go wrong that topples over. The principles involved
are the same when the position of the parties is reversed so that the people desire to maintain the existing
status while the special interests demand action for
their own relief or for the enlargement of their privileges.
In this case the legislators may attach a referendum
to the proposed measure as a concession to popular
opposition, and thus, without actually refusing to confer the benefits sought by the special interests, tack
on a condition that may make their action nuga-
tory. Then the people have a sort of grateful feeling
for having been permitted to triumph over the inclinations of their legislative servants, and forget to be
angry with them for their primary failure to resist
the demands of those who would prostitute government
to the service of private interests. But under these
circumstances the disgust and rage of these interests
exceed, if anything, what they feel when the legislature
yields to the pressure of public opinion for progressive
legislation. This difference is easily explained. New
legislation may be evaded in practice or it may be over-
thrown in the courts. At any rate, in the enactment
of unfavorable measures by the legislature, the special
interests feel that they have merely lost the first skirm-

ish. They can fight on with a good chance of snatch-
ing victory from defeat somewhere along the tortuous
mountain road that leads from the first step in the
legislative process, which is taken by the legislature
itself and is purely tentative, to the final step, which
is taken by the United States Supreme Court and
from which there is no practicable appeal. But where
it is a case of promised boons withheld, where after
long and careful planning the prize comes within
reach only to be snatched away, where effort and
expense are lost, where excited lust of golden benefits
is thwarted, where misplaced confidence ends in humiliation, causes both material and spiritual unite
to foster rage. It is no wonder that the Referendum is unpopular at such times with those who have
been thwarted by it. How much better it would be,
from their standpoint, if the legislators were required
to stand up and be counted, and show how many of
them dare to refuse to fulfill their part of the bargain
by virtue of which they got their seats!

If the Referendum is used because of the legislature's
unwillingness to decide between two factions of the
people, the objection to it cannot be stated very forcibly,
for under these circumstances there is no charge of dis-
loyalty toward secret masters, but merely of desire
to avoid the consequences of taking action contrary
to the will of a large number, perhaps a majority of
their constituents. It is hardly demanded, even by
the most stubborn reactionary, that general measures
affecting the people, in which they take an active interest and which merely involve questions of governmental policy in relation to the common activities of

life, should be arbitrarily settled against the will of
the majority by the representative body. If a Referendum vote is the only way of determining how the
majority feel about such measures, few people would
have the spirit to oppose it on theoretical grounds.
It may be regarded, however, as much safer for the
stability of our institutions and as better comporting
with the dignity of the representative principle for the
legislature to take a chance at guessing the will of the
people rather than humiliate itself by asking them for a
definite, mathematical demonstration of it at the polls.
Wise legislators are supposed to have ways of feeling
the public pulse and of divining the people's will without the formalities of arithmetic. There are the letters
and petitions that flow in from constituents. There
are the editorials in the local newspapers. There are
the week-end conferences with the leading lights in
local politics. There are the casual conversations on
the street and in the train. There are the appearances
at public hearings before legislative committees. There
are the persuasive whispers of the cloak-room and the
illuminating confidences of the convivium. With all
these sources of enlightenment, why should the legislative body have recourse to anything so vulgar as the
Referendum? Still, the opposition is not bitter. It is
mainly a question of good taste, and of what will
ultimately come of these first flirtations of legislative
youth with the siren of democracy.

A more serious condition is revealed where the
Referendum discloses the incompetence of the legislature. Even the crude results that spring from existing legislative practices would often be more crude if the

legislature had to depend entirely on itself for guidance.
It is now attended by skilled mentors who try to save
it from some of th·· follies of inexperience and give its
work a semblance oi intellectual respectability. When
the Referendum cuts down the rewards of legislative
tutoring, so that experience and wisdom desert the
lobby, the graduates of the corner grocery and the
novitiates of the law who respond to roll-call in the
legislative halls may find themselves somewhat be-
wildered by the intricate problems of legislation for a
great state or a populous city. It is not strange
that a representative assembly, freed from one of its
masters, should feel the need of turning to the other.
The Referendum under these conditions might have
the effect of revealing the incompetence of the legislature, but it could not truthfully be charged with
increasing this incompetence. It is not to be wondered
at that incompetent persons should shrink from accepting responsibility when all their secret props are
removed. If, under the Referendum, the legislators
disclosed their incapacity for leadership, the people
would have cause to regret the fact of this incapacity,
not their knowledge of it. The natural tendency of the
Referendum, when joined with the other instruments
of democracy, is to dignify the representative function
by freeing it from the paralyzing effect of secret control
and by giving legislators a better opportunity for the
development of individual leadership. As issues tend
to be separated and settled on their merits, instead
of being inextricably tangled in personal and party
platforms and confused by partisan organizations,
there is greater encouragement for the use of brains

by legislators and for their acceptance of responsibility.

The legislative timidity induced by the Referendum is, therefore, partly a wholesome respect for the will of the rightful master, partly a revelation of present incompetence, and partly an earnest of better conditions in the future, when singleness of purpose, free play of mind and responsible leadership of the people shall, we hope, characterize the activities of representative assemblies.

CHAPTER XV

WHEN the Referendum, invoked on account of opposition to a particular item in the appropriation bill,
or to the increase in a particular item, has the effect of
holding up the entire budget of a state for six months
or a year, or even longer, the inconvenience of the
institution cannot be denied. When the constitution,
in order to make the Referendum effective, provides
that no act of the legislature, without exception, shall
go into effect until ninety days after the legislature adjourns, and not then if a five per cent petition is filed
against it, thus effectually preventing the legislative
body from adopting prompt measures for public relief
or protection in times of sudden crisis, there is ample
reason for denunciation of the institution in the form
in which it lends itself to such obstructiveness. But
these results are not the necessary concomitants of the
Referendum. In order that regular appropriations may
not be held in suspense and the established organs of
government starved to a standstill, the Referendum
section of the constitution should be so drafted as to
require petitions calling for a vote on appropriations
to be aimed at specific items or the increases in specific

items, leaving the general budget to go into effect without unusual delay. Moreover, the executive should be authorized, as he sometimes is, to call a special election if in his judgment the interests of the state will suffer by the appropriations covered by the petition being left long in a state of suspense. So far as general emergency legislation is concerned, the Referendum often leaves too much leeway for the legislature, instead of too little. No doubt there should be provision for quick action in emergencies, but the door should be closed as tightly as possible against the jocose evasions of constitutional limitations often practiced by legislatures.

Aside from appropriations and genuine emergency legislation, both of which are specially provided for in well-devised schemes, comparatively little harm can result from the delays incident upon the use of the Referendum. True, measures enacted by the legislature and even supported by a strongly preponderant public sentiment may be held in abeyance for the period between their enactment and the next regular election. It is hardly to be expected, however, that hopeless minorities will habitually go to the expense and trouble of invoking the Referendum on measures which are certain to be approved by the popular vote in the end. This may happen a few times when the Referendum is new or even occasionally afterwards when minorities have large financial interests at stake or when their consuming partisanship makes them spiteful. But this slight disadvantage is the more easily to be tolerated as it is incident to a mild conservatism which involves only a moderate delay and time for second thought before the final step forward in legislation is taken. After all, it is not long till the next regular election and if the urgency is great a special election can be called.

In some cases it may be found that the people are less progressive than the legislature and particular measures which seem very desirable to those in charge of administrative departments may be vetoed by the people out of lack of sympathy or lack of understanding. It is to be observed, however, that in these days of governmental extravagance when public expenditures and public indebtedness are increasing by leaps and bounds, it may not be altogether amiss for the people to put on the brakes occasionally, even though they cause the government engine to slow down a bit on a stretch of track where high speed would be safe.

The Referendum is fair to the conservatives. It gives them another chance. They, at least, should not object to it where it is used as a companion piece of political machinery to the Initiative. Perhaps, after the Referendum has been tried, if it is found to interfere unduly with the smooth forward march of progressive policies, the radicals may invoke the Initiative to do away with it! Then we shall see how the tyranny of the majority is going to develop in an untrammeled democracy!

CHAPTER XVI

FIRST ARGUMENT IN FAVOR OF THE REFERENDUM—THAT
IT WOULD REMOVE TEMPTATION FROM THE LEGIS-
LATIVE BRANCH BY WITHDRAWING ITS ULTIMATE
POWER TO BESTOW SPECIAL PRIVILEGES

In this book and everywhere in the serious discussion
of American political institutions, a great deal is said
about the temptations of aldermen, state legislators,
and members of Congress, arising from the desire of
certain persons or corporations to secure special privileges in the form of irrevocable grants, and from the
power of the legislative bodies to confer such privileges.
It is pointed out that these temptations, manifold and
subtle in their forms, tend in two ways to degrade the
representative assemblies. In the first place, they develop and bring to fruition any germs of corruptibil-
ity that lie latent in the characters of the individuals
who are temporarily clothed with privilege-granting
powers. In the second place, the knowledge that these
temptations exist itself starts a selective process among
the people tending to keep back those who pray the
Lord not to lead them into temptation and to bring
forward those who importune the Devil to tempt them.
The power to use governmental authority to grant
special privileges having monetary value which, under
the doctrine of the Dartmouth College case, im-

mediately take on the form of vested rights, irrevocable without full compensation, is a natural source of corruption. It invites men corruptly to seek governmental favors. It invites corruptible men to seek positions where they will have a chance of being corrupted. Between this upper and this nether millstone the honor of the legislative body is ground to dust. This indictment of our legislative system, if true, could not be more fatal. Here is the cancer that is gnawing at the vitals of representative democracy. Only heroic treatment can save the body politic.

But the temptations of the legislature are not confined to the granting of irrevocable privileges. In most of the states the effect of the Dartmouth College decision has been somewhat weakened by the adoption of constitutional amendments reserving to the legislature the right to alter or repeal its acts, especially those relating to corporations. While the temptation is still strong in the granting of special franchises, which become contractual rights, there is also a constant, though less acute temptation in connection with special privileges that are not irrevocable. The very power to repeal or amend corporate charters; the very power to regulate the rates and practices of corporations, continuing as it does from legislature to legislature; the very power to tax property, privilege, and enterprise, and once having laid the tax, to remove it, to lighten it or to increase it, make the temptations to corruption more constant. Franchise-granting comes by spells. A corrupt bargain between a public service corporation and a board of aldermen or a state legislature at a critical time is apt to stink to heaven. But the constant, unremitting application of corrupt influence to control the action of legislative bodies comes to be expected, almost tolerated. This vice is regarded as an inevitable incident of government, and we have a tendency, first, to endure it, then, to pity it, and finally, when the chance comes, to embrace it. That politics should be a school of corruption is enough to make the angels weep. What can be more deadly to democracy than this? What plague can equal this plague of political leprosy?

The Referendum is offered as a remedy, a specific for legislative corruption. Vaccination for smallpox, antitoxin for diphtheria, and rat-killing for the plague are generally accepted as efficacious remedies, although their application is sometimes attended by considerable inconvenience. If the Referendum will check corruption, it can be forgiven a few vagaries. Every remedy receives its final proof from use. But it is not the purpose of this book to sift the evidence of experience and present a digest of it to the readers. I leave that task to others or to time itself. We are here concerned with the theoretical soundness of proposals, viewed as still being in the experimental stage. Our question is, do they appeal to reason? If they do, and still prove failures in general practice, we may then be driven to the conclusion that the fault lies not with the proposals themselves but rather with the practitioners, as is notably true with reference to the Golden Rule.

How does the Referendum attack the problem of corruption? It does not of itself abolish franchises. It does not necessarily substitute public ownership for public regulation of franchise utilities. It does not by a stroke of the ballot do away with a protective tariff, or a beet sugar subsidy, or railway mail contracts. It does not drive the fruit-stands from the side-walk, slice off the bow-windows that project into the street or compel the Hebrew merchant to keep within the property line when he solicits patronage. The Referendum simply withdraws from the legislative body the final authority to grant these privileges, making its action subject to review by the electorate, on the theory that if a special privilege is improvidently bestowed or if in its nature it runs counter to the public interest, the people will veto it. It is obvious, as a general proposition, that the majority cannot benefit by special favors. It is only the minority, and usually a very small minority, that benefits from them. The interest of the mass of the people lies in a government of equal justice to all, of special privileges to none. It is, therefore, assumed that where the Referendum is invoked, the use of government for private ends will be vetoed. If privilege-seekers should attempt to corrupt the electorate, they would not only find them too many but would find the cost too great. The value of the privilege sought would not be sufficient to compensate the majority of the people for the disadvantages they would suffer from its being granted, and still leave enough profit to the privilege-seekers to finance their motives. The Referendum, therefore, is a natural check upon the legislation that runs counter to the general interest and can ordinarily be secured from the legislature only by corruption, including in that term the whole array of improper influences which give legislators what may be called a double eye. It cannot be claimed for the Referendum that it will directly cure the corruption of inaction. For that, the Initiative and the Recall are needed.

In so far as the Referendum would have the effect of stopping the grant of valuable special privileges, it would remove the motive to corruption at both ends. The privilege-seekers would see the futility of spending money and favors upon legislators who could not give good title to the privileges sought. With the rewards for legislative treason withdrawn, would-be traitors would be less forward in their candidacy for legislative honors. With corruption eliminated or greatly diminished, the field would be left open to men with normal and honorable ambitions for public service. Secretly corrupt men would not be so anxious to go to the legislature, and secretly weak men would be better able to keep their secret when there. Until the lesson of the Referendum had been learned, there might be some confusion in the legislature and some desperate attempts to revive the failing fortunes of corruption. But in the end the result would be a higher quality in legislators and a better spirit in legislation. Under existing conditions, there is nothing quite so baffling about a legislative body as the fact that its members do not keep their minds on their work. They are thinking of something else. For where their treasure is, there will their hearts be also. By cutting off the hope of illegitimate rewards, the Referendum would encourage single-mindedness in representative assemblies.

CHAPTER XVII

SECOND ARGUMENT IN FAVOR OF THE REFERENDUM—
THAT IT WOULD CONDUCE TO THE CONSERVATION OF
PUBLIC RESOURCES

THE resources of the state—what are they? First
of all comes a healthy, intelligent, self-restrained citizenship. But let us pass this item. The resources that the
Referendum will tend to conserve may be classed as the
property, the prerogatives and the credit of the government. Public property includes the public domain,
with its mines, its forests, its water powers, its reservoirs
of oil and natural gas, its harbor and terminal facilities.
It includes the country highways and the city streets,
the parks and boulevards, the public buildings, the
municipal utility plants and all the varied holdings
of the city, state, and federal governments. The prerogatives of government include the right of eminent
domain, the power of taxation, the right to regulate
the rates of common carriers and all public utilities,
the right to protect the lives and limbs of citizens in all
industrial pursuits, and many other powers not rightfully possessed by private individuals. The credit of
the government is its ability, within the limits fixed
by constitution or statute, to borrow money for public
improvements and to sell its bonds at a reasonable
rate of interest. Public credit is based on public prop-

erty, public prerogatives and faith in public integrity. All of these things are well worth conserving. How will the Referendum help?

In early colonial days the corporation of the City of New York was given title to all the unoccupied land on Manhattan Island. The city sold off this land from time to time for small sums which were used to pay the expenses of the municipal government. If a leasing system had been adopted the rentals from the city's real estate might now be sufficient to make local taxation unnecessary. Philadelphia owned a gas plant which was nearly wrecked by corrupt officials and then turned over to a company to be operated for private profit. When the city's legislative body was ready to extend the company's lease on extravagant terms a few years later, the resistance of the people would have been futile except for the unexpected conversion of the mayor to the reform point of view. They had to pray to God for help, being unable to help themselves. Luckily the unfamiliar sound pierced the portals of Heaven, and they were succored. In St. Louis not many years ago, the enterprising members of the municipal assembly put a secret price on everything the city had to bestow. They even plotted to sell the courthouse. Their activities were finally checked by the circuit attorney and yawning prison doors. At an earlier date Congress bestowed untold riches upon the transcontinental railroads in the form of land grants from the public domain. Now the railroads seek to compel the public to pay dividends on the present value of these gratuities. We have seen in most recent times by what a tiresome and unseemly struggle the United

States government has been prevented from alienating the best resources of Alaska. And so it has been throughout the period of our national history. Representative assemblies, whether city councils, or state legislatures, or Congress itself, have seemed eager to despoil the people of their heritage and turn it over to private individuals for development and exploitation. The streets of many cities have been mortgaged with perpetual franchises. The property of the nation and the states has been frittered away. Undoubtedly, some of these legislative extravagances have been popular at the time and would not have been prevented by the Referendum. The people themselves have not been fully awake to the necessity of the conservation policy until recently, and yet there have been many occasions when the Referendum would have saved the people's property. The usefulness of this check is already recognized in the numerous provisions of constitution and statute requiring the submission of franchise grants and the alienation of municipal utilities to popular vote. For some reason, representative assemblies seem to be more deeply impressed with the impotence of government to retain and develop public property and more strongly convinced of the necessity of encouraging private enterprise by public gifts so long as there remains anything to give than the people themselves are. Perhaps this is due in part to a consciousness on the part of legislators of their own unfitness for the management of public business. It is certainly in part due to the sinister influence of special pleaders who raise a chorus of defamation against the state and under cover of their own clamor use more material

persuasions to convince the legislators of the infinite
superiority of private enterprise over public husbandry.
To these influences the electorate is more nearly im-
mune, and for that reason the Referendum would tend
to prevent the alienation of public property.

At various times and in varying degrees representative bodies have attempted to parcel out the prerogatives of government to private interests and by contract
to strip the state of some of its powers. Railroad, telegraph, pipe line and water companies, and other public
service agencies have been clothed with the sovereign
power of condemnation. Efforts have been made to
contract away the state's power of taxation. Contracts have been entered into abrogating the state's
continuing authority to regulate rates. These attempts
of the legislators temporarily occupying the seats of
power to curtail the prerogatives of their successors
do not always succeed, owing to the unwillingness of
the courts of justice to give judicial sanction to them.
Yet, in many cases they do succeed in large measure,
and the state finds its action handicapped by previous
acts that have taken on the nature of contracts and are
held to be sacred against the future touch of government. That the Referendum would operate as a check
upon these tendencies cannot be doubted. The people,
who are compelled to live continuously subject to the
laws, cannot regard with favor the attempt of this
year's board of aldermen, this year's state legislature
or this year's Congress to hamstring its successors,
and deprive the people of the future benefits arising
from a government fully armed and continuously free
to exercise all its legitimate functions.

The Referendum has long been applied in many
American communities as a check upon legislative
indifference to the public credit. The issuance of state
or municipal bonds is often made conditional upon the
approval of the electorate, sometimes even by a two-
thirds affirmative vote. Sometimes it seems as if the
people's usual conservatism in regard to public debt
had been displaced by a careless liberality in the use
of the public credit. But observation tends to prove
that the people are not so much concerned about the
amount of public indebtedness as they are about the
use made of the proceeds of bond sales and the extent
and value of the public property on account of which
the debt was incurred. For example, the people do not
manifest alarm at the bulk of debt incurred for public
utility purposes, where interest and sinking fund charges
are to be met out of the revenues of the undertaking.
The people are not slow to approve bond issues for
parks and playgrounds or for other public improvements for which there is a pressing need or which promise to be of benefit to the community generally. They
are most likely to reject bond issues where they have
reason to expect that the money will be squandered
by corrupt or inefficient government in extravagant
contracts, or that it will be diverted in whole or in part
from the uses for which the bond issues are asked.
Who can deny that precisely here lies the chief danger
of increasing debt? If the city has permanent improvements to show for every dollar of debt incurred, if
outstanding bonds are secured by great and profitable
municipal undertakings, a large debt does not impair
the city's credit. It is a well-known paradox of business

life that the more a man borrows the better his credit is, for the habit of borrowing cannot be maintained except as a companion to the habit of paying debts when due. Capital runs to meet the man or the city that puts it to profitable use.

Conservation of the state's resources is not merely a doctrine of negation. It often demands the adoption of a bold, aggressive policy of development. Conservation both in its obstructive and in its constructive applications is a policy that affects the welfare of the whole people in a peculiarly intimate way and that vividly appeals to popular interest and imagination. For this reason, it is especially fitting that the people should hold the reins on the legislature in all conservation matters, for they are pretty sure to tighten them against reckless driving on a dangerous road and to slacken them again when the road is clear and safe.

CHAPTER XVIII

DISRESPECT for law is fatal to democracy. The dead letter marks a partial paralysis of popular government. The statute-books need to be alive in every section. They should present a well-knit, vital body of rules that are actually in force, unencumbered with obsolete or unenforceable legislative dicta. Clearly, the Referendum will not of itself help to remove from the statute-books provisions that originally were in line with public sentiment, but that have ceased to express the popular will by reason of changed conditions. To get rid of these out-of-date laws, the Initiative is needed. But there are many cases where laws are enacted which do not at the time of their enactment represent effective public sentiment and which are dead letters or half-dead letters from the beginning. Some unenforced laws are kept on the statute-books and some unenforceable ones are put there out of deference to formal respectability. There is a strong element of hypocrisy in American law-making. The legislatures, and even the people, are sometimes more anxious to have laws written in the books than in the hearts of men. Nevertheless, there can be no doubt that the Referendum would often prevent the enactment of unenforceable legislation, and so tend to maintain the integrity of the state. Sometimes petitions would be filed against new restrictive legislation of a controversial nature, but if the Referendum vote showed a strong preponderance of public sentiment in favor of the measures voted on, this fact would tend to give them stability and to induce the minority to accept them as the established law of the state. A restrictive measure overwhelmingly ratified at the polls would not be subjected to the persistent efforts that are now often directed toward the emasculation of reform laws passed without the specific sanction of the people. In other words, the Referendum not only would tend to prevent the enactment of unpopular and meddlesome legislation, but would also give stability to new legislation that is in accord with public sentiment. While the Referendum would not prevent laws from becoming obsolete, it would hinder the enactment of measures that are in advance of public sentiment and would hinder the repeal or the weakening of legislation that is abreast of the times. The clamor of loud-voiced minorities would have less effect upon the people at large than it now has upon their representatives. From the eye of the legislator at the state capital prevailing sentiment is often hidden by the mist arising from the fierce breath of the militant few who fill the corridors either insisting that all men shall conform to their standards of life or demanding that they themselves shall be exempted from the necessity of conforming to the general standards of the community. The Referendum removes the ultimate control of legislation from the artificial storm center at the capital to the wider fields of common life where average weather conditions prevail.

There is good reason to believe that the Referendum would prevent many of the legislative outrages now perpetrated by temporary partisan majorities in the representative assembly. The people are often shocked by the bold violations of the principles of local self-government where the state legislature interferes in municipal affairs for partisan purposes. Even the members of the party in power do not generally approve the tyrannical grabs of the party leaders for patronage that does not belong to them. The masses of the people are not in favor of gerrymandering apportionments, no matter which party they are intended to benefit. The electorate is strongly against legislative measures devised for the purpose of perpetuating by artificial means the predominance of the faction or party temporarily in control of the government. The people resent the passage of laws that make promises to the ear and break them to the hope. Legislation drafted for the very purpose of defeating its professed objects would not fare well under the Referendum. Reform measures devised by the known enemies of reform are not over-popular. Half-way measures are advantageous when they serve as the opening wedge for complete reforms. But when they are designed, not as cautious and experimental beginnings, but as mere futility-demonstrations to be conducted under the personal supervision of reactionaries, half-measures are likely to be worse than none at all. The people are keen to discern the motive of political legislation in matters of general popular interest, and they can generally be depended upon to accept the half-loaf that is better than no bread and to reject the half-loaf that has been purposely spoiled in the baking.

In a democracy the importance of keeping the statute-books clear of unpopular and unenforceable legislation and of legislation enacted in bad faith can hardly be overestimated. The stability and success of popular government depend in an especial degree upon the citizen's respect for law and the orderly adaptation of legislative means to popular ends. The Referendum offers the means of rebuking legislative tyranny, the prostitution of legislative power to partisan ends and standpat chicanery.

CHAPTER XIX

THE REFERENDUM ON JUDICIAL DECISIONS

As ordinarily understood the Referendum applies only to acts of the legislative body. Inasmuch, however, as judges in the United States exercise the prerogative of declaring legislative acts unconstitutional or of interpreting them to mean something less or something else than they were generally supposed to mean, it has been suggested that certain judicial decisions be subjected to the Referendum. This might take the form of a general optional Referendum on all decisions relating to statutory law or it might be an optional or an obligatory Referendum on all decisions declaring statutes void as being unconstitutional. It would naturally be limited to the decision of the court of last resort in the particular case or to the decision of the highest court in the political subdivision directly concerned. In so far as the Referendum was limited to judicial decisions setting aside statutes, it would be within its natural scope as a check upon legislative action; for the unmaking of a statute is legislation as clearly as the making of it. It would seem to be an especially appropriate procedure to appeal to the people as final arbiter in these cases of conflict between two branches of the government. As I have already said elsewhere in this book, there are strong reasons for not depriving the American judiciary of its peculiar jurisdiction over the constitutionality of statutes, and with the Initiative available for the amendment of the constitution in the light of new judicial interpretations, it cannot be said that the Referendum on judicial decisions is strictly necessary. Yet its regular use as a means of finally settling a disputed interpretation between the legislature and the judiciary would furnish a more direct and less cumbersome method of enforcing the people's will than would be available under the Initiative. At the same time the people would still be able to go to the judiciary as a ready protector against the usurpations of the legislature. In fact, the courts would merely have power to suspend the operation of a statute pending an appeal to the electors. A judicial decision would have the same effect as the filing of a Referendum petition against a law, except that the decision need not be made within a specified time or before the statute went into effect. In this way, the procedure would not be so much a Referendum on the court's decision as a judicial mode of applying the Referendum to legislative enactments. In other words, the courts would then have a suspensory veto or repeal of statutes instead of the absolute veto or repeal now vested in them. Who can rightfully speak of this suggestion of Mr. Roosevelt's with derision, as if it were the product of a disordered imagination? There is nothing about it that is contrary to the genius of American institutions, and it offers a possible remedy for a political condition that has become acute. A recent investigation shows that during the seven years from 1902 to 1908, inclusive, no less than 468 different

statutes were declared unconstitutional by the highest
courts in the several states of the Union.[1] Such a
condition of affairs cannot be ignored. If the Referendum is to be applicable to all legislation, it should lie
against these judicial decisions. "If the courts have
the final say-so on all legislative acts," says Mr. Roosevelt, "and if no appeal can lie from them to the people,
then they are the irresponsible masters of the people."
Again he says: "The power to interpret is the power
to establish; and if the people are not to be allowed
finally to interpret the fundamental law, ours is not a
popular government."

If, however, all decisions affecting statutory law,
involving mere secondary interpretation as well as
repudiation, were to be made subject to the Referendum, confusion would be likely to result. The Initiative
and the Recall are more appropriate remedies than the
Referendum, for the misuse of purely executive, administrative, or judicial powers.

[1] Herbert S. Swan, in "The Public" of February 9, 1912.

PART IV
THE RECALL

CHAPTER XX

THE Initiative and the Referendum are instruments of pure democracy. In so far as they are put into actual use, they supplement representative government by the direct participation of the people in the legislative function, either by complete legislative action under the Initiative or by the exercise of the veto power under the Referendum. The Recall is a procedure of an entirely different order. It is the complement of popular election of representatives. It does not involve direct participation by the people in the exercise of governmental functions. It is simply the guaranteed right of the people to discharge their public servants when these public servants cease to be satisfactory to them. While the Recall does not involve the direct participation of the people in the primary functions of government, and therefore is less radical than the Initiative and the Referendum, it nevertheless has a wider application than either of these institutions. It is not limited to the legislative department. It affects the entire field of government, legislative, executive, judicial. It is as wide in its application as the representative system, and it may even be extended beyond the scope of popular elections to office. It may be made to apply to judges and administrative officials appointed by the executive or the legislature, and to executive and legislative officers chosen by indirect election.

The Recall introduces us to a great theoretical controversy about the nature of representative government. It has been held in some quarters that the principle of representative institutions does not involve popular sovereignty at all, but merely the right of the people to elect their rulers at stated intervals. According to this theory the President is a monarch with a limited term, and governors and mayors are temporary princes and potentates of subordinate jurisdictions. The people do not rule, but they select representatives to rule over them. To be sure, if they are not pleased with their rulers, they can select others at the expiration of the stated terms of office, but during those terms public officials hold irrevocably the prerogatives of government. Under this theory, the people are regarded as incapable of self-government, as not qualified to express or have an opinion on specific governmental policies, but only to pass upon the efficiency of their government in a general way. Are they happy? Are they prosperous? Are crops good? Do the burdens of government feel light? Do war and pestilence keep at a safe distance? Is the community free from famine, fire, and flood? If so, the people, naturally, will be satisfied with their rulers and reëlect them. If not, they will try others. But the people are not supposed curiously to examine into causes; they are to judge by general effects. The Recall does not accept this theory of the underlying principle of the representative system. It holds that a representative is a servant, an agent, not a master. To be sure, like an ambassador pleni-potentiary, he is a servant with power, but he has had his specific instructions or is presumed to be acquainted with his master's will, and if he fails to recognize his responsibility or if he misinterprets his instructions, he may be recalled at any time. He holds an indetermi-nate franchise, or what is sometimes called a tenure during good behavior, within the limits of a max-imum fixed term. The Recall does not necessarily involve the lengthening of terms of office, but it natu-rally leads to that, or even to the entire abandonment of the fixed-term idea. It is a continuing control, calculated to preserve at all times the relation of master and servant between the people and their representa-tives. While the avowed purpose of the Recall is to preserve in the people the right to discharge faithless, inefficient or insubordinate servants at any time, the natural obverse of this purpose would be the reserved right to keep a good servant indefinitely in order that the people may profit by his experience.

As applied to elective officers the Recall takes several forms. It may simply involve the automatic submission to the people, in the midst of an established term of office, of the question as to whether or not there shall be a Recall election at that time. Under this very limited application of the principle, the people do not enjoy the right to initiate Recall proceedings by petition, but simply to vote in the middle of a fixed official term upon the question of shortening the term. If they vote to have a new election, the effect is the same as if the official involved had been elected for the shorter term in the first instance. He may stand for reëlection if he chooses to do so and if he can secure a nomination under the regular procedure for making nominations. Other candidates may be nominated in the usual manner and in every respect the election procedure may be the same as at the beginning of a regular term of office. Indeed, the law may provide that an election called in the middle of a term of office shall be for an entire new term instead of being for the remainder of the unexpired term. If so, the person elected, whether the incumbent or some new candidate, would have the right to serve for a full term from that date, subject to the right of the people again to order a Recall election in the midst of the new term. This adaptation of the Recall principle is designed merely as a recognition of the advantages of a long term of office when the people get a satisfactory public servant and the serious disadvantages of a long term when they get a public servant who disappoints them.

In its more usual form the Recall provides that upon the filing of a petition signed by a certain number or percentage of the voters demanding the removal of a public official during his term of office an election must be held at once to determine whether or not he shall be permitted to fill out his stated term. The petitioners are usually required to state in general terms their reasons for invoking the Recall against the official involved. Sometimes Recall petitions may not be filed against an official until he has been in office for a specified period. Naturally, in the case of legislators, whose active service is usually limited to a comparatively brief period at the beginning of their term, the time required to elapse before the Recall can be invoked against them is likely to be shorter than in the case of an executive or judicial officer, who renders continuous service and generally for a longer official period. The petitioners asking for the Recall may be required to name in their petition a candidate to be voted for at the Recall election. Or the nomination of one or more candidates may be left to the regular political agencies after the filing of the petition has determined that an election is to be held. The incumbent against whom the Recall is directed is entitled to have his name placed on the ballot unless he resigns his office or expressly declines to allow his name to be presented to the voters. This right of the incumbent is irrespective of the source of his original nomination, and irrespective of whether he is again supported by the same party or group or a new candidate is named by such party or group. Sometimes, the voters at a Recall election are required to determine separately the question whether or not the official involved is to be recalled. In that case, his name does not appear on the ballot as a candidate. If a majority votes against his recall, he continues in office unmolested. If a majority votes for his recall, he is thereby removed from office. Under this scheme, the electors vote separately for the other candidates, and in case the Recall is effective the candidate receiving the highest vote is elected to fill the vacancy. This is the California plan, and under it candidates at Recall elections are nominated only by petition, not by the regular party methods. The number of signatures required for a Recall petition has ranged in the practice of different cities and states from twelve per cent of the vote cast at the last preceding election

for officials elected at large in the state of California
to seventy-five per cent as provided in a recent Illi-
nois statute authorizing the adoption of the commission
form of government in cities. The most common requirement is twenty-five per cent. It is considered
essential to the conservative use of the Recall that the
number of signatures required on the petitions should
be sufficiently large to protect elected officials from
the spite of mere partisan opposition. Moreover, experience shows that a larger number of voters are
usually interested in candidates than are interested in
measures such as come before the people under the
Initiative and the Referendum. In case of flagrant
cause for public dissatisfaction with an official it should
be easier, therefore, to get signatures to a Recall petition
than it is to an Initiative or a Referendum petition.
On the other hand, unless the cause for his recall is
serious or even if it is, if his power is feared, citizens
will naturally hesitate to give their signatures to petitions against an individual. On the whole, it would
seem that even where nearly half of the electors voted
against an official when he was a candidate for office,
once elected he will be practically secure against annoyance by the Recall where the signatures of as many
as twenty-five per cent of the electors are required to
start Recall proceedings, unless subsequent to his
election he has given special cause for offense to the
citizens. Not only the trouble and expense of frequent
elections, but the general sense of fair play will act as a
check upon the wanton use of the Recall. In some
cases the law does not allow an official to be subjected
to Recall proceedings more than once during his term

of office, or, it may be, more than once every six months
or every year. Sometimes a new official elected at a
Recall election cannot be recalled during the unexpired
term which he is chosen to fill out. Sometimes the
reasons given by the petitioners demanding the recall
of an official are printed on the ballot together with his
reasons for asking a vote of confidence. Naturally,
the statements on either side have to be closely limited
as to length. It is not the theory of the Recall that
reasons given for its use should be subject to review
by the courts. In no sense is the Recall limited to cases
of malfeasance or misfeasance in office. The petitioners
are not required to prove their case and the official
concerned is not required to answer any charges. The
Recall does not involve removal for cause in the legal
sense, but removal purely in the discretion of the people
for any reason which may appear to them sufficient.
For this reason the Recall does not necessarily involve
the disgrace of the official removed from office by its
use. It may involve simply a difference of opinion
in matters of public policy.

The Recall is not usually applied to appointive
officials whether judges or administrative officers. But
there is no conclusive reason why it may not be so applied. It might properly be used to terminate the
official tenure of an administrative official whose term
of office has not expired, in order to give a new executive
a better chance to carry out the policies which he was
elected to carry out. Under this plan, administrative
officials whose work is satisfactory to the people would
be left undisturbed, and it would be unnecessary
either to give the executive arbitrary power of removal

or to handicap him by keeping in office important department heads who cannot be removed for cause but whose service and policies are unsatisfactory to the people. The Recall might even go to the extent of electing a substitute for an unsatisfactory appointive officer, on the theory that the executive, having made one failure, should not be trusted to try again during that term of office. These two ideas could be combined by providing that in case the Recall is instituted against an appointive officer during the term of the executive who has made the original appointment, the place should be filled by election; otherwise, by the new executive. Under many existing forms of city government, a Recall provision of this kind might prove very convenient and useful to the people. The same principle might be applied to the Recall of appointed judges, though with the judiciary there would be stronger reasons in precedent and established public opinion for leaving the vacancy to be filled in all cases by the executive.

The principal objections urged against the Recall in general and the principal arguments in its favor, together with its special application to appointive officers and to the judiciary, will be considered at greater length in succeeding·chapters.

CHAPTER XXI

FIRST OBJECTION TO THE RECALL—THAT IT WOULD TEND
TO WEAKEN OFFICIAL COURAGE AND INDEPENDENCE

In the program of fundamental democracy the Recall
is something of an afterthought. It was not indis-
solubly linked with the Initiative and the Referendum
until within the last few years. But its appeal to the
popular imagination and the striking effect produced
by the mere suggestion of it upon the emotions of the
office-holding class have brought to it a prominence that
is, perhaps, somewhat out of proportion to its relative
ultimate importance. It seems quite possible that with
the Initiative and the Referendum in good working
order, democracy could get along very well in many,
perhaps most, cases without the Recall. But the people
enjoy baiting the politicians. Anything that brings
consternation into the camp of the power-mongers
immediately awakens popular enthusiasm. Moreover,
the Recall being in a sense a more logical next step in
the development of the representative system than its
companion measures are and being more personal, direct, and hard-hitting, it has proved to be a source of
great practical strength to the general program of which
it is a part.

The popularity of the Recall and the circumstances
under which it has come to be a great nation-wide

political issue have a curious interest in connection
with the question of the value of courage and independence in public office. The opponents of the Recall are not slow to point out that it would have a most
deteriorating effect upon public officials, suppressing
in them the very qualities most needed for successful
public service. The changes are continually rung upon
the official timidity and time-serving that would result
from tenure during good behavior with the electorate
as the judge of what behavior is good. It is a patent
fact, admitted by everybody, that public officials cannot render the highest service if they are afraid to stand
up straight and perform their duties with an eye single
to the public welfare. American political history is
replete with evidences that the people love a fighter.
In many cases their admiration for a man's courage
will make them tolerate him even when they think
him to be wrong. But in the long run the value as well
as the popularity of official courage depends upon its
uses. Is it courage to do wrong that marks the highest
conception of official duty? Is it courage to turn on
the people and combat their interests? Is it courage
to set up individual opinions and ride roughshod over
public sentiment? What kind of official courage is good
for public service? Are the Americans a servile people,
happy only when they are browbeaten by officialdom?
Are they a roystering crew who need to be clubbed into
decency and self-respect? Are they children that their
ways should be ordered for them by the political elders?
It may be admitted that there is some possibility of
timorousness in public servants who are subject to discharge at any time. But this timorousness is based

either on the vagaries of the master or on the conscious
inefficiency of the servant. So far as the master is
concerned, we can either deny that he is subject to
vagaries or affirm that, if he is subject to them, it is his
own lookout. The people, when acting under responsibility, are not half so fickle and unreasonable as some
individuals would have us believe. In particular places
at particular times they may go wrong, but this is the
exception and not the rule, and it is the people themselves that have to suffer for it. They soon recognize
their own limitations and are willing to yield to the
advice of their official servants, if the intelligence,
faithfulness, and reasonable patience of these servants
have been proven in experience. The trouble in ordinary practice is that elected officials, secure in the
possession of public power for fixed periods, are often
tempted to repudiate their constituents and serve the
special interests from which continuous favors may be
expected. In fact, the representative system has so
far broken down in America that many legislators and
other public men have come to regard the electorate
merely as a sentry set to guard the gate of power and
keep men out who do not have proper credentials. If
they can catch this sentry asleep, or get him drunk, or
cajole him, or bribe him, or club him aside, or pass off
forged credentials on him, and so get into office, they
have nothing more to do with him. They have got
past him and can loot the city at their leisure. In
other words, election has come to mean to many men
simply a way, perhaps a disagreeable, inconvenient or
dangerous way,—but still a way of getting into office.
Now, when the sentry not only guards the gate but

sends his emissaries through the city to watch the behavior of those who have passed in and, if any of them behave like enemies, does not hesitate to bind them and cast them out again, treachery becomes dangerous and traitors lose their nerve. The people admire courage, but they do not look with favor upon men who ride into office on false pretenses and then flout the electorate whose powers have been exhausted by a single exercise of the right to vote. Under the political conditions that have developed in America it usually takes more courage, infinitely more, to represent the people after election than to betray them or to neglect them. Conditions have become so bad that it is now almost the normal habit of the voters, having elected men to office, to look upon them as public enemies, from whom nothing good can be expected unless it is cudgeled out of them. The city hall, the state house, and the national capitol are looked upon as the enemy's country, or, to speak more accurately, as the fortresses of the people which have long since been captured by the invaders that overrun the land and take tribute from the people. Sometimes, indeed, *all* Gaul seems to be pacified, but usually a desultory warfare is being carried on outside of the walled towns by the irrepressible lovers of liberty.

It is urged by some that while under the Recall an honest and able public official would have nothing to fear from the majority of the people, yet he would be subjected to the annoyance and expense of defending himself against the attacks of special interests offended by the strict performance of his duty. Great corporations have power to foment disturbances. They have agents and money with which to start Recall petitions. The liquor trade and the vice industry have ways of attack and are not always overscrupulous as to the means they use to discredit the officials they do not like. It is said that the Recall would put a weapon in the hands of the various disgruntled elements of the population with which to overawe executives and judges and keep them from the fearless performance of their duties. This argument may not be altogether without force, but its importance is greatly lessened by the number of voters whose coöperation is usually required for the initiation of the Recall. Special interests, with all their money and all their influence, find it difficult to secure the coöperation of one-fourth of the entire electorate in a procedure of this kind. There is some danger that if the necessary petitions are secured and a Recall election is ordered the incumbent official may be removed by his enemies on a light vote where inconvenience or apathy keeps large numbers of satisfied voters from going to the polls at a special election. This danger is minimized by the widespread interest that naturally is taken in a movement so radical as the attempt to remove a high public official from his office. It may be guarded against absolutely by a provision that no elected official can be recalled by fewer voters than a majority of the entire number cast at the time of his election, or if he was not elected by a majority of all the votes cast, then that he cannot be recalled by fewer voters than supported his original candidacy. But there is no good reason to believe that a public official courageously performing his duty to the satisfaction of a clear majority of the people, would be allowed to lose a Recall election through public apathy.

Sometimes the full performance of official duty necessarily involves the adoption of policies that are temporarily annoying and unpopular. Almost any large plan, whether it be for the reconstruction of a street, the overhauling of a school curriculum or the reorganization of an official staff, arouses hostility. Children often have to be forced to take medicine or submit to operations necessary for their welfare, perhaps even essential for the preservation of their lives. Are the people like children? Will they revolt at the first prick of the needle or at the first taste of bitterness of the drug, and recall their political doctor? "Only under a democracy can a nation commit suicide," says Dr. Weyl. Will the people do it under the Recall system? I think not. A far-seeing statesman may occasionally be driven from office for proposing remedies too painful for endurance. But, on the whole, statesmen are more likely to be recalled for temporizing, inadequate policies than for thorough-going measures that appeal to the imagination. The only thing needed to win popular support for a policy is to show the people that the policy is necessary for the permanent welfare of the state or the city even though it involves temporary hardships. The American people have almost too much imagination. They are almost too ready to postpone present comforts for expected future benefits. The very genius of their restless, progressive life, of their unremitting toil, of their tolerance of unpleasant and unwholesome conditions, is the dream of future achievement. The people at large are not half so likely to be sordid and to resent rugged statesmanship as are the minority who have wrecked the representative system in order to get control of government and who are now busily engaged in taking the profits.

In the end, the discussion of the Recall simmers down mainly to the fundamental differences of attitude and opinion between those who believe in popular government and those who do not. To those who believe in it, manhood suffrage is an existing condition, merely preliminary to universal adult suffrage—which is the theory of democracy. To those who do not believe in it manhood suffrage is a condition tolerable only on account of its failures, tolerable only as it can be diverted in practice from democratic theory and made an instrument for carrying out the will of the aristocracy. So long as the electorate can be influenced, can be bought and sold, can be driven or led, can be overawed or manipulated into the support of the vast structure of privilege and vested rights which constitutes the Powers-That-Be in American society, manhood suffrage is accepted by them, not as a theory, but as a condition. Are the people as a mass sane and self-reliant? Are they capable of intelligent and consistent political action under leadership that has only public ends in view? Are they, or are they not? Here is the nub of the controversy that rages about the Initiative, the Referendum, the Recall. To be sure, there are legitimate differences of opinion about the practicability of certain specific forms of these measures; there is doubt in regard to some details. But when the discussion wages hot, the big party lines stand out. On one side are those who do not so much disbelieve in these specific things as they instinctively oppose the acceptance of them and array themselves against those who are aggressively for them.   On the other side are those who do not so much believe in the necessity of the Recall as they resent the opposition to it.   They want to know why all this hullabaloo about it, why all this paralyzing fear that public officials will lose their independence as against their constituents.

CHAPTER XXII

SECOND OBJECTION TO THE RECALL—THAT IT WOULD
MAKE PUBLIC OFFICE LESS ATTRACTIVE TO HIGH-
CLASS MEN

At the present time public office, especially high
office, is in itself sufficiently attractive to men of calibre,
but they are often deterred from seeking or accepting
it by the terms imposed upon candidacy. There are,
indeed, plenty of fairly capable men who would be
willing to serve as aldermen and legislators even at the
meagre salaries now usually paid, if the conditions
of nomination, election, and subsequent service were
conducive to self-respect and free action. There can
be no denial of the fact that Americans like to hold
office. Perhaps one of our troubles is that too many
of them have political ambitions at the same time. It
is the unseemly striving, the expense of the competitive
canvass for votes, the secret obligations to the political
machine and the business interests that finance it, the
insufferable dullness of legislative stagnation while the
official performers mark time waiting for the political
impresario to nod, the innumerable checks devised under
our government to prevent decisive official action,—it
is these things that deter so many high-class citizens
from seeking careers in the public service. Even in
our efforts to dethrone the political boss and give the

control of nominations to the people in the direct primaries, an offensive emphasis has been put upon the ex-
pectation that men who are to have office must throw
themselves at it by filing petitions or paying fees and
making formal declaration of their own candidacies.
The recognition in the law that the man must seek the
office, rather than the office seek the man, throws a
wet blanket over the aspirations of men who wish at
least to observe the forms of modesty.   Even if modesty
is not quite so deep as receptive candidates would
have the public believe, yet the fiction is a useful one,
as it preserves the ideal that public office is primarily
an opportunity for public service rather than for self-
advancement.

That high-class men are now too scarce in the city
council, in the state legislature, in Congress, in the
executive and administrative departments of government, and even upon the bench will be freely admitted
by the most eloquent advocate of the status quo.   When
it comes to considering the effect of the Recall upon
the situation, we are compelled to resort to analysis.
We must look into the nature and disposition of "high-
class" men.   We must inquire whether they constitute a homogeneous element of the population or are
themselves liable to sub-classification.   Are appearances
ever deceiving in relation to them?   Then we must
inquire more fully into the underlying causes that have
created the conditions which now moderate the political ambitions of these best-qualified persons.   Is it
necessary and inevitable in the very nature of society
that high-class citizens, apparently in robust health,
should suddenly become "sicklied o'er with the pale

cast of thought" the moment it is suggested that they run for office? Would the Recall accentuate the disagreeableness of candidacy, or might it remove some of the existing hindrances to the free union of public service and personal distinction?

A great many people seem to regard men as distinguished in their fitness for public office in proportion as they have been successful in making money in private enterprises. Leading business men are looked upon as of the very highest class of citizens. It was at one time a widely-accepted slogan of municipal reform that city government is business, not politics. There is some truth in this view. Public office ought not to be an asylum for people who have too little energy or too little intelligence to make a living in private life. The head of a great department of city, state, or national government charged with the construction of public improvements, with the operation of a public utility, or with the organization of an army of clerks and accountants, needs business ability and experience. But mere ability to accumulate money through devious channels of commerce or by distorting the law for rich clients does not constitute a qualification for public office. Indeed, the spirit of money-grubbing, insatiate for the irresponsible power of great wealth, unfits a man for public service no matter how exceptional his ability may be. And so, many men who pass for high-class citizens are not in reality eligible at all. They are not attracted by public office except as they can use it for their own benefit or for the benefit of their allies in the business world. When they aspire to political power, it is to make government a branch

of private business. The fundamental distinction between public and private business is that the former
cares nothing for income except to meet necessary
expenditures, while the latter seeks income without limit, expenditures following after it.   The
motives that actuate the two kinds of business are
distinct and even conflicting. The result is that a
business man trained in the hard school of money-
making feels ill at ease in public life. He is like a fish
out of water, unless he takes the water with him. He
is used to looking upon people as raw material to be exploited for selfish ends, not as beings entitled to participate on an equal basis in the pursuit of life, liberty, and
happiness. Under his guidance government becomes
at worst an engine of oppression to enrich the strong
and at best a benevolent despotism to ameliorate the
condition of the poor. The spirit of coöperation in
service is foreign to the typical man of this class. He
may be a high-class captain of industry, but he is not
a high-class citizen. And only citizens in the ultimate
sense are eligible for public service. Moreover, aside
from his motives, a successful business man is quite
likely to prove a failure as a statesman. His training
is apt to give him narrow views and stereotyped methods
which are wholly unadapted to the conditions of governmental functioning. A man of this description is
seldom attracted to office at the present time except
when the nomination is handed to him on a silver plat-
ter by the political leader who controls the party organization. Then he is willing to subscribe liberally
to the campaign fund for the titular honor incident to
the holding of public prerogatives. He is generally

more or less of a figure-head in office, leaving the details of government to the underlings provided by the dominant organization. When such men enter upon campaigns for election, they simply open a barrel of money and pour it into the hands of the practical politicians who know how to use it. If men of this character found themselves in office held to a strict accountability to the people, it would be irksome. They cannot make up their minds to treat government as a major interest. They are in office to enjoy the honor of it, not to make it honorable.

On the other hand, there are men in almost every community who take an interest in public affairs as such. Sometimes these men are successful in private business, sometimes not. They have a broader outlook than the mere business man. They keep themselves informed on questions of public policy. They often initiate constructive schemes of public improvement. It may be that they start a movement for new parks or for better paving; possibly they interest themselves in tax reform or franchise restrictions; perhaps they work for the establishment of the merit system, or for the enactment of progressive legislation relating to labor. Such men have two important qualifications for public office. They have an interest in public affairs as such, and they know something about them. Sometimes these men are highly educated in academic political science; often their education has been wholly derived from the practical school of citizenship. If in addition to public motives and knowledge of public affairs, they have native ability for organization, for construction, for performance, they constitute the true high class among the citizenship of the community.

Men of this stamp are, for the most part, kept out of office now. Representative government does not choose the fittest men in the community for responsible positions. They would have to change their nature in order to be nominated and elected. Sometimes they go into practical politics, convinced that they can achieve reform only by fighting the Devil with fire. The next time we see them, their hands are black and their faces lurid. They are looking and acting just like the Devil himself. We are sometimes forgetful of the fact that the Devil is the Devil chiefly by reason of his using fire. He is evil because he has the appearance of evil. If reformers are going into politics to fight him they should use water, not fire, and often the pressure is low or the pipes broken. Invariably they fail to extinguish the Devil's conflagration when they can do no better than organize a bucket brigade. Observation and experience generally keep the faithful reformers on the outskirts of politics. One of the chief reasons they cannot be nominated and elected is the ignoble competition of cunning men whose nostrils are keen for the scent of spoil. When the unscrupulous jostle at the entrance, the scrupulous have no chance of getting in unless they become as they. And even if the reformers could be nominated and elected to office they would often find themselves bound hand-and-foot by the red tape intended for the rogues who were expected to win, or in the legislative assembly they would find themselves isolated and baffled by invisible influences. The interests that often control government do not want honest or even able men in official positions. They fatten upon governmental duplicity, inefficiency, and shortsightedness.

Now, if we are right in believing that the Referendum would lessen the opportunities for corruption in public office, by the same token it would remove in part the causes underlying the conditions that now make it impossible for high-class men either to be chosen to office or to render effective service when they are chosen. With the control of government by special interests broken down, with corrupt men deterred from seeking office by reason of its unprofitableness for them, the two principal difficulties that have stood in the way of the selection of truly high-class men for public positions would be removed. The Recall would not deter this class of men from accepting office. Responsible leadership, dependent upon the continued good will of the people, would be meat and drink to them. The opportunity for honorable public service and a direct appeal to the constituencies for support is just what they have all along been wanting. Big business men who have been trained to regard government as a secondary function of society might be further deterred by the Recall from the acceptance of office. But men trained for public service, with capacity for democratic leadership, would not be deterred. They would merely come into their own.

CHAPTER XXIII

THIRD OBJECTION TO THE RECALL—THAT IT VIOLATES
THE MORAL RIGHT OF THE OFFICIAL TO HOLD OFFICE
DURING THE FULL TERM FOR WHICH HE WAS CHOSEN

ALTHOUGH the law does not regard an election or appointment to public office as a contract formally binding upon the state, although it is a well-established principle that official positions may be abolished by the power that created them without any liability for damages to the dispossessed incumbents, it is nevertheless urged that the Recall would violate a moral and practical obligation which the people owe to their official representatives. It is pointed out that public officials are poorly paid, that candidates always have to spend a lot of money to be elected, that in office the expenses of necessary travel and entertainment are heavy, that public officials are mulcted for contributions to all sorts of philanthropic schemes (since beggars love a shining mark), that they have had to give up the jobs they previously held or make special arrangements for taking care of their private business before accepting office. For these various reasons, it is said that a public official is clearly entitled to enjoy the emoluments of office during the full term for which he was originally chosen and upon the basis of which he has made his financial calculations. Moreover, from another angle it is shown that a man sometimes accepts public office only because it promises him time and opportunity to work out certain reforms to which he is pledged. In such cases, it is as if a man were hired to do a certain job within a given time, or were hired to see what he could do with it in a given time. To take the job away from him before the time has expired or to cut short his experiment before he has had time to prove its value is regarded as both unfair to the employee and unprofitable for the employer.

Curiously enough, the opponents of the Recall have not been heard to object to the right of public officials to resign before the expiration of their terms. Yet if there is a moral obligation that militates against the right of Recall, it would seem with equal force to forbid resignation. The trouble is that in our political philosophy we have exalted the individual at the expense of the state. If sacrifices are to be made by either party, we instinctively feel that the state should make them for the individual, instead of *vice versa*. This is an unintelligent and false paradox, which has grown out of our excessive individualism. Why should we always pity the office-holder, and never sympathize with the people? Why should we feel that public business may be neglected, postponed or even sacrificed for the benefit of the private undertakings of the very men selected to attend to public affairs? Is it not a monstrous thing that public offices should be created for the benefit of the officials who are to fill them? When shall we be rid of this notion that government is a mere incident, a social diversion, a graft to be parceled out among the lucky ones?

The public can afford to be just to its servants. In fact, it cannot afford to be otherwise. The legitimate emoluments of an official subject to the Recall are a mere bagatelle in comparison with the stake the people have in the manner of his use of the prerogatives of office. By holding on to the reins of government for six months, or a year, or two years, after his inefficiency has been shown or after his official policy has deviated from the policy favored by the people, an official may work irreparable injury to the public interests. The mere question of his salary for the remainder of the term for which he was chosen is of feather weight to the public. It is proper that the individual should take this risk of personal inconvenience and loss in case he fails to retain the confidence of his employer, the people. Nevertheless, as a concession to prevailing sentiment, it might not be amiss to provide in the Recall for the payment to the recalled official of a portion, say one-half, of the salary he would have earned, if he had filled out his term. The public is not much concerned in keeping him from drawing the salary. It is gunning for bigger game. But in order to prevent abuse of public leniency, the question of the payment of this pension might be voted upon as a separate proposition at the Recall election, or it might be left for judicial determination by some public tribunal on the merits of each case. It might even be feasible under certain exceptional circumstances to allow the recalled official the full amount of his unearned salary. The state can well afford to court the gratitude as well as the respect of its citizens.

When we come to the question of the propriety of

curtailing a public official's experiments in government, no serious argument against the Recall can be made on the score of its unfairness to the individual. His disappointment may be great, but it is a trivial matter compared with the right of the people to control the policies and experiments of their public servants. If the exercise of the Recall in a particular case is contrary to their own best interests, the people will have to learn by experience. Ultimate discretion must be lodged somewhere, and the whole fabric of popular government in all its variations is founded upon the theory that the self-interest, the intelligence, the conservatism of the electorate are the best guaranty against the abuse of this discretion.

It is absurd that the private interest of any individual or set of individuals in continuing to hold office should be permitted to interfere for a single day with the execution of the public policies formulated by the underlying organs of the state. The government belongs to the people, does it not? If they would recall their agents, who shall gainsay them?

CHAPTER XXIV

FIRST ARGUMENT IN FAVOR OF THE RECALL—THAT THE
PEOPLE SHOULD HAVE A CONTINUING RIGHT TO
CORRECT MISTAKES IN THE SELECTION OF THEIR
PUBLIC SERVANTS

IN private affairs it is a well-established rule that the
principal has the right to discharge his agent whenever the latter proves unsatisfactory. In special cases
where employment has been given by contract for a
definite period, the rights of the employee in case of his
dismissal are limited to the compensation agreed upon.
He acquires no vested right to continue in the performance of particular acts as the servant of the employer,
and especially is this true where under the terms of his
service he acts as a discretionary agent.

In public affairs, in the field of legislation, a law, if it
proves to be wrong, can be amended. The tremendous
shock given to the entire country by the Dartmouth
College decision was due to the enunciation by the
Supreme Court of the rule that a legislative act granting corporate powers, without an express reservation
to the contrary, was irrepealable. The states almost
unanimously responded to this decision by making
constitutional provision for the reservation of the right
to repeal any corporation law, and Congress has adopted
the policy of expressly reserving this right not only in

laws governing corporations but in acts granting special franchises. Indeed, any right or property granted by the government may be resumed for public purposes upon payment of proper compensation to the grantees or their successors.

Upon these analogies, an argument for the Recall is founded. If it is the recognized practice in the every-day affairs of life to permit the master to discharge his servant when he wills, compensating him only in cases where a time contract has been made, and if it is thought to be essential to public welfare that the people or their representatives should always have the right to correct legislative mistakes by amending or repealing laws which have proven disappointing in practice, it seems to be equally reasonable and necessary that the people should have the right to correct mistakes made in the selection of their agents. That public officials frequently are chosen through a misunderstanding of their capacities or of their purposes is undeniable. That legislators deliberately betray their constituents and that executives do what they were not expected to do and fail to do what they were expected to do, are common experiences of our political life. If terms of office are very short and expire simultaneously so that the people can strike every obstructive official at one blow, and if the people have the rights of Initiative and Referendum, they may be able to minimize the dangers of irreparable damage to the public welfare arising out of fixed terms of office. But why should they be compelled to take an official for better or for worse, promising to love, honor, and obey him till his life or his term of office expires? Sometimes the delays or the readjustments of public policy caused by one refractory official occupying a strategic position in the governmental scheme and irremovable until his fixed term runs out one, two, three, or four years in the future, work a permanent injury to the public. Checks and balances among the departments of government may do very well, but why should one official be able to thwart the people's will and overbalance the people's power? It seems too absurd for defense that a city, a state, or the nation itself should be compelled to retain in its service for a period of two, or four, or six years an official who no sooner enters upon the performance of his official functions than he makes his unfitness for the office he holds manifest. This unfitness may take the form either of administrative incapacity, or of repudiation of policies he was elected to carry out, or of general misunderstanding of the people's will or lack of sympathy with it. The trouble may come in regard to old established policies of government, with reference to reforms that were at issue in the campaign preceding his election, or in connection with emergencies that arise subsequently. In any of these cases it is monstrous that government should be such a great, lumbering, unadaptable machine, as to prevent the people from meeting the occasion with the same free hand that characterizes private enterprises.

It may be urged that the people, having had opportunity to examine into the qualifications of candidates for office and to choose the most fit, should be compelled to stand by their selection. To this there is the practical answer that often the candidates are all unfit. If it be said that the people might themselves find fit men, irrespective of party nominations and individual canvasses, the practical answer is that the machinery provided by the legislature for the easy organization and the free expression of the will of the electorate is often defective and unworkable. Even if it be granted that by the Initiative, the Referendum, direct nominations, and other devices, a better machinery is provided, giving the people the fullest possible freedom in the selection of public officials, still they would make mistakes. Men are many-sided, mystery-enshrouded creatures. No electorate, especially in a populous district where long and intimate personal acquaintance with potential candidates for office is impossible, can be certain of its choice. What is more elusive than the character and fitness of a candidate in the heat and haste of an electoral campaign? Who can know the secret weaknesses of his nature? Who can see the invisible strings that are attached to him? Who can foresee the emergencies he may have to face during a term of office? After all other means for assuring the steady, reasonable fulfillment of the people's will in government have been exhausted, the need still remains for a practicable means of discharging public officials who no longer enjoy the confidence of the electorate. The Recall is such a means.

CHAPTER XXV

DEMOCRACY does not consist in rotation in office or
in the selection of a myriad of officials by popular vote,
but in the continuous responsiveness of government to
the needs and will of the people. True, under simple
conditions such as originally existed in the New England towns, where each community had a separate life
and distinct local needs, it was convenient and bene-
ficial to parcel out the functions of government to
many petty officials chosen annually at town-meeting.
The general participation of the people not only in the
determination of local policies but in the actual administration of them, was of great educational value
to the citizenship and did not seriously interfere with
efficiency. Local problems were comparatively simple
and did not require expert knowledge for their solution.
Local tasks were also simple and did not require technical experience for their performance. But conditions
have changed even in the towns of New England.
Cities have grown up and populations have run together. Roads, drainage systems, water supplies,
transportation lines, parks and boulevards, telephones,
electric light and power plants, great newspapers, trade

organizations, and an endless list of interurban and inter-town services and interests have touched local public affairs as with a wand. The old system of town politics has become progressively less efficient even though its forms survive. At every point local policies are connected with the affairs of a larger community. Everywhere even town administration calls for special knowledge, experience, breadth of view and coöperation on a large scale. Under the new conditions constant rotation in office and the selection of every official by popular vote have become causes of confusion and inefficiency. If this is true with reference to the town, which is the smallest important political unit, it is much more strikingly true of populous cities, widespreading states, and the nation itself. The general participation of the people in public affairs is no less important than it was in other days and under conditions that have passed away, but the old forms of participation have become ineffectual and obsolete.

Short terms of office and a multiplicity of elective officials impose a double burden both on the electorate and on the officials themselves. A political campaign in these days, even if it be only for the office of alderman, member of the legislature or city clerk, calls for the expenditure of much time and energy in making the acquaintance of the voters and considerable money in presenting the candidate's qualifications and principles to them. The less important the office, the heavier is the proportional burden of the campaign. The shorter the term, the less worth while is it to undertake the campaign at all. On the other hand, the people assume impossible burdens when they attempt to

discriminate between hundreds of unknown candidates
for scores of obscure offices. It is no impeachment of
the capacity of the people for self-government to allege
that they cannot do such an absurd and unnecessary
thing. The long ballot is the result, in part, of the
people's jealousy of irresponsible power. They have
demanded the right to retain over many public officials
the only sort of popular control that, until recently, has
been thought possible. But the device has failed, in
many cases utterly and ignominiously. The development of irresponsible party organizations with complete
control of the nominating machinery has turned the
long ballot into an instrument of tyranny, inefficiency,
and corruption. It has come to be a standard trick of
the political machine to place at the head of the ticket,
whenever it appears necessary for success, some respectable and well-known citizen who will be content
to be a figurehead, or even, if pressed by an active
public opinion, a man of the militant, progressive type,
and then to load up the rest of the ticket with undesir-
able henchmen who can be depended upon to conduct
their offices according to the dictates of the organization and to distribute the favors and the patronage
at their disposal for the further entrenchment of corrupt
politics. In most instances this trick succeeds, for
the attention of the people is concentrated on the principal offices and in the nature of the case they have
to depend upon the say-so of the party organizations
as to the fitness of minor candidates. The result is
that respectable men generally fill the big offices, while
inefficiency and favoritism run riot among the rank and
file of officialdom. Even when a militant reformer,

conscientious, able, energetic, with all the qualifications for rendering the highest type of public service, gets to be governor, or mayor, he finds himself checkmated and the practical working out of his plans hindered and perhaps stopped entirely by the leaden unresponsiveness of the men lower down in office whom he cannot remove and who cannot possibly be galvanized into the life of reform. In this way, administrations that start out with promise and glowing hope often end in disappointment and sometimes in dismal failure. The people do not get what they voted for. Not only is government kept ineffectual and wasteful, but the citizens' courage to strive for better things is checked and dissipated. Moreover, by short terms and frequent elections, the people find themselves breaking into the continuity of public policies and in danger of losing officials whose service is satisfactory and whose experience makes it more valuable than new officials could possibly render. If government is not for the office-holder but for the people, then short terms of office are a serious disadvantage.

One of the most conspicuous and promising democratic movements of the time goes under the name of the Short Ballot. It proposes to cut down the number of elective officers to a minimum and to concentrate their responsibility. By this means it is hoped to give the people a fair chance to be careful in the selection of the two or three or half dozen important officials voted for at one time, and to secure the full benefits of this more careful choice by giving to the few officials so elected authority to appoint all the others whose names now confuse the ballot. One of the means of shortening the ballot is by the lengthening of the terms of elective officials. Now, experience shows that concentrated responsibility and long terms are dangerous to democracy where there is no effective means of correcting mistakes in the choice of men to carry the responsibility. That mistakes will sometimes be made is clear enough from the fact that often now they are made in respect to the most conspicuous offices. When we get a mayor or a governor to suit us, we wish that the term of office was at least four or six years. When we get one who is a failure, we would be willing to undergo the hardships of a new election within six months. When the executive is honest, able, and aggressive, we rejoice that he has power, and are tempted to load more upon him. We are willing to put almost everything into his hands. But when the executive is weak, wily, or witless, we straightway would diminish his powers, deeming him hardly fit to appoint his own private secretary.

The long term and concentration of responsibility are swords that cut both ways, unless we can dull one of the edges. The Recall is a device for doing just that thing. With it in good working order, the people may safely remove the shackles from their executive and legislative servants and allow them official tenures consonant with the expert nature of their functions. One of the most distressing spectacles in American politics is the people painfully curtailing at every possible point the powers of the boards of aldermen and the state legislatures,—the very bodies which spring most directly from the people and whose free functioning is most essential to orderly political progress. The

Initiative, the Referendum, and the Recall furnish a well-knit system of rational popular control, devised for the very purpose of supplanting the expensive handicaps that have been imposed upon public officials by the popular jealousy and distrust of irresponsible and frequently-abused power.

CHAPTER XXVI

THE RECALL OF APPOINTIVE OFFICERS

IT has already been suggested in a preceding chapter that the Recall may be extended beyond its original scope and made to apply to public officials not elected, or not elected directly by the people. If the President or the members of the United States Senate were to be brought within its purview, the exercise of the right of Recall would probably be entrusted to another authority than the one originally responsible for the selection of the official to be recalled. When it is proposed to make Federal judges subject to the Recall, there is no thought of merely making them subject to removal by the authority that appointed them. They are to be recalled either by vote of Congress or by vote of the people.

Now, the opponents of the Recall principle, even when they are forced to admit the logical strength of the arguments in favor of the right of Recall of elective officers by the people or by the bodies who first elected them, deny absolutely any logical basis for the extension of the system beyond the scope of elections. They say that, bad as the Recall is in its practical effect when confined to the establishment of the people's right to revoke their own appointments, it would bring absolute chaos into government if the Demos were authorized

to stride about the sacred precincts with club in hand
and strike down at pleasure any official, no matter by
whom appointed. This, they say, would be utterly
demoralizing to the public service. It would give every
public official affected by it a two-faced responsibility.
Besides looking to the source of his original appointment for instructions, he would be compelled to take
orders directly from the populace. The horror-stricken
conservatives pray to be delivered at least from this
last wonder of the political nostrum-fakirs. If the
President *must* be recalled, let the Electoral College be
reassembled. If senators are to have their official
terms cut short, let it be by vote of the state legislatures.
If Federal judges are to be removed from office, let it
be by the President with the consent of the Senate; or
if it be state judges or city magistrates who were originally appointed by the governor and council or by the
mayor, let them be removed by the same authority.
If Cabinet officers, members of state boards, and administrative officials in cities are to lose their heads, let
the executive be the executioner.

There is great force in these objections to the extension of the scope of the Recall. And yet, if the Recall
cannot now be made applicable to these cases, it may
be necessary to prepare the way for it by extending the
system of popular elections. Already there is an overwhelming public sentiment in favor of making United
States senators elective by the people, in order to round
out the system of representative government under
which the members of the legislative branch are regarded
as in a peculiar sense the delegates of the electorate.
But, on the other hand, there is a strong move-

ment, backed by sentiment that is not altogether opposed to democracy, for the restriction of the elective
principle as applied to administrative and judicial
officers. The bewildering confusion of the blanket
ballot spattered all over with the names of obscure
candidates for obscure offices has proven to be one of
the chief causes of the irrational results that often come
out of the ballot-boxes. The glamor of facile speech,
friendly hand-shaking and convivial generosity often
wins for the unfit election to places of grave responsibility where expert knowledge is a primary qualification.
It is generally held, at least by the political scientists,
that the elective principle should not extend to the
choice of administrative experts. On the question
of the election of judges there is a sharp difference of
opinion among men who belong in the same party of
political thought.

Out of this welter of conflicting views, may we not
evolve a new theory? Is it not possible that the effective control of the people over government will be
helped along by the curtailment of the application of
the principle of popular election and by the extension
of the principle of the Recall? Obviously the people
have better opportunities to judge the fitness and
efficiency of a public official after he has been in office
for a time than they could possibly have had when he
was a mere candidate. In other words, the Recall
as applied to executive, administrative, and judicial
positions has a better basis in practical theory than
the Election. The Recall is an occasional procedure
based upon public knowledge and experience. The
Election is a sort of recurrent guessing-match. Cen-

tralized responsibility is often regarded as necessary
for efficiency in government and in business. But we
are learning that the boasted economies of centralization are likely to be more than offset by the loss of
individual initiative in the ranks and by the impossible
strain put upon the man at the center. It is organization of responsibility, not concentration of it, that makes
for efficiency. And so it may be that the appointive
power could well be left in the hands of the executive
on account of his better facilities for examining into
the special qualifications of men for particular administrative or judicial duties, while the power of
removal could well be given to the people through the
Recall. An executive has multifarious duties to perform. If he makes a mistake in a single appointment,
it may have serious results for the public, while to recall him for one mistake in one department may put
an over-emphasis on that particular branch of the
public service and bring about the selection of a new
executive who will be just as likely to make mistakes
in connection with other departments. If the executive
is regarded as in truth the servant of the people, why
should not the people have the right to overrule him
in a particular act as an alternative to discharging him
altogether?

While the principle of direct election is unquestionably sound as applied to legislative officers the practical
importance of changing the present method of choosing
United States senators would be greatly lessened, if
the people of the several states had the right of Recall
on them.

It would appear, therefore, that the application

of the Recall to public officials not originally elected by the people, if it is used merely as a mode of removal from office and does not include the direct election of their successors, is not wholly illogical and confusing after all. It may prove an effective means of organizing responsibility and of relieving the executive from the overstrain of centralized administration while at the same time removing the handicap that now rests upon individual department heads who dare not take any important action without first running to the executive and waiting for him to find time to examine into the matter and express his approval of the proposed act.

It hardly needs to be said that if the Recall is applied to appointive officers, the sufficiency of the petitions by which it is invoked will have to be determined either by the absolute number of the signers or by the relation of the number to the total number of registered voters or to the number of votes cast at some recent election held in the district in which the official's jurisdiction lies. The number cannot be a percentage of the total number of votes cast at the last preceding election for all the candidates for that particular office, for the office was not filled by election. In some cases, as for example in that of a United States judge, there may not be any officials elected at large in the district over which his duties extend. But the determination of the sufficiency of a Recall petition and the provision of the machinery for a Recall election under such circumstances are details that could readily be worked out.

CHAPTER XXVII

THE RECALL OF JUDGES

THERE are many men who are not seriously opposed to the Recall as applied to executive and legislative officers,—who, indeed, might be persuaded to tolerate the Recall of administrative officers holding by appointment,—who, nevertheless, are violently opposed to the Recall of judges even where the elective principle prevails in their original selection. President Taft's message in support of his veto of the resolution of Congress for the admission of Arizona to the sisterhood of states with a Recall provision in its constitution applying to all elective officers, including judges, was immediately recognized as a classic in our political literature. Yet it is somewhat difficult to analyze and restate his argument. Fundamentally, the objection to the judicial Recall is that, unlike the executive and the legislative departments of government, the judiciary is not supposed to be representative of the popular will except as it is definitely formulated in the constitutional or established law. While it is admitted that executives and legislators may properly respond to the progressive sentiment of the majority for the time being, it is held that the judiciary represents only the majority that has already grown old and become fixed. In other words, the judiciary is properly a conservative force in the state, representing the will of the permanent rather than that of the fleeting majority. It is urged that the permanent majority in reality constitutes the whole people, for every man finds it to his interest in the long run that the temporary minority should be protected against the hasty oppressions of the temporary majority. The whole people may be regarded as made up of a series of temporary minorities, or of a great mass of individuals every one of whom is sometimes in a minority.

"A popular government," says Mr. Taft, "is not a government of a majority, by a majority, for a majority of the people. It is a government of the whole people, by a majority of the whole people under such rules and checks as will secure a wise, just and beneficent government for all the people."

While it is true that the people can always be trusted to do justice when they all agree, as a matter of fact they seldom do all agree, and the mere numerical majority cannot invariably be trusted to do justice. "No honest, clear-headed man, however great a lover of popular government, can deny that the unbridled expression of the majority of a community converted hastily into law or action would sometimes make a government tyrannical and cruel," urges the President. "Constitutions are checks upon the hasty action of the majority. They are the self-imposed restraints of a whole people upon a majority of them to secure sober action and a respect for the rights of the minority, and of the individual in his relation to other individuals, and in his relation to the whole people in their character as a state or government.

"The constitution distributes the functions of government into three branches—the legislative, to make the
laws; the executive, to execute them; and the judicial,
to decide in cases arising before it the rights of the individual as between him and others and as between him
and the government. This division of government into
three separate branches has always been regarded as a
great security for the maintenance of free institutions,
and the security is only firm and assured when the
judicial branch is independent and impartial. The
executive and legislative branches are representative
of the majority of the people which elected them in
guiding the course of the government within the limits
of the Constitution. They must act for the whole
people, of course; but they may properly follow, and
usually ought to follow, the views of the majority
which elected them in respect to the governmental
policy best adapted to secure the welfare of the whole
people.

"But the judicial branch of the government is not
representative of a majority of the people in any such
sense, even if the mode of selecting judges is by popular
election. In a proper sense, judges are servants of the
people; that is, they are doing work which must be
done for the government, and in the interest of all the
people, but it is not work in the doing of which they
are to follow the will of the majority, except as that
is embodied in statutes lawfully enacted according
to constitutional limitations. They are not popular
representatives. On the contrary, to fill their office
properly, they must be independent. They must decide every question which comes before them accord-

ing to law and justice. If this question is between
individuals, they will follow the statute, or the unwritten
law, if no statute applies, and they take the unwritten
law growing out of tradition and custom from previous
judicial decisions. If a statute or ordinance affecting
a cause before them is not lawfully enacted, because it
violates the Constitution adopted by the people, then
they must ignore the statute and decide the question
as if the statute had never been passed."

Referring to the early establishment of the right of
the American judiciary to set aside particular statutes
on the ground of their unconstitutionality, Mr. Taft
asserts that "this power conferred on the judiciary
in our form of government is unique in the history of
governments and its operation has attracted and de-
served the admiration and commendation of the world.
It gives to our judiciary a position higher, stronger, and
more responsible than that of the judiciary of any other
country, and more effectively secures adherence to the
fundamental will of the people."

Taking up the specific Recall provisions of the Arizona constitution as originally adopted, Mr. Taft
points out that any judge "who has the courage to
render an unpopular decision" may be removed "arbitrarily and without delay" by majority vote. "We
cannot be blind to the fact," says he, "that often an
intelligent and respectable electorate may be so roused
upon an issue that it will visit with condemnation the
decision of a just judge, though exactly in accord with
the law governing the case, merely because it affects
unfavorably their contest. Controversies over elections,
labor troubles, racial or religious issues, issues as to the

construction or constitutionality of liquor laws, criminal trials of popular or unpopular defendants, the removal of county seats, suits by individuals to maintain
their constitutional rights in obstruction of some popular improvement—these and many other cases could
be cited in which a majority of a district electorate
would be tempted by hasty anger to recall a conscientious judge if the opportunity were open all the
time.

"No period of delay is interposed for the abatement
of popular feeling. The recall is devised to encourage
quick action, and to lead the people to strike while the
iron is hot. The judge is treated as the instrument and
servant of a majority of the people and subject to their
momentary will, not after a long term in which his
qualities as a judge and his character as a man have
been subjected to a test of all the varieties of judicial
work and duty so as to furnish a proper means of
measuring his fitness for continuance in another term.
On the instant of an unpopular ruling, while the spirit
of protest has not had time to cool and even while
an appeal may be pending from his ruling in which he
may be sustained, he is to be haled before the electorate
as a tribunal, with no judicial hearing, evidence, or
defence, and thrown out of office and disgraced for life
because he has failed, in a single decision, it may be,
to satisfy the popular demand."

We are even told that the Recall would put a dangerous power in the hands of political bosses, muckraking
newspapers and "those who have money enough to
employ the firebrands and slanderers in a community,
and the stirrers-up of social hate." Under such cir-

cumstances, what kind of judges could we expect to get? "Would not self-respecting men well hesitate to accept judicial office with such a sword of Damocles hanging over them?" The predicted effect of the Recall as applied to the judiciary is summed up in this one forlorn prophecy: "The character of the judges would deteriorate to that of trimmers and time-servers, and independent judicial action would be a thing of the past."

This Presidential message on the Recall of judges seemed to have considerable effect upon the public sentiment of the country. It crystallized conservative opinion and served as a rallying point for those who had been hard-pressed for arguments to meet the onset of this dynamic political idea coming out of the West. In the House of Representatives even Mr. Cannon was content to rest upon the President's statement of the case against the Recall. And yet, strange to say, possibly some may think as a first-class illustration of the soundness of the President's opinion of the majority, California made quick answer to the Arizona veto message and to the President's speeches in the Far West, by adopting the Recall by an overwhelming affirmative vote. Out of more than a score of constitutional amendments submitted to the people of that state by a reform legislature, the Recall, including the Recall of judges, proved to be by long odds the most popular. Evidently, the voice of the President, eloquent as it was, sounded to the Californians like a voice from the past. It seemed to be repeating a beautiful tale handed down unrevised from a century ago. It seemed unreal. It did not describe the judiciary as

California knew it. And if the truth must be told, the President's message does not describe the judiciary as Cincinnati, where Mr. Taft was born and reared, knows it, or as New York City knows it, or as Pennsylvania knows it, or as the state of Washington knows it, or as Colorado knows it, or as Missouri knows it, or as many other states and cities know it. Mr. Taft assumes that judges, no matter how they may have been selected, straightway, at least in the great majority of cases, become independent. He assumes that the judicial ermine falling upon the shoulders of a corporation lawyer or of an intriguing politician transforms him into a wise and just public servant. He admits that "in treating of courts we are dealing with a human machine, liable like all the inventions of man to err, but," he adds, "we are dealing with a human institution that likens itself to a divine institution, because it seeks and preserves justice." Did Mr. Taft really say that? and is it the same Mr. Taft who introduced his administration to the American people with a description of the delays and defeat of justice in our courts and announced the reform of judicial procedure as the public policy that lay nearest to his heart, as the chief addition that he hoped to make to the political repertoire inherited from his distinguished predecessor?

Upon what theory and upon what facts does the demand for the extension of the Recall to judicial officers rest?

In the first place, this demand rests upon the theory that the judicial department of the government is not a thing apart, more sacred than other departments and different from them in its accountability to the will of the people. While the judges are bound to act in accordance with the established law and to interpret and apply that law to specific controversies, they ought to be just as responsible to the people for the manner in which they perform this function as the executive and the legislature are for the performance of their respective functions. In adapting the law to the demands of justice, they should not forget that the letter killeth but the spirit giveth life. The people this very day of this present year may be assumed to be as fully aware of the necessity of preserving the fundamental rights of the minority as they were on the particular day of the particular year when they established a constitution to define the organization and limit the functions of the several governmental departments. Constitutions are not supposed to be frames of government handed down to the people by some superior being or class or generation gifted with exceptional wisdom, or even to be self-imposed restrictions adopted by the people in a lucid moment of a generally mad career. The fundamental laws of the land are assumed to be not merely what a wise generation some time in the past thought they should be, but what the people now and at all times believe they ought to be. The constitution of the United States and its amendments as well as the constitutions and constitutional amendments of the several individual states were beaten into shape on the anvil of practical politics. They were the subject of hot and passionate controversy. They were the crystallization of the will of a majority as fleeting as any majority that goes to the polls in these latter days.

There is no substantial reason to believe that the people of a past generation were wiser and less susceptible to mob influences than the people of the present. Indeed, the very fact of the immense circulation of the daily newspapers, the fact that the whole nation is simultaneously, almost instantaneously, informed of the events of the day, the fact that the discussion of any public question is immediately as wide as the interest in it, are favorable to intelligent conservatism. The people, so to speak, have become hardened to sensations.ˈ They are not easily aroused to radical action. Now and continuously they are as able to judge between constitution, statute, and passing whim as they were a hundred and twenty-five years ago. Our somewhat mythical Fathers were not so different from ourselves that we need to defer our judgment to theirs in matters that affect us, not them. If it is claimed that the majority is getting less and less self-restrained, more and more in need of guidance by the dead hand, this fact in itself would only add to the proof that the political institutions established by our forebears were inadequate. Has representative government, the characteristic product of the sacred constitutions of the past, been so egregious a failure that under its beneficent sway the people are daily becoming less fit for self-government, less capable of intelligent conservatism in political action? Upon what theory must the minority look to the past for the protection of its legitimate rights more than to the future? If the judiciary were to be set apart as a special department of government not responsible to the present majority but charged primarily with the protection of the minority, the few, the weak, the unfortunate, the under-dogs, why should it be compelled to follow the obsolete dicta of the passionate and unenlightened past? The protagonists of the minority might argue with better logic that the judiciary should look to the future and enforce rights which the blundering and truculent majority has not yet been induced by reason or experience to grant in the form of positive enactments. In other words, if the judiciary is to be the special protector of the minority, we have no reason to assume that individual rights have been more fully guarded by the majorities of the past and the constitutions and statutes they have enacted, than they will be by the public sentiment of to-day and the laggard laws to be enacted by future majorities in response to it. On the contrary, political development is more and more in the direction of protecting the individual against the aggressions of power and of hedging about effectively the rights of the weak and the unrepresented. But the theory that the minority needs a special organ of government to protect it from the oppressions of the majority, on the ground that the majority now is less solicitous of human rights either than it was at some time in the past or than it is going to be at some time in the future, is fundamentally fallacious. It is sufficient that the courts, like the other branches of the government, enforce the will of the contemporaneous majority.

De Tocqueville was astonished, eighty years ago, at the stability already manifested by the American democracy. With the eagerness of a true discoverer he explained it as resulting in large measure from the silent, but persistent influence of the bar and the bench, which he characterized as the real aristocracy in America. De Tocqueville represented an old-world point of view. He was surprised to find democracy succeeding so well. We, who believe in it, have been surprised to find it succeeding so ill. We are not so much afraid of the instability of our democratic institutions as we are that they will lose their fluidity and harden into a mere confining shell. We do not feel the need of the restraining influence of the judicial aristocracy whose actual functions were so acutely described by De Tocqueville. . The spirit of American democracy is better represented by the immortal stanza of Dr. Holmes:

> Build thee more stately mansions, O my soul,
>   As the swift seasons roll!
> Leave thy low-vaulted past!
> Let each new temple, nobler than the last,
> Shut thee from heaven with a dome more vast,
>   Till thou at length art free,
> Leaving thine outgrown shell by life's unresting sea!

If Mr. Taft's theory of the special function of the judiciary in fundamental American polity is a true reflection of the spirit and purposes of the founders of our government, that spirit and purpose have become obsolete. They shut us from heaven with a dome less vast than our present needs require. In this discussion we come again to the basic cleavage between parties. Do we fear democracy and wish to shackle it and keep it from interfering with our private enterprises? Do we regard government as useful only as it lends itself to the support of private undertakings? Or do we believe in democracy and wish to enlarge its scope and participate in its activities? Do we regard government as a

great coöperative enterprise, not confined to keeping
the peace and protecting the strong in the pursuit of
wealth, but extending to the communal activities necessary for the furtherance of the general welfare under
conditions as they exist from time to time? Again
we come upon the old confusion between majorities
of men and majorities of dollars. When the voice of
the past speaks of the protection of the minority, it
refers to the Few. When the voice of the present
speaks of the minority, it refers to the Weak. If
present industrial tendencies are not speedily checked,
the voice of the future proclaiming the rights of the
minority may, by a strange paradox, refer to the
Many. If the judiciary were to have a special kind of
independence and responsibility, should we not recall
judges for failure to anticipate and apply in advance of
their formal enactment the laws of justice that lie in
the public mind, rather than shield them from the
Recall when they obdurately apply the obsolete, but
unrepealed injustice of the past?

If we turn from the realm of pure theory to the realm
where theory and fact are mixed, we find a second
ground upon which the extension of the Recall to
judges is demanded. It is still proclaimed by many
who oppose the judicial Recall that judges have no
law-making functions, that they merely perform the
expert service of telling what legislative English means
and of fitting each new enactment into the garment
of legal precedent. It is strange that intelligent men
should still insist on proclaiming this interesting fiction.
The facts are known, and believers in the Recall as a
general instrument of democracy maintain that its

extension to the judiciary is logical and necessary, at least so long as the courts exercise the right to declare statutes unconstitutional and thus participate, even though negatively, in the legislative function. If the Supreme Court of the United States is in reality the supreme law-making body of the nation, restrained in any particular instance only by the fears or the opinions of the "fleeting majority" of its members, the argument for making the justices subject to the Recall cannot be less strong than the argument for the Recall of senators and representatives, unless the objection be raised that the justices are appointive, not elective officials. In answer to that objection, the Recall may be made generally applicable to high public officials not originally elected by popular vote, as was suggested in the preceding chapter, or the Recall as applied to the Supreme Court judges may take the form of a joint resolution of the two houses of Congress or of an order of the President approved by the Senate. The courts must either give up their policy-determining functions or else submit to the same forms of popular control that apply to the executive and the legislative departments.

If now we put theories entirely aside, and confine ourselves to an examination of the facts regarding the practical workings of the American judiciary, we shall find still further reasons in support of the demand for the extension of the Recall to judges. The judiciary is now generally recognized to be the bulwark of vested interests, of property rights so called. Indeed, on numerous and sundry occasions it has found the opportunity and has had the courage, I had almost said the effrontery, to proclaim this fact. The essentially anti-democratic functions assumed by the American courts have become so notorious that Dr. Hadley, in his justly celebrated Berlin lecture, discarded the classical distribution of powers in the American government and set up a new division—the forces of property on one side, the forces of democracy divided between the executive and the legislature on the other, and the judiciary as arbiter between the two.[1] It is this alignment of the judiciary as a buffer to protect property against the assaults of people, and its practical effects upon the welfare of the state, that give greatest force to the popular demand for some effective means of rebuking the presumptions of the courts. The "independence" of the judiciary is seen to be for the most part mere independence of the people. And the case is made worse through the faults of judicial procedure by reason of which justice is so delayed and becomes so expensive that it is practically non-existent for little men except as they are able to catch some of its reflected light from the litigation of big men whose interests happen to be identical with theirs. Wrongs go unrighted, crimes go unpunished, while our judicial fates spin, spin, spin, spin on forever. In their hands red tape has become the thread of life. The people see that something is radically wrong with the courts. The judges shunt the blame on to the lawyers and the lawyers shunt it back. The legislature might take action, but being composed for the most part of lawyers it is deeply impressed with the impracticability of in-

[1] "The Constitutional Position of Property in America," by Arthur Twining Hadley, published in "The Independent" of April 16, 1908.

voluntary reforms. While the judges sleep in security on the bench, the processes of justice drag out their lengthening train. Every judge has some excuse. By unanswerable logic he can prove himself not guilty. President Taft himself, in a message to Congress only eight months prior to his veto of the Arizona Recall, used these words: "One great crying need in the United States is cheapening the cost of litigation by simplifying judicial procedure and expediting final judgment. Under present conditions the poor man is at a woful disadvantage in a legal contest with a corporation or a rich opponent. The necessity for the reform exists both in United States courts and in all state courts." He pointed out that the equity rules of procedure in the United States courts, which affect much the more important and much the more expensive portion of their business, are practically the same to-day as they were in 1789 when the Supreme Court was organized, although that court is charged under the law with the duty of framing these rules and has full power to revise them. The believers in the judicial Recall are of the opinion that, with it as a goad, the people might induce a judge here and there to find a way of accepting responsibility for the reform of judicial procedure. What becomes of the so-called "independence" of the judiciary when the executive, a coördinate branch of the government, in an address to the legislature, another coördinate branch, dares to prod the Supreme Court of the United States in such language as Mr. Taft used in his message to Congress of December 6, 1910? "Several of the Lord Chancellors of England and of the Chief Justices," said he, "have left their lasting impress upon

the history of their country by their constructive
ability in proposing and securing the passage of reme-
dial legislation effecting law reforms. I cannot conceive
any higher duty that the Supreme Court could perform than in leading the way to simplification of
procedure in the United States courts." If conditions
are as bad as Mr. Taft says they are, and if the courts
do not respond to the admonitions of the coördinate
branches of the government, why should not the judges
be subject to Recall by the people, who are the source
of power of all the departments and should be the ultimate arbiter between them?

But not only do the courts stand as the bulwark of
special interests and spin red tape that binds the poor
to their poverty; they also distribute political and
personal favors from the bench that represent one of
the most subtle forms of corruption known to American
public life. Receiverships, and commissionerships, and
trusteeships, and refereeships, handed out by the courts
at the behest of unseen powers, often carry with them
the right to rob bankrupt properties or to mulct the
public under the guise of salaries, fees, and expenses.
Smug and tranquil, clothed with arbitrary powers, responsible to no one for their discretionary acts, the
judges support practices that are essentially corrupt
and that sometimes even break the spell of interested
silence laid upon them and create a public scandal.
The lawyers do not correct or expose the abuses of the
courts, either because they participate in them or because they are afraid of the judges who try their cases.
It needs a rude strong arm from the outside to enforce
the standards of common honesty upon the courts

themselves when they have the control of funds and the fixing of fees.

The Recall may not be a necessary or even the best remedy for the practical abuses that flourish in the courts. The chief danger, however, is that it might not prove effective as a remedy, not that it would degrade the courts and make the judges mere puppets of the people's will. The people at large are more interested in fairness than any set of irresponsible officials can possibly be. The people are conservative in their attitude toward justice between man and man, and it is more important that they should continue to be so, than that conservatism should be imposed upon them by an inflexible institution. Powers unexercised are ultimately lost. Discontent, ultra-radicalism, and even smashing windows may easily result from the imposition of arbitrary restraints upon the people and from the refusal to let them assume continuous responsibility for the protection of individual rights and property rights. It is unsafe to assume that the citizens of the United States are becoming progressively inexperienced in politics and progressively unfit for self-government.

PART V

MAJORITY RULE—THE INITIATIVE, THE
REFERENDUM AND THE RECALL
COMBINED

CHAPTER XXVIII

FIRST GENERAL OBJECTION TO MAJORITY RULE—THAT
IT IS DESTRUCTIVE OF THE REPUBLICAN FORM OF
GOVERNMENT GUARANTEED BY THE FEDERAL CON-
STITUTION

No other argument against the Initiative, the Referendum, and the Recall, which, for brevity's sake, we
may call Majority Rule, has caused such a waste of
statesmen's breath as this one, that these institutions
are unrepublican and, therefore, in violation of the
Federal constitution. The question has become wholly
academic since the recent decision of the Supreme Court
in the Oregon case, remanding to the political branch of
the government entire jurisdiction in the matter. Inasmuch as two Presidents and two Congresses have
admitted states to the Union, declaring their constitutions to be republican in form, although they included
provisions for the Initiative and the Referendum, and
since Congress has accepted the credentials of senators
and representatives from nearly a dozen different
states which have established Majority Rule more or
less completely, it seems safe to regard these instruments of democracy as no longer in danger from the
Federal constitution. Whatever the framers of that
instrument may have meant by the word "republican,"
we have practically settled it that the present meaning

of the word is broad enough to include a government
in which the representative system is supplemented by
the reserved right of the people to take direct action
in legislative matters.

The Recall has not at any time been in real danger
of being considered unrepublican, for it is nothing but
the obverse of popular election, and that is an essential
element in any definition of a republic which has ever
been seriously propounded. The Initiative and the
Referendum, however, have been in some danger, on
the theory that Madison's distinction between a republic as a representative form of government and a
democracy as a direct form was the commonly accepted
distinction when the convention of 1787 was in session.
The authorities show that opinions differed then as
they do now on the question as to whether or not a
democracy is also a republic. The founders of the
Republic were not required to pass upon the political
legitimacy of the Initiative and the Referendum, for
these institutions were practically unknown in their
day. "Nevertheless, from the tone of the Constitution
one may reasonably infer," says Professor Beard, "that
they would have looked upon such a scheme with a
feeling akin to horror. Everywhere in the laconic
record of the proceedings of the Convention preserved
by Madison there are evidences that one of their chief
purposes in framing the Federal Constitution was to
devise a system of checks and balances which would
effectively prevent direct majority rule in any form." [1]

There is no doubt that the constitutional argument

[1] "Documents on the State-Wide Initiative, Referendum and Recall," by Charles A. Beard and Birl E. Shultz, p. 28.

against Majority Rule gained considerable force from the spirit of the constitution and of the men who framed it.   Nevertheless, the argument sprang mainly from opposition to the thing itself.   This opposition hoped to make itself more effective by hiding behind a dictum of the eighteenth century.   It was voiced by men who do not believe in direct government or in the right of the majority to enforce its will in public affairs.   Even though the Supreme Court has refused to take jurisdiction, and Congress by its acts has already determined that Majority Rule is not unrepublican in the constitutional sense, those who oppose it will still be entitled to speak of it as inconsistent with the spirit that presided over the Republic at its birth, and to gain for their position whatever strength this allegation may give.   They may argue that Majority Rule is in fact unrepublican, revolutionary, and un-American.   But they can no longer hope to check its progress on the theory that it is unconstitutional.   The argument from now on will have to be on the merits of the question, not on the technical definition of a word as it was used by the Fathers.

Majority Rule unquestionably effects a radical change in the organization of the state.   It is to be noted, however, that even in Oregon where it has been used most extensively, the number of measures submitted to the people under the Initiative and the Referendum combined is insignificant in comparison with the number enacted by the representative legislature without reference to the electorate.   Majority Rule is not designed to destroy representative government and does not do so.   It merely checks and supplements the work of the legislature, and, if the contentions of its friends are sound, perfects and strengthens the representative system which has become perverted without it. Thus it is held that a little leaven of pure democracy makes republican bread light, porous, and palatable. It is still wheat bread though yeast has been used in its making.

CHAPTER XXIX

SECOND GENERAL OBJECTION TO MAJORITY RULE—THAT IN REALITY IT IS RULE BY THE MINORITY

It is said that the acts of the legislature are more representative of the will of the majority than laws passed by direct vote of the people, for the reason that almost invariably a greater number of electors participate in the choice of public officials than express themselves on measures submitted to the Referendum. Indeed, sometimes only a small percentage of the voters take the trouble to register their will on uninteresting or obscure propositions that are placed upon the ballot. It is said that even in Switzerland, the alma mater of modern democracy, laws are sometimes passed by the legislative body representing a large electorate and then vetoed on the Referendum by vote of a much smaller number. If, for example, the legislators elected receive 500,000 votes, while only 300,000 voters all told take part in the Referendum election, a law passed by the legislature may be rejected by a total negative vote less than one-third as large as the affirmative vote by which the legislators were entrusted with power. Perhaps, even, the legislators are subsequently re-elected by a larger vote than before. Where measures proposed by the Initiative are adopted by a majority on a light vote, there is not the same apparent reversal of the mandate of a more numerous majority, but nevertheless laws are passed affecting the rights and duties of the whole people by vote of what may be a small minority of them. Under the Recall an officer who was elected by an overwhelming majority on a heavy vote may be removed by a bare majority on a light vote. It is even urged that the petitions filed to invoke the Initiative, the Referendum, or the Recall do not in reality represent the will of the petitioners themselves. The abuses characteristic of the circulation of petitions for ordinary purposes are well known. It is said that even in matters of such transcendent importance as the Recall of public officials or the initiation of weighty legislative measures, men sign petitions because they are asked to do so, without really understanding or caring about their contents. Under such circumstances not only may important policies of state be determined by a small minority of the people who are entitled to vote, but the very election itself may be forced upon the people by a spurious demand. Almost anything is possible as a product of this system, if the petitions themselves are no guaranty of popular interest and if the majority of the people refuse to be dragged to the polls at inconvenient times and seasons to pass on questions about which only a very few have any accurate knowledge or care.

These are grave indictments. Unless they can be fairly met, the system of Majority Rule will be in large measure discredited.

We may remark at the beginning, however, that the relative size of the majority at a Referendum election as compared with the majority at an election for the members of the legislature has no necessary significance, even where legislators whose measures have been rejected by a small vote are themselves reëlected by a larger one. In the election of representatives the people do not pass directly upon any specific measures, nor even remotely on the great mass of measures that subsequently pass the legislature. One candidate having many planks in his platform may be voted for by one citizen on account of one of them and by another citizen on account of another. In one legislative district a candidate may be elected on account of his position on a local issue even though the majority of his constituents are against him on certain general issues. It is safe to say that almost never does the election of a particular set of legislators in separate districts establish any clear record of the people's will on any specific policy. It may also be said that the reëlection of a legislator seldom proves that the majority of his constituents agree with him on any specific measure which he has favored or opposed. Under these circumstances the veto of an act of the legislative body may not be at all a reversal of the majority by which the members of that body were elected.

It may also be urged with much force that in all probability the result arrived at on a light vote is usually representative of the sentiment of the entire body of citizens; for what reason is there to suppose that there is more apathy on one side of a question than on the other? If a great multitude of people do not trouble themselves to go to the polls, it is probably because their interest in the result of the election is not very keen. Of course, this cannot be urged in the case of referenda taken, either by accident or by design, at times when it is inconvenient for large numbers of the people to go to the polls. It may be an election called in the dog days when many of the well-to-do people are away on vacations. It may be at hours when the factories are running and workingmen have difficulty in leaving their work to vote. But on ordinary occasions the people most interested on either side of the question at issue will go to the polls, while those who are only feebly interested on either side will fail to do so.

The danger of government by the minority through the forms of Majority Rule may be guarded against absolutely by a provision that Initiative measures shall not be adopted or Referendum measures be vetoed except by a specified number of votes or by a majority of the registered electors or of the electors voting at a regular election. This remedy is considered so drastic as practically to prevent the successful use of the Initiative or the Referendum except on rare occasions, unless the number of votes fixed as a minimum requirement is considerably less than a majority of all the citizens having the right to vote. It is urged that indifference should not always be thrown into the scale of conservatism and every stay-at-home or blank vote be counted against positive action by the electorate and in favor of sustaining the legislature. The friends of Majority Rule refuse to be disturbed by the objection that under this system the electorate is smaller than in the election of officials. They say that even if the number of voters is smaller, their character is more select. They say that the submission of measures to popular vote results in the automatic disfranchisement

of the unfit. To their minds, if a man is too ignorant
on general principles or does not know enough about
the particular measure at issue to cast his ballot intelligently, it is perfectly proper that he should not be
counted one way or the other in the settlement of the
question. While ignorant or venal voters are mar-
shalled at the polls in favor of some candidate who
wants office very badly, it is said that measures are
impersonal and have no interest in their own fate one
way or the other, and that consequently the motive
for corruption is absent. This is unquestionably true
in many cases, though in some, where large private interests are affected, corrupt methods may be employed
even in connection with a vote on measures. Nevertheless, corruption is undoubtedly more difficult and
less likely to take place where the vote is on measures
than where it is on men. The venal vote is generally
indifferent to anything except the price of venality.
Hence it abstains from recording itself where no price
is offered. Likewise with the ignorant vote, it takes
less interest in abstract measures than in concrete
persons. And so it is that Majority Rule appears
to be rule by the minority, while as a matter of fact
it is rule by the majority of the fit. Even the advocates
of pure democracy are not interested in mere numbers,
except as every unit that is counted represents a live
opinion.

It seems to me that the theory of the self-disfranchisement of the unfit coupled with the normally
representative character of a popular vote even where
only a portion of the entire electorate goes to the polls,
presents a satisfactory answer to the objections to

Majority Rule here under consideration, except in those cases where the petitions are insufficient in size or too defective in quality to guarantee the existence of a widespread general interest in the measures to be voted on. It may be well as an extra precaution to require a certain minimum vote for the enactment or rejection of laws or for the removal of public officials, but attention should be mainly directed towards the petitions. In one Western town the ease with which the Recall was recently worked provoked the suggestion that a provision should be enacted requiring all would-be petitioners to go to the city hall to sign their names. In a small town this might not be altogether unreasonable, but in any place of considerable size a sufficient number of other convenient places would need to be designated in order to keep the Recall in any sense a workable instrumentality. For Initiative petitions, it is possible to devise a plan for taking signatures at registration and election places under the supervision of the regular precinct officials, and as for the Referendum the dangers incident to defective petitions are much less vital. Of course, all signatures to Majority Rule petitions should be properly verified and carefully checked against the registration lists, but it is impracticable and unnecessary to guard against signatures that are given as the result of solicitation rather than out of self-expressing eagerness. Votes as well as signatures are influenced by solicitation and argument but we do not refuse to count them. Indeed these votes furnish leadership its opportunity, and without that democracy would be confused and helpless. Neither does it seem wise to raise the required percentages or absolute numbers, as the case may be, to any great extent as a concession to the abuses of professional petition-mongering. The better way is to insist upon the genuineness of the signatures and a fullness of statement that will discourage citizens who have no special interest in the matter from lending their names merely out of good nature or to satisfy importunity. The extension of the suffrage to women, though greatly increasing the number of signatures required where petitions are based on percentages of the entire electorate, may nevertheless make a rational canvass for signers easier. The women can be found at home during the daytime and with their coöperation it should be less difficult to circulate petitions according to residence and voting district than it is where only men enjoy the suffrage.

CHAPTER XXX

THIRD GENERAL OBJECTION TO MAJORITY RULE—THAT IT INVOLVES THE FURORE AND EXPENSE OF FREQUENT ELECTIONS

POPULAR elections are very unpopular with some people. Expensive, ineffectual, disturbing to business, productive of excitement and exaggeration, attended with outbursts of vulgarity and ill-will, frequent elections are regarded as an inconvenience, even as a public curse. The cost and the clamor of elections are one of the arguments most frequently urged against Majority Rule, and most widely credited. Bad as conditions now are with one year out of every four spent in preparation for a Presidential election and another in recovering from its effects, with state elections every second year and in some commonwealths annually, with city and judicial elections thrown in for good measure, and our basket of woes actually heaped up and running over with bond elections, and charter elections, and franchise elections, and what-not elections, it is urged that the adoption of the Initiative, the Referendum, and the Recall would be an inexcusable running after folly. Many people do not enjoy the sound or the sight of democracy at work. Its noise grates upon their nerves. Its interferences are disconcerting. The mountain labors mightily only to bring forth a mouse. Then why all this turmoil and expense? With a Recall election invoked every few weeks by the political malcontents, with an Initiative election every little while to satisfy the demands of the political dreamers and with a Referendum election after every session of the legislature and almost after every meeting of the city council to give the minority another whack at the way things are going, what hope can we ever again have of enjoying even a modicum of peace and prosperity?

In considering this objection to Majority Rule, attention should first be called to the fact that under it precautions may be and usually are taken to discourage the multiplication of elections. The Recall, to be sure, always involves a special election, but this may be more than offset by the lengthening of terms of office, and the consequent diminution in the frequency of regular elections. Moreover, the number of petitioners required to invoke the Recall is usually so large as to discourage its use except at times when the people are glad to incur the expense and trouble of an extra election for the sake of correcting a grave political mistake. A man who employs a servant or appoints an agent is often greatly irritated by the necessity of stopping in the midst of important or interesting work to discharge him and find another to take his place. The employer grumbles at the time lost and the bother of the thing, but he would much rather undergo these annoyances than be compelled to put up with bad service or fraudulent representation for a long period. To discourage the multiplication of elections for Initiative purposes, the law usually provides that a much larger number of signatures shall be required to call a special election than to submit a proposition at the next succeeding regular election. Such a provision has a powerful effect, for the expense and trouble of securing additional signatures will prevent the proponents of any Initiative measure from trying to get a special election unless they deem their proposition to be of an emergency character, which is seldom the case. The Referendum is more likely to be an emergency measure, and then the emergency is past when the petitions are filed and the legislative act aimed at suspended. Therefore, there is no call for a special election unless the executive, in his discretion, issues one. So we see that Majority Rule aims to be conservative in the matter of elections, though not absolutely preventing an increase in their number. Sometimes a further provision is made, limiting the number of measures that may be submitted to the people at one time. This limitation, if devised in good faith, is intended to simplify the issues and prevent disorder and confusion, but few advocates of Majority Rule are willing to accept it. They prefer to take their chances on the people's good sense preventing or overcoming the disadvantages of a laborious and complicated election.

It is to be noted, further, that Majority Rule is calculated to modify the characteristics of popular elections. The relative importance of persons is diminished and that of measures is increased. Now, while a campaign on a franchise question or a question of issuing bonds or of consolidating areas of government may give rise to bitterness and exaggerated statement, it cannot be doubted that in the majority of instances a discussion of measures is likely to be more dignified and enlightening than a discussion of candidates. With the adulation of personal friends or hopeful followers as well as the unjust personal attacks of individual or political enemies eliminated, and with the people relieved of the sickening spectacle of eager candidates throwing themselves at the heads of the electorate by effusive bragging and the tapping of beer-kegs, we might certainly hope for a toning-up of the processes of democracy so that they would become less offensive to people with delicate sensibilities. While there will still be candidates for office and popular elections to select representatives, the whole theory of Majority Rule looks to a large reduction in the clamor of campaigns. This result, it is expected, will be brought about by a reduction in the number of elective officers, by the lengthening of their terms, by the diminution of the opportunities for official corruption and the consequent discouragement of office-seeking by unscrupulous men who are willing to make an election canvass a ribald riot if thereby they may win votes, by the greater relative weight given to platforms and measures as compared with persons, by the inducements offered to men of character and dignity to enter public life and to participate in public discussions, and by a hundred other influences tending to redeem democracy free, from the characteristic absurdities of democracy with its feet tangled in the ropes.

And, finally, if Majority Rule makes popular elections what they ought to be, namely, the means by which an enlightened people registers its will after full and fair discussion of questions intimately affecting the welfare of every citizen, then the objection to them on the score of expense and bother falls to the ground, be they few or be they many. In the nature of things, there is nothing more worth while to everybody than real politics. There is nothing of more entrancing and persistent interest. It is only when elections are futile that their cost is wasted. In cities, especially, where the conditions of life tempt men and women, particularly the young, to dissipation and folly, frequent elections, if conducted in the true spirit of democracy, are a cultural influence of the highest value. They are a means of practical civic education. No money effectively spent in the training of the citizenship and the organization of the processes of democracy is ever wasted. To withhold the expenditure is the fatal extravagance.

CHAPTER XXXI

FOURTH GENERAL OBJECTION TO MAJORITY RULE—THAT IT LAYS TOO HEAVY A BURDEN UPON THE TIME AND INTELLIGENCE OF THE ELECTORATE

IF the people are unable to do such a simple thing as to elect the best men among them to perform official functions, how can it be supposed that they will be able to pass intelligently on complex legislative measures which only experts can understand? If representative government has failed because of the sheer neglect of the people to attend to little duties, why should we expect them to take care of great ones? If the people's political back is so feeble that it bends double under a hundredweight of obligation, how shall it rise upright under a ton? The disbelievers in popular government develop a case of acute sympathy for the over-burdened electorate. The trouble with our country now is, so they say, that the people have already been given too much to do. They have to earn a living anyway. They have families to care for. They must have some amusement, for nature demands that labor be followed by relaxation. They do not wish to be bothered with a multiplicity of public duties. It is because the people cannot attend to public affairs directly that the representative system has been devised to clothe selected men, who have both time and knowledge, with discretion in governmental matters. Why, then, shall we attempt to require of the people "the intolerable toil of thought"?

"If you would have your business thrive, go; if not, send," is a good old adage with many applications. One of them is to the affairs of government. There is a fatal element in the sympathy for the people that would relieve them of political responsibility and allow them to lapse into civic lethargy. In America, since the Declaration of Independence was issued, government has always been regarded, theoretically at least, as the people's business. It is a business that they cannot shirk with safety to the state. Democracy can live and grow only by exercise. It may be necessary for the people to send representatives on the public business, but once in a while they need to go themselves in order to see that their interests are being properly looked after. It is not altogether inexplicable that there should be found those in the state who are perfectly willing to relieve the people at large of the responsibilities of government. The comparatively small segment of the population from which the official class is mainly recruited and which lays hold of the problems of government with interested avidity, is not at all averse to the exercise of power, unrestrained by the meddlings of the populace. Agents of wealthy men are pleased to be given a free hand in the management of their masters' property. They are satisfied to have the owners spend their time yachting or dabbling in philanthropy or patronizing chorus girls, leaving their money affairs in experienced hands that are not required to render an account of their stewardship. The lawyers, who supply all the raw material for the judiciary and the bulk of it for the legislators and the important executive and administrative officials, and the powerful few who do not find it very difficult to enlist the services of lawyers whether in or out of office, naturally enough are content to have the government left to themselves. They can then establish customs that make bribery venial, peculation from the public treasury a mere matter of precedents, and franchise-grabbing eminently respectable, even meritorious. If the ignoramuses who compose the mass of the people can only be induced to keep their hands off the affairs of state, everything will go along smoothly, business will prosper, the wealth of the country will flow into the hands of the thrifty ones who best know how to use it, and how much better it is for everybody!

But when these Greeks come bearing gifts, the people may well beware.

The argument that if the electorate has failed through neglect to choose honest and able men to office, it has thereby proven its unfitness for larger tasks and graver responsibilities is sufficiently plausible to demand a careful examination. When the radicals say that the cure for the failures of democracy is more democracy, they may be stating a truth, but, if so, it is one that needs to be established with proof. This whole controversy rages around three questions—first, are the people indifferent to public affairs? second, are they too busy with other things to attend to them? third, are they too unintelligent to be concerned with them profitably? These three questions go to the very root of democracy. The answers to them will reveal the capacity for self-government possessed by any given people at any given time.

Let us first consider the question of popular indifference in the United States to-day,—its extent, its causes and the probable effect of it upon Majority Rule and *vice versa*. At Presidential elections the number of votes cast runs from about 60% to about two-thirds of the total number of males of voting age residing in the United States. When we take into account the great numbers of unnaturalized immigrants included among the males of voting age and the colored men, who are practically disfranchised in most of the Southern states, the popular interest taken in Presidential elections as indicated by the vote cast seems to be reasonably acute in all portions of the country except where political life has been blighted by race prejudice. It is true that the number of votes cast at state and local elections is almost always considerably smaller than at Presidential elections, and that the vote cast on Referendum measures is still smaller, occasionally approaching the vanishing point. It is also true, or at least it appears to be so from a long series of experiences, that the electors generally take a more extensive interest in men than they do in measures. In spite of the widespread participation of the people in elections, popular apathy is generally heralded as the despair of political reform. Some of the causes of such apathy as exists have been mentioned in previous chapters. We need only say here that apathy in regard to candidates seems to arise largely from the sense of the futility of elections where the issues are clouded and the people have reason to expect betrayal by their representatives, no matter which set of nominees is elected. In so far as popular indifference is the result of disgust at this futility, it is hoped that Majority Rule by making elections less futile will remove the cause of this indifference. The indifference sometimes shown towards measures submitted to popular vote is explained in many cases either by the absurd triviality of the questions at issue or by their special relation to a much narrower constituency than the one that is asked to vote on them. Whether time and experience under Majority Rule will fully establish the fact that measures are inherently less interesting to the people than men, cannot be foretold with certainty. It is a demonstrable fact, however, that the affairs of government, especially those of city government, affect all the people vitally, constantly and at many points. Here are the elements of intense practical interest reaching into the very homes of the people and gripping the housewives and the growing children as well as the men who now have the ballot. Although measures are impersonal and appeal primarily to the intellect rather than to the senses, there is every reason to believe that under Majority Rule they would command a much greater absolute and relative interest than they now do. Popular indifference to politics becomes more and more inconceivable as the functions of government expand and as the people's intimate dependence upon coöperation for the rendering of necessary services increases. What can be more interesting than the character of the roads we use, the amount of the taxes we have to pay, the efficiency of the schools where our children are educated, the purity and abundance of the water supply, the quality and price of gas and of the electric and telephone services, the removal of garbage and ashes from our doors, convenience of street-car transportation, the reliability and promptness of the postal service, the maintenance of adequate fire and police protection, the prevention and cure of disease by the health department, and other things like these? One would suppose that under conditions permitting effective action through governmental agencies to protect the people's interests in such matters, popular indifference to them would not long continue to be possible. At any rate, no conclusive case has yet been made out against the people on the score of their permanent indifference to public affairs. We cannot assume such indifference as inevitable, for the assumption would remove the very foundation stone of democracy.

The next question is, are the people too busy to take on the added obligations proposed by Majority Rule? Is their time so much occupied with more important things that they cannot devote any more of it to public affairs? We shall have to admit that the American people are busy. They work like mad. They rush about like mad. They play like mad. But this feverish activity is not permanently essential to their welfare and happiness. If by the introduction of Majority Rule we are able to change the conditions that now make the typical reformer "a beautiful and ineffectual angel, beating in the void his luminous wings in vain," if we are able to minimize the discouraging waste of energy incident upon the futile efforts now made to push the creaking car of government along, the same amount of time that is already given to public affairs would bring marvellous results. And when we consider the general trend toward a shorter work-day and more numerous holidays, and the immense amount of leisure now busily expended on matters much less interesting and much less useful than government, we are forced to the conclusion that busy America has all the time needed for the consideration of public affairs, if only the channels of political activity can be cleared out so as to prevent waste in its use. I do not mean to assert that Majority Rule might not be misused to encumber the ballot with a multitude of projects too technical or too detailed to be mastered by the voters within the time reasonably at their disposal for this purpose. But that is a possibility which can be met and overcome as the necessity arises.

Lastly, we come to the question of the people's intelligence. In spite of occasional displays of stupidity in the election of unfit men to conspicuous offices where a better course lay clear before the people, the desperate failures of the long ballot are not to be charged up to lack of intelligence on the part of the voters. The work of selecting a score or two of public officials from an army of candidates, is not a problem of intelligence at all. It is a mere guess, a flipping of coins, and in the nature of the case can be little or nothing more. How can native intelligence or acquired wisdom help any man, a citizen of a state or of a large city, to pick out competent officials from a haphazard list of names published in the newspapers or appearing on the ballot? He cannot have the candidates call upon him for a personal conference. He cannot ask them for

references and then investigate the references. He
cannot look into the personal history and characteristics
of each candidate. He must depend on the party label
or the sound of each man's name, and neither of these is
a safe guide. The candidate may be a drunkard or a
libertine without his knowing it. These little personal
characteristics are not usually published, either because
the newspapers fear the libel law or because there is a
tacit understanding between them and the candidates
not to indulge in personalities, the agreement being
guaranteed by the proverbial honor among thieves.
How different it is with a measure, printed in full and
distributed to all the voters weeks or months in advance
of the election! It can be put under examination by a
million different voters at one and the same time. A
candidate is only one. He cannot be copied and
scattered broadcast. But a measure is quite different.
Every citizen can take it home with him, read it, sleep
over it, discuss it with his wife if he has one, talk about
it on the car or in the field or wherever he meets a
fellow-citizen with a minute to spare, write letters about
it for the local newspapers, and never let it go until he
has mastered it. I do not say that all the electors will
do this or that any of them will always do it, but the
task is not one that is beyond the powers of numerous
citizens of every community. It is not expected that
every voter will read each submitted measure and then
shut himself up in a dark closet to pray over it and
ponder upon it in isolation and free from all worldly influences. Many citizens, perhaps a majority of them,
will depend upon the neighborhood specialists who are
equipped for local intellectual leadership and delight

in it. So far as intelligence goes, a citizen can arrive
at a safer judgment on thirty different measures than
he can upon thirty different men. By devoting some
time to the work, he can find out what the measures
mean unless they happen to be choice samples of legislative bill-drafting thrown out to foil the intelligence of
the judiciary. A citizen slightly above the average in
intelligence ought surely to be able to master thirty
different measures as fully as a legislator can master a
thousand within the same period of time. Of course,
thirty is an extreme number and there are few advocates
of Majority Rule who would not deplore such an excessive use of the Initiative and the Referendum, except
under very unusual circumstances. But it seems fairly
clear that on important issues, interesting throughout
the political unit where the vote is taken, the intelligence
of an average American electorate would surprise those
superior persons who look upon the voters as a mere
misguided mob. One thing is certain—we cannot have
too much intelligence among the people on all questions
affecting the public welfare, and if Majority Rule would
make the electors exercise their wits a little now and
then, we need not be consumed with sympathy for
them. The back that bends will have to grow strong
under its load. It is a precious load, and any other back
would be pretty sure to make off with it.

CHAPTER XXXII

FIFTH GENERAL OBJECTION TO MAJORITY RULE—THAT
IT IS BASED ON THE IDEA OF EQUALITY WHICH IS
A WILL O' THE WISP

SINCE the reactionary party in America has got its second wind, largely as a result of the "fearless independence" of the courts in applying handicaps to the radicals, we have discovered in our midst orators, authors, and journalists who with the bravado of cheap convictions assert that the Declaration of Independence is mere buncombe. They say that all Jefferson's talk about men being born free and equal is twaddle. They point out that some men are born black and others white, that some enter the world as five-pounders and others as fifteen, that some inherit constitutional weakness and others strength, that some grow to be five feet four inches tall and others to be six-feet-six, that some have a genius for making money on a large scale while others hardly know enough to spend it on a little one, that some have a native knack for constructive work while others are constitutional blunderheads. Sometimes in mere zeal of proof they even mention the idiots and the insane to show that Jefferson either did not know what he was talking about or took deliberate advantage of the credulity of the primitive age in which he lived.

Upon reflection we can hardly avoid the conclusion that Thomas Jefferson and his associates must have known of the natural inequalities among men and could not have hoped to convince their contemporaries of the non-existence of these inequalities. What, then, does the Declaration mean? What is the doctrine of political equality and how does it form a basis for Majority Rule? In other words, why should the one-man-one-vote principle be extended from the election of representatives to the determination of specific policies of state? Why, should these important matters be settled by a mere count of noses, when the noses vary so much in size and color? Is it, indeed, one of the deep, dark designs of democracy to reduce all men to a dead level, to iron out all their differences, to eradicate genius, to forbid culture, to divide wealth equally among all the people, to make wine and love free to everybody? What do the much-used phrases "equality," "equality of right," and "equality of opportunity" mean?

The Declaration seems to mean that all normal human beings should be guaranteed as nearly as possible equal opportunities for self-development and, when they have arrived at maturity, equal political rights. This is the fundamental postulate of democracy. It is based upon the fact that in spite of all the physical and intellectual inequalities natural to human beings, all men have the fundamental experiences of life in common. They are born as helpless babes needing care, nourishment, shelter, social training. In childhood and youth they love play and exciting exercise. They love, they marry, they procreate, they work, they suffer, they grow old, they die. The normal

panorama of human life is essentially the same for all
men. The differences are matters of detail or of special
development. No man can claim any better natural
right to seek happiness than any other. The function
of democratic government is to see that every individual
born into the state has as good an opportunity for the
full development of his powers as the circumstances
over which the state has no control will permit. In
the performance of this function, the state begins with
adult men, giving each an equal vote to be used as his
own intelligence, self-interest, and patriotism dictate.
This does not level the powers of men. This does not
destroy the opportunities or the influence of gifted men.
It merely saves to the state the unearned increment
of native ability. It merely socializes leadership. It
merely compels the man of special ability to exercise
his influence through persuasion. He has only one vote
to cast, but if his talents are devoted to the public welfare thousands of men in the exercise of their sovereign
rights will accept his leadership and fill the ballot-box
with their reënforcing votes. But democracy finds
that the mere application of the ballot to the election
of representatives does not guarantee sovereign rights
to the individual. It is the purpose of Majority Rule
to extend this application to the direct performance of
primary governmental functions, so that every vote
shall count one in a fundamental sense. The equality
thus to be established is not a will-o'-the-wisp, but a
practical aim of democratic statesmanship.

True, we find that men cannot be made wholly free
and equal by the gift of suffrage even under Majority
Rule. Taking them at twenty-one, we find them al-

ready unfairly handicapped. Hereditary inequalities
may have been accentuated, or they may have been reversed by the influence of early environment. Democracy is not satisfied to take men as they may be turned
over to the state as adults, and leave their previous
opportunities unregulated. How far it will be able
to fight inequality back to its origins, only the future
will disclose, but democracy will not be satisfied until
it has reached the utmost boundaries of the world
that is subject to political influences. Already it is
pushing the battle against inequality back to youth,
back to childhood, back to the cradle, even back to the
womb. It may even attempt some day to equalize
the opportunities of its citizens by a eugenic selection
of grandparents for them. Even so democracy will not
deny inequalities, but will strive to forfend the horrible
wastes of lunacy, imbecility, crime, and hereditary
disease. Democracy has no patience with the theory
that the world's life is enriched and made picturesque by
glaring inequalities. It is not necessary to have a room
full of dunces in order that one prodigy may shine.
It is not profitable that three-fourths of a city's population should vegetate in congested squalor in order
to make Fifth Avenue and Riverside Drive resplendent.
It is horrible to maintain an underworld peopled with
outcast women in order that the dames of the middle-
class may flaunt their protected virtue. Democracy
does not pine for a flat monotony of life and character,
but it is quite willing to tone down many of the existing contrasts.

CHAPTER XXXIII

SIXTH GENERAL OBJECTION TO MAJORITY RULE—THAT
IT WOULD MEAN GOVERNMENT BY NEWSPAPER

THE abuses of irresponsible power are not confined
to the formal agencies of government. Tyrannies
social, religious, industrial, intellectual, are practiced
by institutions that are so organized as to resist growth
and readjustment to the changing conditions of life.
There is a certain community of interest amongst
oppressors everywhere. Likewise, the spirit of In-
surgency is essentially the same whether it manifests
itself in politics, in ecclesiastical organizations, in
educational activities, or elsewhere. As tyranny driven
from one lodgment immediately seeks another, so the
forces of democracy victorious in one field break over
into others.

The climate of America during the last hundred years
has been tropical for the growth of institutions. The
titanic social and industrial forces at work have gen-
erated heat that has caused enormous growths to
spring up out of our fertile soil almost overnight. The
modern newspaper as an institution is one of the most
marvellous developments of this gigantic age. Founded
as a guaranty of liberty, it has developed such vast
power and is so little subject to control that it often
seems to endanger the very freedom it is in honor

bound to defend. Having the means to blazon a man's
name and projects simultaneously in every village and
hamlet of the country or to carry a distortion of the
truth about them into millions of homes and offices
in a single day, the press enjoys a sheer, downright
power for favoritism or oppression that far surpasses
the power of presidents and rivals that of absolute
princes. Statesmen are made and unmade by the
newspapers. Fame, honor, wealth, power are given
or withheld by them. It requires only monopoly control of the press to make its power superlatively
dangerous to the state.

In former times, when any man with journalistic
ability and the most meagre capital could found a newspaper, actual and potential competition kept the press
from serving as a lodgment for irresponsible power.
The newspapers may have been more partisan and less
scrupulous then than they are now. Certainly their
news service was much less efficient. But side by side
with increasing efficiency has come monopoly control
of the general news service and a tremendous increase
in the complexity and size of individual newspaper
plants. It is no longer possible to establish successfully
a new daily paper without large capital for immediate
use and the permanent backing of great financial interests. Naturally, the newspapers are not as free
in dealing with political policies affecting special interests as they once were, or if they are, it is in spite
of great temptations. Moreover, students of journal-
ism tell us that more and more the advertisers pay the
running expenses of the papers and exercise a restraining influence on their editorial policy. From the finan-

cial standpoint the papers have become primarily advertising sheets, with the news function as a subsidiary
incident. If the postal laws admitted free papers to the
mails, the price, which has generally gone down to
a penny, might be removed altogether. The papers
must have circulation in order to get advertising, and
so they must make themselves acceptable or necessary
to the people. They are already so necessary, as practically the sole source of information which the people
have with regard to current events and the men and
measures of the time, that if the newspaper monopoly
were complete and secure it would hardly need to cater
to the good will of the public at all. Monopoly is not
yet complete, but a very large proportion of the leading
dailies are owned or controlled by men whose interests
prompt them to suppress or distort the truth in regard
to certain matters which vitally concern the people.
Sometimes public officials are abused and robbed of the
popular support without which they cannot succeed,
because they will not take orders from the proprietors
of powerful journals. Sometimes progressive measures
are denied publicity and progressive men are mis-
represented or ignored because certain newspapers
have secretly become organs of those who are opposed
to progress. While there is still considerable competition among newspapers and while there are many
journals that appear to be independent and fearless on
most public questions, there is beyond doubt a peril-
ous dominance of personal and selfish interests in the
control of the press to-day.

The reactionaries who hate the radical press for its
interference with the quiet enjoyment of their special

privileges and for its attacks on complaisant public officials, join with the progressives who fear the obstructive power of the subsidized press, in questioning the effect of Majority Rule upon the power and responsibility of the newspapers. If already they are a mighty instrument of government, driving legislatures to do what they would not and preventing them from doing what they would, lording it over mayors of cities and governors of states, nominating candidates for public office and forcing men they do not like into political retirement, what limits can be placed upon their usurpations under Majority Rule? Then will they not be supreme? Through them the passions of the omnipotent majority may be fanned into a flame, its prejudices aroused, its intelligence cunningly perverted. Then, it is said, irresponsible government by newspaper will prove to be more unbearable than the worst tyrannies of representative assemblies and the most maddening obstructions of out-of-date judges. Can it be that Majority Rule, clothed in all the habiliments of popular freedom, will prove to be a mere plaything in the hands of the publicity trust?

We cannot deny that the dangers of newspaper domination deserve to be seriously considered, but there are two factors in the situation which tend to relieve our fears. In the first place, the normal use of all means of communication is to convey truth, not to conceal it. Language, the printed page, the report, are for truth-telling. Unless a person's mind has actually become perverted, he will lapse into truthfulness even against his will. A newspaper filled with falsehoods is a prodigy. No one cares to read mere lies. They are not interesting. The newspaper has a great power over its readers. By constant iteration, unless the readers drop off, it can finally induce them to accept as true what they originally knew to be false. But a newspaper that does not play an honest game has hard work to get itself read. Its good repute is a very delicate thing, and cannot long survive the poison of secret control. The hunger of the readers for truth and their keen sense for detecting the spirit of double-dealing in the papers they read have a strong reciprocal influence upon the papers themselves. The pressure of truth to be told is hard to resist. With all its apparently irresponsible power, with the dominance of the business office over the editorial policy acknowledged, with its actual ownership by the greediest of special interests conceded, the newspaper finds itself paralyzed as a power for evil. Like a lazy beast, it may lie down in the path and refuse to carry its master farther in the right direction, but it cannot carry him far the wrong way. The master knows the way. If he cannot ride, he will plod on afoot. The newspaper is the natural organ of democracy. It deals in intelligence and sells its wares cheap. If it refuses to function, it dies.

Moreover, democracy is not absolutely dependent on the newspaper for publicity. Under Majority Rule the state itself may issue publicity literature and send it to every voter, thus enabling him to dispense with the newspaper so far as actual knowledge of the issues before the people is concerned. If necessary, the state itself can publish an official gazette devoted to public affairs. This possibility will tend to hold the newspapers in check and to make them accept, even though it should be against their will, the function of democracy's publicity agents. As a matter of fact, the more they address themselves to this function under Majority Rule, the more they will prosper. So long as they keep to their true function of truth-telling, no matter how great their influence on politics, it will be only for good. Through them democracy will be expressing itself, and to speak of government by newspaper will be only another way of saying self-government.

CHAPTER XXXIV

FIRST GENERAL ARGUMENT IN FAVOR OF MAJORITY
RULE—THAT IT WOULD SIMPLIFY POLITICAL ISSUES

EVEN under the parliamentary system as it exists
in Great Britain, which is especially designed to keep
the government in harmony with public sentiment, the
appeal to the people is sometimes so confusing as to
leave grave doubt as to the meaning of the people's
reply. Some of the electors are trying to say no to
tariff reform, while others are trying to say yes to
Irish home rule, and still others are voting to curb the
power of the House of Lords. It is a curious anomaly
that the Referendum should have been made an issue
in England by the Tory party, but it is explained by the
fact that in the form proposed it would have given an
appeal to the electorate to stop radical legislation but
would not have given an appeal to prevent reactionary
legislation. This incident of recent British politics is
illustrative of the tactics of privilege-holders everywhere. In their perennial struggle with the democracy
they consent to the use of any political device, no matter how democratic its form, when they think it can be
turned to their own advantage. They are strict op-
portunists. They do not stand on mere political
theories. Time and again in America we find the
political machine accepting under pressure some new

device of democracy, the only condition being that it shall be introduced gradually and in such form as to facilitate the readjustment of machine politics to the new rules before the independents are able to do anything effective with them. This is one of the sources of greatest political confusion among us. We almost never have a clear-cut issue to vote on. Whatever the result of an election, the elected representatives have a wide leeway in the interpretation of the meaning of the popular verdict. The result is disputation and recrimination while the wheels of legislation are blocked altogether or the car is steered on the wrong course.

The establishment of the Initiative, the Referendum, and the Recall, as one of its chief practical results, would enable the electorate to render discriminating and unmistakable verdicts. It is not easy to argue this point. The love of confusion in politics seems so absurd that we are tempted to question the good faith of those who advocate it. They remind us of pickpockets. About all that can be said on this score is by way of explanation of the specific ways in which Majority Rule will simplify issues. Once we establish the facts, we can leave this matter to the jury without argument on the law.

It is admitted that single measures, simply worded, are not always simple in their effects. One law dovetails into a whole system of laws, or butts into it. The very appearance of simplicity that comes from the separation of issues may sometimes be misleading. This is a fact that has to be considered in connection with the enactment of laws whether it be by vote of the legislature or by vote of the people. But the advantage of having acts separate and distinct is often recognized in the constitution itself in a clause requiring that every bill shall have a single object which shall be clearly expressed in the title. One of the great abuses of legislative procedure, where the legislative body is not restricted by such a clause, is the practice of tacking "riders" on appropriation bills or other necessary legislation. In this way one house sometimes forces the other to accept unwelcome measures, or both houses force the executive to approve vicious provisions in order to avoid the inconvenience or positive disaster incident to the stoppage of the regular functions of government. In some constitutions and charters this difficulty is partially met by the extension of the executive's veto power to specific items in appropriation bills, but he is seldom, if ever, permitted to separate other measures into their parts in the exercise of his legislative functions. As already pointed out in a preceding chapter of this book, the power of amendment during the process of legislation is frequently abused to bring the issues into confusion, with the result that even in the small compass of the legislative body itself, individual legislators are compelled to vote against what they approve in order to defeat what they disapprove, or to accept what they believe to be wrong in order to get what they believe to be right. The result is not only confused legislation but a confused record. Men elected to office pledged to a certain principle are found recorded against measures that profess to embody it. If these men are honest, their action may be justified, but their legislative record lays them open to misrepresentation and attack. If they are dishonest or have changed their minds, they can set up the claim that the measures against which they voted were not the same as the measures to which they pledged themselves. The bare record often lies, and since it is the highest visible test of the faithfulness of a legislator to his constituents, they have to depend on false or distorted evidence in passing judgment upon him. And so, under the irresponsible representative system, with its existing perversions and abuses, legislation is often illogical and confused, and an ill-blown vision-distorting glass is held up between the legislator and his constituents.

But this is not all, by any means. Not only are the people uncertain as to what they get in actual legislative results and in representative faithfulness, but they do not even know what they voted for. The confusion of legislative processes runs back to the polls, the pledges, and the platforms. An elector cannot vote at all without voting in favor of a dozen or a hundred different things some of which he may favor but some of which it is morally certain that he opposes. Even where political parties are at their best, representing organized differences of opinion on great questions of public policy rather than degenerate rivalries for the perversion of government to personal ends, it is impossible to maintain the necessary fluidity in the policy-determining forces of the state so long as every legislative influence must be directed toward the enactment or defeat of a set party program. Where a bare majority of a bare majority of a legislative body is enabled to enforce its will upon the whole people because party lines are held taut and caucus rule is invoked, we may get flagrant miscarriages of the people's will. Democratic government in a real sense is impossible unless any important question of public policy can be released from the entanglements of partisanship and the obligations imposed by party solidarity, and decided on its own merits by a free expression of the public will. In a modern state, with the immense complexity of its interests and the rapidly changing conditions incident to increase in population and industrial development, it is unthinkable that there should be at any time only one important issue. But upon every important issue there is and must be a different alignment of opinions. It is a function of Majority Rule to make these realignments easy and effective, to make possible the decision of each separate issue by the actual majority on that issue.

Under Majority Rule the Referendum may be invoked against specific legislative acts or against specific parts or sections of such acts, or if good and evil are so interwoven in a legislative act as to be inextricable, the entire act may be rejected and a new one substituted by the Initiative. When parties are degenerate or unresponsive to the genuine distinctions of public opinion, the Initiative permits the formulation of separate issues to be submitted to the people. On one measure Republicans who cannot control the organization of their party may be reinforced by Democrats, Socialists, and Independents acting in a non-partisan capacity to form an overwhelming majority in the state. In another case Democrats whose power as a majority party is frustrated in the legislature by the refusal of a few of their representatives to abide by the party program may at the polls be enabled to carry out the mandate by which they were entrusted with political power at the preceding election. The Socialists with a lone representative in Congress or the state legislature may on some specific measure submitted to the people rebuke and overturn the indifference to the public welfare manifested by the representatives of the dominant parties. Under the Recall a single official elected on a party ticket or appointed by a partisan executive may be separated from the factitious support of a political organization and made to stand or fall on his own merits as a public servant. Even where many measures, some of them conflicting or inconsistent, are submitted to popular vote at one time, and even where one Recall election applies to several officials, every voter indicates his will specifically and in detail. The particular men and the particular measures of which a majority disapproves are beaten and those which the majority approves are sustained. It is a different majority that acts on each separate issue, but the result is the enforcement of the public will at every point, and that is democracy.

CHAPTER XXXV

THERE are some who think citizens can be too well educated, but we need not argue with them. We can outvote them. There are also some who think that too many people may participate in public affairs or that the people as a whole may participate too much in them. Their position, when analyzed, is that it is not good to mind one's own business. Public affairs are the people's business. That is what the term means. We may assume in this discussion that the spirit of democracy with which the modern world is pregnant not simply tolerates but demands the best possible education of citizenship, extending to the entire electorate, and the fullest practicable participation of the people in the affairs of government. Participation must be organized, of course, just as an individual's activities in furtherance of his private interests must be organized in order to be effective. Full participation in a coöperative project does not mean that everyone interested in it must perform the same functions, do the same things. It means, rather, that everyone interested in it should have knowledge of its purposes and should be conscious of the significance of his share

in its benefits and of his contribution to its success.
The indifferent, non-participating citizen is, in the body
politic, what the dead letter is in the body of the law.
In so far as the people do not participate in government,
the state is sluggish, sick, in danger of sudden collapse
in times of stress.

Though we all admit the inadequacy of the civic
education of the people in this country, nevertheless
there are many educational agencies already at work,
some of them with conspicuous success. The jury
system, which was once counted as a great school of
citizenship, does not occupy as high a position as it
once did. The excessive legality that is characteristic
of our present judicial procedure, resulting in delays
of judgment and miscarriages of justice, is not particularly useful in cultivating loyalty among the citizens
who serve as jurors or in imbuing them with an intelligent respect for the state and its ways. In important
cases the jurors are often treated almost like convicts,
kept in isolation for weeks at a time, and marched out
once or twice a day for an airing under guard. In the
selection of juries the questions asked and the standards
established are often calculated to weed out all intelligent men, unless, moved by some secret passion for
jury service, they cunningly dissemble their intelligence. In the rural districts the jury system doubtless
still has considerable educational value; for outside of
the cities and beyond the sphere of influence of local
dailies it is less a mark of unintelligence to be qualified
for service through not having an opinion of one's
own.

Then we have the civil service, which under the United

States government and under many state and city
governments is filled by appointments from lists of
successful competitors at public examinations. The
merit system opens a considerable field for public
service and appeals to the interest and intelligence of
young men and women. It stimulates the study of
public affairs and tends to create a large body of citizens
who are specially well informed in regard to certain
details of public work. But this system falls short of
the perfect school of citizenship, not only because it
is still quite limited in its application, not only because
it is often administered faultily, but also for the very
reason that it imposes on the citizens who take advantage of its benefits the obligation to abstain from the
more active forms of political work. After all, the civil
service under the merit system offers few opportunities
for the development of leadership and the display of
exceptional powers. In part on account of the protection from arbitrary removal usually guaranteed
to employees of the classified service, they tend to
become sluggish in the performance of their duties,
to regard themselves as a class apart and to exalt their
jobs above their functions.

Rotation in office is another educational device characteristic of American politics. In small rural communities where public functions are simple, there is
considerable advantage in passing the offices around
so that every citizen will have some practical experience
in administration. It is like the general education by
which all children, no matter what their predilections
and special abilities may be, are subjected to a common
course of intellectual training for a few years. They

must all learn to read, write, and cipher, whether they like it or not,—though in the matter of spelling, concessions are made. This breaking every citizen in as constable, pathmaster, school inspector, or town clerk at some time in his life may also be likened to the training of children in the home, where good policy requires that girls be taught all the practical phases of housekeeping and the boys how to drive a nail and tend a furnace, irrespective of their special leanings towards art, music, or baseball. But rotation in office is impracticable in populous communities except on a very small scale. True, the effectiveness of the old system of rotation can be preserved to a considerable extent by the appointment of citizens to unsalaried positions where they can coöperate with the regular public officials in the details of civic administration. School committees, probation officers, special advisory commissions, juvenile street cleaning leagues, all open the door of civic education to the people. And yet here the work of each particular participant is narrow and offers less than the highest interest. It is only in the details of helping that he can be effective, and often he finds his work largely wasted on account of the policies that permeate the public department with which he is coöperating, policies that are determined higher up under influences which he cannot overcome. In the happy city or state that is blessed with excellent government, efficient, progressive, intelligently adapted to the needs and the will of the people, this kind of participation in public affairs is a quiet but effective means of civic education. Under less favorable conditions the citizens are apt to "play hooky." If they cannot be taking part in the big things, they at least do not wish to dawdle over ineffectual trifles.

The voluntary civic bodies, such as law and order leagues, city clubs, voters' leagues, and taxpayers' associations, offer still another means of civic education. Sometimes they become powerful agencies of public opinion and attain a dominating influence in local public affairs. Their unofficial investigations of the qualifications of candidates for office, of the merits of proposed legislation, of the actual practices of government, of the opportunities for municipal improvement, enlist the interest and a portion of the energies of a considerable number of the so-called public-spirited citizens. But this work, valuable as it is in keeping the spirit of civic patriotism alive, is in most cases rather futile and discouraging. Working without financial reward and it may be at considerable material sacrifice for the public welfare, men often find themselves a target for abuse on the ground that they are self-constituted guardians of the people with no mandate to speak for them. As reformers these men are often either hated, if they have influence, or despised if they have it not. This is fine educational work in many instances, but exceedingly costly.

In recent years the necessity for civic training, especially in view of the enormous influx into this country of foreigners ignorant of our institutions whose children must be initiated into the mysteries of American government through the public schools, has caused the introduction of special courses in civics in the school curriculum, even below the high school, and in many instances the matter has been pushed even further in

an effort to organize the school children into minia-
ture cities or republics for self-government. Often one
trouble with the civics teaching is the fact that it is
given by women instructors who have no practical
knowledge of public affairs, while the school-city suffers
from the disrespect all generally feel for the actual city
which the children are taught to imitate. Progress has
been made in many places toward vital instruction in
civics in the schools, but the work is just begun. School
civics still tends to instruction in forms of governmental
organization, not to a vital understanding of the activities of government and its relations to life.

Political parties, which theoretically furnish the
best of all the agencies for civic education, have largely
fallen under the domination of influences that have
deadened them to this function. The caucus and the
convention have come to be, in large measure, mere
schools of political trickery. Citizens who merely
"learn the game" do not thereby become properly
educated. They learn things that are not so, and they
learn methods that tend to unfit them for serious participation in the affairs of the city or the state. Direct
primaries offer a measure of relief from this condition,
but even they may prove to be futile if they degenerate
into mere running-matches of self-selected office-seekers.
Parties, no doubt, still do something as a means of
civic education, but when they are so hidebound as
to exclude from their working membership all the
citizens who aspire to a free use of their own intelligence,
they cannot be said to be performing their educational
function in a satisfactory way.

As a last means of civic education we have the widely-

heralded ballot-box and the voting-machine. It cannot
be denied that the successful manipulation of an average American ballot is a mechanical achievement of
which the electorate may justly feel proud. To mark
it without voiding it is something. To fold it is also
something. To sign your name to the roll proves that
you can write. To tell the clerks every time you register
when you were born, where you voted last and how
long you have lived at your present address, keeps the
memory of your past history green. To be able to pull
the levers of a complex mechanical apparatus and make
it cast your vote is, indeed, a badge of civic distinction.
But the very finest educational product of the election
process comes with the ability to vote a split ticket.
How pitiful it is that the educational value of the
ballot should so largely consist in learning this difficult
sleight-of-hand!

Majority Rule does not supersede any existing means
of civic education. It does not curtail any existing
participation of the people in public affairs. Where
these means have broken down, it restores them. Where
they are imperfect, it improves them. Where they are
inadequate, it supplements them. The jury, the civil
service, the voluntary civic association, the public
school, the party, the ballot-box, all are vivified as
educational agencies by the touch of popular responsibility. For those who love to serve the state without
thought for general policies, there is room. For those
who have imagination, there is opportunity for the
free play of their intelligence upon great public issues.
Civic education resulting from the adoption of Majority Rule is dynamic; it is self-education, not the mere

doing of tasks under direction. What can be better for the state than to have its citizens everywhere discussing the work of the legislature under the Referendum, debating the merits of new public policies under the Initiative, or critically examining the efficiency of the administrator and the justness of the judge under the Recall? After their long tutelage in public affairs by numerous well-recommended instructors, the people need, as the crowning feature of their education, the privilege of making independent use of the knowledge they have so acquired. The finishing touches can never be put upon knowledge except by the actual doing of things. Responsibility assumed as the result of free participation in the affairs of government, big and little, confers the degrees and issues the certificates of proficiency in civic affairs.

CHAPTER XXXVI

THIRD GENERAL ARGUMENT IN FAVOR OF MAJORITY RULE—THAT IT WOULD MAKE PARTIES AND POLITICAL ORGANIZATIONS MORE ADAPTABLE TO THE NEEDS OF THE TIME

POLITICAL parties are generally regarded as a necessary means of organizing and putting into effect the public will in a democracy. Even the reformers who desire to exclude party organizations entirely from municipal affairs grant the necessity of party government in state and nation, and there are many intelligent men who do not recognize the practical possibility of conducting the government of cities on strictly non-partisan lines. They say that every great mass of voters must be organized to be effective. There must be some means of formulating issues and presenting candidates for office in such a way as to secure intelligent and decisive action by the people at the polls. If the nomination of all candidates were left entirely to petition and the formulation of all policies to the Initiative, unaided by any party organization, popular elections might fall into confusion, being nothing but an awkward choice in a welter of personal and factional candidacies and of unrelated and discordant political suggestions. Where nominations are free and easy there is no certainty that the will of the majority will prevail unless a more or less complicated machinery for second, third, and fourth choices or for double elections is provided. Even then the successful candidates are responsible solely, each to a different unorganized majority of the voters, without the mediating and sobering influence of a recognized group of coöperating citizens. An exaltation of the individual and an over-emphasis of the qualities of personal popularity are likely to result. Public officials who ought to coöperate find themselves pulled apart by conflicting personal interests and responsibility to different, but undefined majorities. In theory at least, government by parties is logical and necessary in city affairs as well as in state and national affairs.

But the abuses of party organization have been so great that it has been necessary for the strong arm of the state to reach out beyond the final elections and take control of what were originally the purely voluntary unofficial processes of private groups of citizens. As the population of political units increases, as the electorate becomes a larger and larger mass of individuals, as the problems of government multiply and become more complex, the government will have to reach farther and farther down toward the individual to keep the channels clear for the organized expression of the public will. The organization of the people for the preliminary formulation of issues and for the selection of leaders becomes a more and more complex and delicate process which must be protected at every stage from the dangers of perversion. Starting with a government in the hands of parties which have already been perverted in large measure from their legitimate functions, we seek to rescue the party organizations from their present control and to protect them for the future against capture by private interests, but the very persons whose power we are attempting to dislodge hold in their hands the processes of legislation which must be used to pave the way for their dislodgment. It is like reasoning in a circle. We can get nowhere unless we can break the circle. Getting Majority Rule is the breaking of the circle and using it is keeping the circle from being reformed .

Party organizations are necessary. It is not absolutely necessary that the same organizations should interest themselves in local government which concern themselves with state government. And yet cities are becoming less and less isolated units. Purely local public utilities have almost disappeared. The city is a terminal of the state. Their interests are inextricably interwoven, and the sphere of purely local affairs is narrowing from year to year. ' The city not only depends upon the state for its governmental powers but requires the coöperation of the state in the exercise of them. Even the national government has to be called in where public utility systems are interstate, and we may not always accept as final the separation of a city into two municipalities because it happens to be divided by an artificial state boundary line. The problems of transportation, taxation, public improvements, protection of health, suppression of crime, conservation of natural resources, and almost every vital problem of government demands the coöperation of city, state, and nation. We cannot, therefore, hope to solve the problem of political parties by drawing an arbitrary ring around the cities and requiring the parties to keep out altogether or even by requiring them to change their forms. What we need is not to destroy parties but to bring them under popular control. They are now too rigid and non-adjustable. The processes for the expression of the people's will must be made and kept more fluid. This is, perhaps, the highest use of Majority Rule. It keeps the door of opportunity open to the citizens for the reorganization of their parties. As it deprives the several departments, legislative, executive, and judicial, of the arbitrary power to turn the government into a means of granting or guaranteeing special privileges, so it removes the strongest motive for the private capture of political parties through which the control of government is secured. Under Majority Rule temporary parties can easily be organized to contest the dominance of the old organizations that obstruct rather than express the public will. In a sense the signers of an Initiative, or a Referendum, or a Recall petition constitute themselves a new party for a specific purpose. By such means the arbitrary power of corrupt or selfish organizations can be wrested from them and the whole process of the formulation and expression of the people's will can be brought under the protection of impartial law. No longer will self-perpetuating party committees be enabled to keep a strangle-hold upon government by the device of the long ballot with its treacherous crew sailing into power under a false flag. No longer will the party leaders be able to make corrupt alliances with great pirate corporations for the conversion of government into a subsidiary branch of private business. No longer will party conventions, caring only for the prerogatives of power, be able to confuse issues and make irreconcilable or meaningless promises, secure in the knowledge that the people have only a choice between two or three separate sets of confusions and hypocrisies. In short, Majority Rule opens the way for the salvation of political parties from the standpoint of the state, which needs them, and for their damnation from the standpoint of the corrupt and arrogant interests, which pervert them when they can.

CHAPTER XXXVII

FOURTH GENERAL ARGUMENT IN FAVOR OF MAJORITY
RULE—THAT IT WOULD BE A MEANS OF PERFECTING
REPRESENTATIVE GOVERNMENT

THE opponents of Majority Rule raise a great hue and cry against it on the ground that it would destroy representative government, which they regard as the last word in human political experience. The friends of Majority Rule retort by alleging that the government we now have is representative only in name, but that under Majority Rule government would be really representative. It is undoubtedly a fine thing to have a ready-made scheme for getting our business attended to with no more trouble to ourselves than is involved in spending a few minutes at the polls once or twice a year, but it is still finer to keep track of our business a little for ourselves and see that it *is* attended to. It is unnecessary to recount here, in detail, the present failures of representative government in America. The preceding chapters of this book are full of references to them. The fact of the people's misrepresentation by our boasted representative system is so patent to everybody, so universally admitted, so often commented on, that to argue about it seems to be casting doubt upon something about which all have long since been agreed. To be sure, we occasionally hear it said

that the people get as good a government as they
deserve, that if they know no better than to elect
fourth-class men to office, they ought to be compelled
to take the consequences. Yet even those who say this
do not make the claim that the people get what they
want in legislation, except perchance after long wanting
it and coming to want something else more. A stitch
in time saves nine. A mild remedy that might be effective if applied when the body politic first begins to
feel indisposed may be of no use whatever later in the
case.

When aroused to argument, the reactionaries tell
us that under our present system the people's will
always prevails in the end, if the people persist long
enough. Of course, they say, the people's thought
must be well seasoned, adhered to under difficulties,
profound, unescapable, overwhelming, before it really
becomes the people's *will*. But even if we should grant
that the people's will does in fact overcome all obstacles
and crystallize itself ultimately into law, we should still
have to inquire whether it is a necessary and beneficent
function of representative institutions to hold off reforms as long as possible and to yield to popular demands only as a last desperate necessity. Is it the
function of representative government to check the
people, to make them ask a dozen times for a thing
before it is given to them, to try to persuade them that
they do not want what they think they want, to re-
strain their enthusiasms for progress, to cultivate their
willingness to remain stuck in the mud?

The friends of Majority Rule admit that representative government is properly cautious about the whole-

sale adoption of new schemes, but they deny that its normal attitude is one of resistance to progress. Rather, its proper attitude is one of alertness for new ideas, of readiness to test their value, of eagerness to find improved ways and means for solving the problems of government. And so we come once more to the fundamental party division between those who believe in going backward and those who believe in going forward. Both parties use certain words and phrases in common and join in professions of loyalty to certain institutions, such as representative government, but when they use the same words they mean different things and when they worship the same gods it is with different thoughts in their hearts. To the progressive party Majority Rule means, not the destruction of representative institutions, but the perfecting of them. It is not proposed to abolish the legislature, the executive, or the judiciary. It is only proposed to connect them vitally with the people and make the connection continuous. The storage-battery method has proven unequal to the constant and heavy demands on government. It is not proposed to do away with representatives but to make them represent their voting constituents instead of their campaign contributors. The checks and balances deliberately adopted in the constitution, the bicameral legislature, the veto power of the executive, the judicial power of interpretation, the restrictions of the fundamental law, are regarded as sufficient guaranties of governmental sobriety of action without the addition of a double-headed allegiance in the breast of the individual representative. To destroy this fatal dualism, the people who stand

back of the representative assume the right to furnish
him with his inspiration and to check him or withdraw
him entirely if he goes elsewhere for it.

Now, one of the strongest points in favor of Majority Rule is its promise of the development of a new type
of leadership. Representative government logically
favors responsive popular leadership, but under the
system that has actually developed in American politics
leaders in the true sense are at a discount. Vote-
getting leadership is in demand, to be sure, but it is
vote-getting on the basis of personal popularity and
ability to make promises that sound well until election
day and that can easily be explained away afterwards.
Under the system that has generally prevailed in this
country until very recent years, and that still prevails
in many states and cities, the best opportunities for
leadership with the greatest assurance of stability even
in public office have been offered to men who would
devote themselves not to the leadership of the people
but to the leadership of the cohorts of corporate wealth.
The new leadership promised by Majority Rule will
necessarily be of a different type. It will not be a
leadership of manipulation and false promises. It will
not be a leadership where the led exist for the sake of
the leader. It will not be a leadership modeled after
the organized brigandage of the high seas or of the
mountain fastnesses. It will be a leadership of political
thought rather than of the strong arm or the glad hand.
Surely this does not spell destruction for representative
government.

The argument in this book has proceeded on the
theory that the devices of Majority Rule would be

ready for use at all times and would in fact be used from time to time. Some of the advantages claimed for them will be secured to the people merely by the possession of them. Others will come only as a result of their practical use. Yet no one, not even the most ardent advocate of the Initiative, the Referendum, and the Recall, contends that these instruments should be regarded as tools for everyday use. The government is not to be conducted mainly by them. They are for emergencies. They are the kit of tools which democracy uses to repair the representative system when it breaks down. The old ladies who have ridden in the vehicle ever since their childhood are afraid to have anyone touch it with wrench and hammer even when they see it lying on its side in the ditch. They even regard the use of an oil-can as an unheard-of and dangerous interference with its natural propensity to creak and to squeak as it lumbers along the highways of the state. But modern conditions demand comfortable, safe, and rapid transit. Even the old ladies will be reconciled when they come to enjoy the benefits of the overhauling.

CHAPTER XXXVIII

FIFTH GENERAL ARGUMENT IN FAVOR OF MAJORITY
RULE—THAT IT WOULD BE A BULWARK OF TRUE
CONSERVATISM

CONSERVATISM is a good word that ought to represent a good idea. It ought to mean thrift as opposed
to prodigality, wise use as opposed to wanton waste,
steadiness in action as opposed to going by jerks, preservation and development of all the resources at our
hand rather than miserly hoarding or careless destruction of them. Those who sit securely in the possession
of vested wrongs and pray not to be disturbed, abuse
the word when they call themselves conservatives. A
surgeon who finds a man sorely wounded and before
sewing up his gashes waits to see whether he is going
to bleed to death, cannot properly be called conservative. A fruit-grower who refuses to trim his trees one
year for fear that they are going to stop growing the
next, and refuses to thin his fruit when it is small for
fear that most of what he leaves will fall off later on
in the season, is a reactionary ignoramus, not a conservative. The statesman who sees corruption in its
beginnings but refuses to interfere with it on the ground
that it may correct itself if let alone or that it is not yet
important enough to bother about proves thereby, not
his conservatism, but his laziness. A street railway

company that runs its cars by horse-power a score of years after electric traction has been proven to be the only practical mode of operation, is stupid, not conservative.

In politics both the opponents and the advocates of Majority Rule claim to be conservative. The former think themselves conservative either because they confound conservatism with fixity or because they sincerely believe that Majority Rule would lead to confusion, hasty and ill-considered action and disaster. If their claim to conservatism is based upon their hostility to change as a general principle, we may fairly dispute their right to use the word. If their claim is based on fear of the specific consequences of the adoption of Majority Rule we may reason with them to show that their fears are unfounded. Their motives are conservative, though their program of resistance to the instruments of democracy may be in its effect quite the opposite. The advocates of Majority Rule claim to be conservative because they regard the mass of the people as necessarily careful to husband and make the best use of what they have, and because Majority Rule puts the people in effective control of the government. They regard the progressive adjustment of governmental policies to the changing conditions of social and industrial life as a necessary element of true conservatism in politics.

To quibble over words is fruitless, but to define them is often necessary. In maintaining that Majority Rule would be a bulwark of true conservatism, I shall assume for the word conservatism the meaning which I have said it ought to have—thrift, wise use, steadiness in action, preservation and development of resources. It hardly needs to be said that conservatism as here discussed relates to public affairs and is defined from the standpoint of the state. It is quite possible that an individual citizen may sometimes find his immediate private interests in conflict with the public interests. If so, he might act conservatively from the standpoint of his private affairs without being truly conservative from the public standpoint. In this discussion, it is assumed that a citizen functioning as such is an organ of the state as truly as the chief executive is one, and that accordingly he should be actuated by public rather than purely selfish motives.

Political thrift—what is it? The state has both prerogatives and property, but the latter is only incidental to the former. The thrift that characterizes true political conservatism jealously guards every prerogative of government. It takes every care not to barter away in the least degree the public powers. It watches closely every franchise grant, every corporation law, every delegation of public functions, every contract for the performance of public work, every partnership in which private interests use in any special way or get the benefit of any special use of public property. Thrift ties a good stout string to every special privilege granted by government. In dealing with public property thrift never gives it away or permits its impairment. For every item of property or easement over it or interest in it, thrift demands a full return. Not only is present use considered, but prospective changes in use and increases in value are also taken into account. Franchises granted and property sold

by a thrifty public will not be good material for specula-
tion. They will be worth what they cost, but no more.
Does Majority Rule tend to thrift? While it is possible
that under special circumstances the people may be
prodigal of public rights and property, the Referendum
is everywhere regarded as a check upon prodigality.
There can be no doubt that the people as a whole, to
whom all the privileges and property of government
are permanent assets, will be more thrifty in the guard-
ianship of these assets than an irresponsible legislature
will be. It is notorious that such bodies tend to be
free in the disposal of the things belonging to the people.
They often are tempted to give such things free or
upon easy conditions because they are individually
profited by money or favors received in return. Majority rule by combining interest with power tends towards true conservatism in this important field of
public action.

Wise use is another element of conservatism. It is
hostile to the folly of providing parks for the people
and then putting fences around them or covering them
with signs to keep off the grass. It is unfriendly to the
policy of investing millions upon millions of dollars in
schoolhouses and school grounds, and then keeping
them out of use except during a fraction of the day five
days in the week and nine months in the year. Wise use
does not hide libraries away in inaccessible vaults and
bury information so deep in dust and documents that
it is lost to the uses of the state. Wise use does not
ignore the special qualifications of particular citizens
and their enthusiasms for service. It does not leave
fertile fields to lie fallow when the people are hungry

both for work and for bread. Can there be any doubt
that in this element of true conservatism the people,
who feel the needs and see the opportunities about them,
will be more insistent than their representatives are?
When the community is perishing politically for lack
of well-distributed places to meet for the discussion of
public questions, would the people open the school
buildings and the field-houses of the public parks as
social centers for everything *but* politics? The instruments of democracy are sharp sticks in the people's
hands to prod their sluggard stewards into beneficent
action. This, too, is truly conservative.

Steadiness in action is not characteristic of irresolute
representative bodies pushed forward irresistibly by
public opinion one day and imperiously pulled back the
next by the invisible cords of special interests. The
statute-books are full of evidences of this dual influence.
Yet its opponents urge strongly against Majority Rule
the claim that the people are subject to fits of passion,
to unreasonable enthusiasms, to fleeting impulses, and
that government would be reduced to chaos and the car
of progress run into the ditch if the irresponsible power
of representatives to thwart the popular will were
taken away. This claim we deny, and we appeal for
proof both to experience and to the inherent probabilities of the case. Have the people in Switzerland been
flighty in the use of the Initiative and the Referendum?
Have the people of Oregon pursued a wabbly course or
upset the state during their ten years of experience with
Majority Rule? No doubt there are isolated instances
of apparent fickleness on the part of the people in the
choice and recall of public officials and in the advice

given and later reversed on public questions.   But these instances are few, and may usually be explained by the clogging of the channels of expression so as to have produced a false verdict at one time or the other, or by the fact that conditions over which the people had no control made a change of advice seem necessary.   An instance of the former was the use of the Recall in Los Angeles a few years ago to remove from office a mayor who had slipped in by minority vote between a divided opposition.   An instance of the latter was Chicago's reversal of itself on the municipal ownership of street railways when the entanglements of law and finance imposed upon it through the workings of our celebrated representative system proved to be insuperable obstacles to the immediate carrying out of the policy originally approved by the people.   If we turn to the inherent probabilities of the case, what do we find?   A people that has a substantial interest in the established order is of necessity conservative.   If a people loses its substantial interest in the maintenance of existing institutions, violence and revolution are sure to come.   The majority may for a time be bought or bullied into respect for property in which they have no share except for the price of their servility.   But the productive energy of the people soon fails under these conditions, the streams that feed the reservoirs of wealth dry up, the greed of the propertyless populace increases until it cannot be satisfied, even the legions of law and order melt away.   Then comes the deluge! Majority Rule in a country like the United States, if it is not deferred until it becomes useless through the people's lack of interest, will tend to steadiness of action.

Property cannot stand unless it has the people back of it. The people will not stay back of it unless the distribution of wealth and the rewards of labor are fairly equitable. Under present conditions in the United States true conservatism demands the readjustment of the disordered relations whose lack of harmony now threatens the stability of the state. Government in America is far behind in the performance of its functions. The red tape that binds it and fritters away its energies needs to be cut away. The entire body of the people has an interest in conserving what is still useful in the ancient polity and in throwing the rest on the scrap heap in order that government may freely function. There is some danger that in communities where the people generally are prosperous Majority Rule may not be progressive enough. It takes intelligence and a certain degree of discontent to overcome the inertia of established ways. Yet we may reasonably expect that American electorates, where property qualifications are not required and where a slight degree of permanence in local affiliations is deemed sufficient, will not generally be reactionary. They are likely to be in most cases responsive enough to the exigencies of progress to constitute a truly conservative force in the state. If perchance they sometimes go a little too slowly, it can be forgiven them on the theory that it is better as a general rule to give the benefit of the doubt to what is old unless the old is so inadequate as to have overcome the ordinary presumption in its favor.

The preservation and development of natural resources are the climax of conservatism. There would be no dispute about it if we were discussing the management of an estate rather than the heritage of the people. The building of roads, the construction of canals, the improvement of natural harbors and water courses, the protection of the forests from wanton destruction, the impounding of waters that otherwise would run to waste carrying destruction with them in seasonal floods, the maintenance of technical schools, and laboratories for scientific experiment, the conversion of arid wastes into fruitful fields by irrigation, the opening of hitherto inaccessible areas by the introduction of railroads and telegraphs are some of the legitimate undertakings of a conservative government. What could be less conservative than the policy America has pursued under the representative system in regard to the great network of national highways now under private control? By its prodigality and recklessness in regard to the railroads, it not only has encouraged premature and wasteful investments, it not only has loaned prerogatives of sovereignty to private use, it not only has permitted corporations organized for profit to manipulate the growth of cities and the distribution of population, but it has nurtured in the bosom of the state a rival authority so large and powerful that it can be resubdued only by tremendous effort and at great expense extending over a long period of years, perhaps only in the end by the repurchase of the prerogatives conferred upon it and the immense property it has built up.

It is a mistake to regard the men who organize a trust and extort for their services a fifty-million-dollar fee from the industry which the trust controls as conservative men. The vaulting ambitions, the daring schemes, the ruthless methods of our financial overlords are not conservative. These men are the reckless radicals who, unless restrained in time, will bring the state to ruin. Majority Rule, the effective expression of the deliberate will of the whole people, untrammeled by constitutional prohibitions or by judicial ultimatums, stands forth the palladium of liberty, the bulwark of true conservatism, the guaranty of the stability of the state, the best possible assurance of the protection of property against the assaults of the madmen of high finance who would transform social wealth into a personal possession and turn the producers of wealth as beggars into the street.

CHAPTER XXXIX

MAJORITY RULE IN GREAT CITIES

MANY men who favor the establishment of Majority Rule in the governments of states and cities generally, are afraid that it would not work well in a great metropolis like New York or Chicago. They believe that the American people in most of their political subdivisions are well qualified for self-government, but that an exception must be made with regard to a few cities where the peculiar characteristics of urban life are sharply accentuated. In the great cities the contrasts between the few who have great riches and the many who have little or nothing are most pronounced. Here also are the babel of tongues, the inequality of political experience, the heterogeneous customs. Moreover, metropolitan populations are favorably situated for responding quickly to the passionate appeals of the press. The volatile nature of metropolitan life, the unstable character of the population, the absorption of the people in superficial and momentary interests, seem to make conditions out of which political disorder naturally springs. No doubt these conditions all have a bearing upon the fitness of metropolitan populations for self-government, but in so far as their special circumstances and characteristics make Majority Rule unsafe they also militate against the success of representative in-

stitutions. Accordingly, it is not so much the adaptability of the Initiative, the Referendum and the Recall
to the conditions of large cities that we have to consider
as it is the adaptability of democracy itself to these
communities. If the theory of this book is correct, the
alleged dangers of Majority Rule in great cities are
additional proofs of their need of it, if perchance thereby
democracy itself may be saved to them.

Take, for example, the extreme disparity of wealth
in great cities, and the segregation of the people into
different residence districts according to differences
in their social status. Here we have conditions that
are hostile to democratic institutions. The masses of
the people have no keen interest in the preservation
of their poverty, and so they do not require proof before
permitting change. Their impecunious condition is
made more unbearable by the immediate proximity
of flaunted riches. Envy, hatred, and willingness to
strike reckless blows at the existing order are a natural
result. The patriotism that attaches to citizenship
where it enjoys the obvious benefits of free government is deadened in the breasts of people who think
they have nothing to lose from the overturning of existing institutions, and perhaps something to gain.
Where vice is a commercialized pursuit, where congested poverty submerges a large percentage of the
people, where humiliation whispers to discontent and
irresponsibility promises immunity to crime, there is
reason to fear the unrestrained authority of the populace. But we must not confuse the issue. These dangerous conditions are proofs that radical measures
are necessary. Democracy does not for a moment ad-

mit that the abuses of life prevalent in great cities are
normal and to be tolerated permanently. Democracy
would be untrue to itself if it did not purpose to lay
a strong hand upon the cities and to uproot the upas
trees that poison their social atmosphere. The conditions of urban life which are said to make Majority
Rule dangerous are themselves deadly. They cannot
be long endured. If Majority Rule would remove
them, even at terrible cost, it would prove itself a beneficent instrument for the ultimate salvation of the state.
The fear that Majority Rule would prove to be a radical
upsetting force in cities should be a hope instead of a
fear. Cities need to be upset. Who of all the staunch-
est defenders of property rights, who that is most
content with the established order, who that is proudest
of our national and civic achievements, dares say aloud
or even whisper in his inmost soul that these monstrous
and horrible aspects of urban civilization, the very
aspects against which enraged democracy would be
most likely to fling itself, *ought* to be preserved?

In the great cities, also, there is the confusion of
tongues that results from the mingling of numberless
nations. In New York and Chicago and many other
American cities the people whose parents were native
to the United States constitute a small minority of the
entire population. Germans, Irishmen, Jews, Italians,
Hungarians, Poles, Greeks, join to make cosmopolitan
communities where diversity of customs and inequality
of political experience tend to unfit the people for governmental coöperation. A great American city, in
large measure, consists of a federation of alien colonies,
bound together, so far as they are consciously united

at all, only by the meshes of governmental organization. This absence of homogeneity, this imperfect fusion of interests, this discrete mass of tendencies, do not hold out a very strong promise of enlightened use of the instruments of democracy. And yet there is no process of political education that can compare with Majority Rule. Here again the conditions that are said to make Majority Rule dangerous are the very conditions which no man wishes to make permanent. The more rapidly we can change them the better it will be. If a fluid democracy will fuse these inharmonious elements and establish a unity of purpose and feeling in city life, gradually developing a nucleus of civic consciousness around which may gather the aspirations and the jubilant purposes of a composite people, then Majority Rule is the very instrument most needed for the purpose.

The dangers that arise from the facility of communication in great cities, from the incitements of street agitators, from the sensational appeals of the omnipresent newspapers, from the shock of great disasters, from the thrill of the crowd, are inherent in the very condition of proximity which is the distinguishing characteristic of cities. These conditions are as permanent as city life. If they militate against the success of democracy, their influence must be overcome by offsetting influences, or else self-government must be denied to cities. But even here we find that popular responsibility is the best corrective. Mobs arise and people act upon sudden impulses when they do not have to take the consequences. The wildest harangue of the demogogue and the most brutal suggestion of an unscrupulous or neurotic press will fall on deaf ears when the people are sobered by the possession of power and when the way lies open to the cure of abuses by prompt and orderly methods. If the people of a great city tend to be volatile and give themselves up to fleeting pleasures, it is largely for the reason that they have leisure, and this very leisure is democracy's opportunity. This enormous energy let loose by the shortened hours of labor, the proximity of neighbors and the ease of communication, is a force that can be turned to account in government. Like the disorderly youth who organize street gangs as a means of self-expression, the people of cities are in need of something more to do.

If we look soberly at the question of the applicability of Majority Rule to great cities, we see, therefore, that unless we are to give up democracy altogether in the case of city populations, we must adopt some means to remove or ameliorate the conditions that now seem to make it dangerous. If the patient's heart is too weak to stand the operation that would save his life, what can be done about it? When things have arrived at such a sorry pass, it is necessary to take some risks in the hope of effecting a cure. One thing seems certain. Majority Rule can safely be applied to cities to as great an extent as Home Rule can be safely applied, and there seems to be every reason for hope that if applied within these limits it will be a great instrument for the betterment of civic conditions and the political education of the people. If democracy can be saved at all, it can be done in this way. In cities people shift their residences frequently, but a mere change from one ward or one voting district or one

street to another does not dislocate to any considerable
extent the citizen's civic interests. Cities also throng
with transients and newcomers and business men who
sleep in the suburbs. The instability of public policy
that might result from the full participation of the
newcomers and the transients in the affairs of government may properly be avoided by restrictions of the
suffrage based upon periods of continuous residence.
So far as the special day population is concerned, the
extension of the suffrage to these men who do business
in the city while they reside in the suburbs, might even
tend to greater intelligence and stability in municipal
policies.   One of the great advantages of Majority
Rule as applied to cities is that it opens the way for
these needed readjustments of the suffrage.

In so far, however, as city electorates are unfit for
self-government and in so far as Home Rule under
Majority Rule would endanger the interests of the
larger community of which the city is a part, the state-
wide application of the Initiative, the Referendum and
the Recall opens the way for the centralization of
administrative functions and the curtailment of the
special powers of cities.   This is suggested merely as an
indication that the distrust of the self-governing capacities of urban populations either in general or in
particular places and at particular times, would logically lead to the curtailment of the right of Home Rule,
not to the denial of the right of Majority Rule within
the sphere of permitted local self-government.   On
the contrary Majority Rule is a necessary means for
enabling cities to make good use of the powers they
have and to fit themselves for greater powers.

CHAPTER XL

SOME of the statesmen who have recently accepted
Majority Rule as the program of democracy in states
and cities regard it as less than a national issue. They
do not think the Initiative, the Referendum and the
Recall well suited for use in connection with the Federal
government. Their conclusion is based upon several
considerations. The nation covers an immense area
and includes an enormous population. It is not homogeneous. The machinery of elections is provided and
even the qualifications of the electorate are determined
by forty-eight separate commonwealths in the exercise
of sovereign discretion. Moreover, under the constitution one branch of the government is wholly appointive
and one and part of another are chosen by indirect election. The very principle of federation establishes a relation between the general government and the several
states as such, and limits the direct relationship between
the government and the individual citizens. Besides
this, the Federal government enjoys only enumerated
powers. Unlike the state governments it cannot embark
upon an unlimited policy of experiment and discovery.
It is also urged that with the various state governments
fully democratized there will be no danger of misrepre-

sentation in Federal government. Moreover, there is a lurking reservation in the professed loyalty of some of the disciples of Majority Rule. They are quite willing to think that there is no need of extending it to Federal matters, because they are not yet quite sure that in the great issues of national life the people should easily have their way. Questions of war and peace, of interstate and foreign commerce, of money and banking, and of the ultimate guaranties of liberty and property, are regarded as too complex, possibly as too important, to be subjected to the arbitrament of the ballot.

As to the great size and population of the country taken as a whole, it is clear that these do not in themselves constitute a bar to the use of the new instruments of democracy. News that is of general interest to the country is read in San Francisco and in Boston, in Duluth and in Galveston on the same day. Many of the weekly and monthly publications circulating in Oregon are the same publications that circulate in New York. While the people in different portions of the country have to depend for the most part on different newspapers, the same thing is true of people residing in different sections of the same state. But communication is so easy and so rapid and the standardizing influence of the big news agencies is so great that the essential elements of a nation-wide discussion are practically the same everywhere. While the bias of locality and the prejudices of individual editors and publishers give the discussion different tints in different places and for different sets of readers, yet in the main the nation can make up its mind on a national issue as intelligently and almost as quickly as the people of a state or a city can come to a conclusion on a local issue. The population of the country is no less homogeneous than the population of a single city, and while proximity in cities helps to fuse alien elements into a new unity, on the other hand dispersion in the country at large tends to soften the prejudices and prevent the irritations that result from racial incongruities in close contact. In proportion to the importance of the issues at stake, it would be just as easy and as inexpensive to get up the petitions, hold the elections and count the votes for the entire country as it is for individual states.

We encounter a more serious difficulty when we consider the fundamental plan of the Federal government. The states have equal representation in the senate, which the constitution promises to preserve. The President and the Vice-President are chosen by the Electoral College in which each state is represented according to its proportionate number of senators and congressmen combined. The senators are still elected by the state legislatures, not by direct vote of the people, except to the extent that the constitution has been circumvented by the new devices of popular government in the various states. In some states Negroes are practically disfranchised though they constitute a large proportion of the entire population, with the result that the number of votes actually cast at the elections in these states is a mere fraction of the number cast in other states of equal population. A few states have enfranchised women, thus practically doubling the potential electorate. One state may adopt a property qualification for the suffrage; another may adopt an educational qualification; still another may limit the number of voters by requiring long-established residence as a qualification for voting. It is obvious that the Initiative, the Referendum and the Recall in their usual forms cannot be made universally applicable to the Federal government without effecting changes or having results ulterior to their immediate purpose. There is no difficulty in applying the Recall to congressmen, and with the advent of direct election of senators the Recall may be applied to them with equal facility. Even now Recall by the state legislatures either upon their own motion or upon the advice of the people would not interfere with the essential constitution of the Federal legislature. The President and the Vice-President might be recalled, as they are elected, by a majority vote of the Electoral College under direct instructions from the people of the several states. So long as the states establish the suffrage on different bases, it is impracticable either to elect or to recall any Federal official by direct majority vote of the people of the country taken as a unit. But the use of the Electoral College is a simple device. Indeed, even this is unnecessary as the constitution might provide for the direct counting of the vote by states, each state being credited with as many votes as it now has in both houses of Congress, all of the votes of any particular state being cast in accordance with the decision of the majority of the electorate in that state. Or a still closer approach to direct Majority Rule could be had by counting only two votes at large for each state and all the rest by individual congressional districts. By such methods the Referendum and the Initiative as well as the Recall could be made applicable to national affairs without the necessity of establishing a Federal electorate and Federal election machinery. Indeed, the Recall of the Federal judiciary by popular vote could be arranged for in a similar way without much more difficulty than would apply to the Recall of appointive judges in state or municipality.

What shall we say to the argument that Majority Rule fully established in the several commonwealths would so transform underlying political conditions as to render its extension to national affairs wholly unnecessary? It is admitted that effective democracy in the constituent localities tends to exert its power over the general government. Back of all free institutions must lie an alert, intelligent people trained to manage their own local affairs. It is not denied that the democratization of state and local governments would tend to liberalize national government and make it responsive to the people's will even if its forms remained unchanged. Yet how often have we seen the spectacle of Federal influence and Federal power reaching down into the localities to uphold the hands of unrepresentative politicians and to prevent the adoption of democratic policies by the people! The offices at the disposal of the Federal government give a powerful leverage for the control and perversion of democracy even in the localities. It is said that pure democracy prevails among the peasants in the villages of Russia, but no one can maintain that this local democracy has sufficient power either to secure justice to the peasants through its own functioning or to liberalize the entire

Russian government. With the Recall in force against
state legislators, what would that avail to keep congressmen and United States senators responsive to
the people's will? With the Recall against all the
governors and all the mayors, how would the President
be affected by it? With state judges subject to removal
by popular vote, the unrecallable Federal judiciary
would get more business than it does now, and would
become even more distinctly the last bulwark of special
privilege. Indeed, people who are concerned with
great progressive issues which are affected by the attitude of the judiciary refuse to take a lively interest in
any judicial body except the Supreme Court of the
United States; for the adjudications of all other American tribunals are written in water, while the decisions
of this court are graven on tables of stone. The Initiative and the Referendum might give the people
of every state perfect control over state and local
legislation, but how would this democratize national
legislation in its sphere apart?

But it is urged that the national government has
only enumerated powers anyway, while Majority Rule
is a device for controlling the exercise of new or hitherto
unused powers such as are lodged in the states. It is
true that all powers not expressly conferred upon the
national government and not expressly denied to the
states are in theory vested in the states. But the
powers of the national government, though enumerated,
are enumerated in general terms and are subject to
constant expansion by changes in conditions and by
interpretation of the Federal tribunal from which
neither the states nor the people can appeal. And even

if the powers of the general government were more rigidly defined and were not actually expanding with the exigencies of time, yet they have to do with certain supreme functions upon which the welfare of the people depends. What can be more vital to the people than the power to declare war, to negotiate treaties, to maintain the army and the navy, to regulate commerce, to control the public domain, to manage the postal service, to establish and maintain the standards of value, to levy taxes without limit as to amount and with few limitations as to method, to carry on internal improvements? Are these things so few in number or so small in importance that the people need not trouble themselves to maintain control of them? There can be but one answer to this question.

The argument against the extension of Majority Rule to national affairs finally comes down to one single point, namely, that the functions of the Federal government are so important and so vital to the nation as to preclude us from safely trusting them to popular control by the direct instruments of democracy. On this point the argument is somewhat strengthened, or, to speak correctly, escapes being weakened, by the fact that Switzerland, where Majority Rule has long been in successful operation, is a country protected from the dangers of war by general agreement of the European powers. But, on the other hand, we can claim almost as much security for America on account of its isolation. Let us waive that claim. A democracy is stronger than any other form of government because it enlists the coöperation and good will of the whole people. It is least likely to submit to foreign invasion,

because the people's own liberties as well as their homes
and their property are at stake. It is least likely to
embark upon a fruitless and unjust war, because the
burdens of war fall heaviest upon the many and the
benefits of a war of aggression do not accrue to them.
There is every reason to believe that the war power
would be as soberly, as intelligently, and as justly exercised under absolute Majority Rule as it is now. The
other special functions of the Federal government are
not such as to give color of reason to the argument
that they should stand in a different relation to the
will of the people than the functions of the states. Surely
the regulation of commerce, the management of the
Post Office, the conservation of natural resources, the
improvement of water ways, and all similar functions
are not beyond the capacities of the people by means
of a representative government supplemented and
strengthened by Majority Rule. When it comes to
the currency, the trusts and the protection of property,
why, these are the very things we are gunning for. If
the people cannot enforce their will in regard to *them*,
there is little use of our going to all this trouble to
invent new tools of democracy.

APPENDIX

THE INITIATIVE AND REFERENDUM CONSTITUTIONAL AMENDMENT
IN OHIO

ON March 27th, 1912, after a long struggle the Ohio Constitutional Convention passed on second reading by a vote of 97 to 15 the following article on the Initiative and Referendum, to be submitted to vote of the people of that state at the November election in 1912:

ARTICLE II

SECTION 1. The legislative power of the state shall be vested in a General Assembly consisting of a Senate and House of Representatives but the people reserve to themselves the power to propose laws and amendments to the constitution, and to adopt or reject the same at the polls independent of the General Assembly, and also reserve the power, at their own option, to adopt or reject any law, section of any law, or any item appropriating money in any law passed by the General Assembly. The limitations expressed in the constitution on the power of the General Assembly to enact laws, shall be deemed limitations on the power of the people to enact laws.[1]

SECTION 1-a. INITIATIVE. The first aforestated power reserved by the people is designated the Initiative, and the signatures of twelve per centum of the electors shall be required upon a petition to propose an amendment to the constitution.[2]

[1] The last sentence of section 1 was regarded as a concession by the more radical advocates of the Initiative. It simply provides that the distinction between constitutional and statutory law shall be maintained by the people under the Initiative the same as by the legislature.

[2] The more radical advocates of the Initiative desired to fix the percentage for its use as low as five, but twelve is not generally regarded as a high percentage requirement for the Constitutional Initiative. If the suffrage is

When there shall have been filed with the secretary of state a petition signed by the aforesaid required number of electors, and verified as herein provided, proposing an amendment to the constitution the full text of which proposed amendment to the constitution shall have been set forth in such petition, the secretary of state shall submit for the approval or rejection of the electors the proposed amendment to the constitution in the manner hereinafter provided, at the next succeeding regular or general election in any year occurring subsequent to ninety days after the filing of such petition. All such initiative petitions, above described, shall have printed across the top thereof: "Amendment to the constitution proposed by initiative petition to be submitted directly to the electors."

SECTION 1–b. When at any time, not less than ten days prior to the commencement of any session of the General Assembly, there shall have been filed with the secretary of state a petition signed by six per centum of the electors and verified as herein provided, proposing a law, or a petition signed by eight per centum of the electors and verified as herein provided, proposing an amendment to the constitution, the full text of which shall have been set forth in such petition, the secretary of state shall transmit the same to the General Assembly as soon as it convenes. The proposed law or proposed amendment to the constitution shall be either approved or rejected without change or amendment by the General Assembly, within four months from the time it is received by the General Assembly. If any such law proposed by petition shall be approved by the General Assembly it shall be subject to the referendum as herein provided. If any such amendment to the constitution proposed by petition shall be approved by the General Assembly it shall be submitted to the electors. If any law or constitutional amendment so petitioned for be rejected, or if no action be taken thereon by the General Assembly within such four months, the secretary of state shall submit the same to the electors for approval or rejection at the next regular or general election in any year. The General Assembly may decline or refuse to pass any

extended to women, however, twelve per cent of the total vote cast in a great state like Ohio will make quite a formidable number.

such proposed law or constitutional amendment and adopt a different and competing one on the same subject, and in such event both the proposed and competing law or both the proposed and competing constitutional amendment shall be submitted by the secretary of state to the electors for approval or rejection at the next regular or general election in any year.

All such initiative petitions last above described, shall have printed across the top thereof in the case of proposed laws, the following: "Law proposed by initiative petition to be first submitted to the General Assembly," or in case of proposed amendments to the constitution: "Amendment to the Constitution proposed by initiative petition to be first submitted to the General Assembly." [1]

Ballots shall be so printed as to permit an affirmative or negative vote upon each measure submitted to the electors.

Any proposed law or amendment to the constitution submitted to the electors as provided in section 1–a and section 1–b, if it is approved by a majority of the electors voting thereon, shall take effect thirty days after the election at which it is approved and shall be published by the secretary of state.

If conflicting proposed laws or conflicting proposed amendments to the constitution shall be approved at the same election by a majority of the total number of votes cast for and against the same, the one receiving the highest number of affirmative votes shall be the law or in the case of amendments to the constitution shall be the amendment to the constitution. No law proposed by initiative petition and approved by the electors shall be subject to the veto power of the governor.

SECTION 1–c. REFERENDUM. The second aforestated power reserved by the people is designated the referendum, and the signatures of six per centum of the electors shall be required upon

[1] It is to be noted that no Initiative on legislative measures wholly independent of the legislature is permitted. This was a concession to the conservatives in the convention. The scheme adopted, however, can have no other effect than a brief delay of measures initiated by the people and an opportunity for their consideration by the legislative body and the submission of competing measures on the same subject in the discretion of the legislature. This plan cannot be regarded as seriously objectionable even from the standpoint of the radicals.

a petition to order the submission to the electors of the state for their approval or rejection, of any law, section of any law or any item appropriating money in any law passed by the General Assembly.

No law passed by the General Assembly shall go into effect until ninety days after the same shall have been filed by the governor in the office of the secretary of state, except as herein provided.

When a petition, signed by six per centum of the electors of the state and verified as herein provided, shall have been filed with the secretary of state within ninety days after any law shall have been filed by the governor in the office of the secretary of state, ordering that such law, section of such law or any item appropriating money in such law, be submitted to the electors of the state for their approval or rejection, the secretary of state shall submit to the electors of the state for their approval or rejection such law, item or section, in the manner herein provided, at the next succeeding regular or general election in any year occurring at a time subsequent to sixty days after the filing of such petition, and no such law, item or section, shall go into effect until and unless approved by a majority of those voting upon the same. If, however, a referendum petition is filed against any such item or section, the remainder of the law shall not thereby be prevented or delayed from going into effect.

SECTION 1–d. EMERGENCY MEASURES. Acts providing for tax levies, appropriations for the current expenses of the state government and state institutions and emergency measures necessary for the immediate preservation of the public peace, health or safety, if such emergency measures upon a yea and nay vote shall receive the vote of two-thirds of all the members elected to each branch of the General Assembly, shall go into immediate effect, but the facts constituting such necessity shall be set forth in one section of the act, which section shall be passed only upon a yea and nay vote, upon a separate roll call thereon. The acts mentioned in this section shall never be subject to the referendum.[1]

[1] Emergency legislation makes one of the most troublesome problems encountered in drafting a scheme for the Referendum. It is universally recog-

SECTION 1–e. The powers defined herein as the "Initiative" and the "Referendum" shall never be used to enact a law authorizing any classification of property for the purpose of levying different rates of taxation thereon or of authorizing any single tax on land or land values or land sites at a higher rate or by a different rule than is or may be applied to improvements thereon or to personal property.[2]

SECTION 1–f. LOCAL INITIATIVE AND REFERENDUM. The initiative and referendum powers of the people are hereby further reserved to the electors of each municipality on all questions which such municipalities may now or hereafter be authorized by law to control by legislative action, such powers to be exercised in the manner now or hereafter provided by law.

SECTION 1–g. GENERAL PROVISIONS. Any initiative or referendum petition may be presented in separate parts but each part shall contain a full and correct copy of the title, and text of the law, section or item thereof sought to be referred, or the proposed law or proposed amendment to the constitution. Each signer of any initiative or referendum petition must be an elector of the state and shall place on such petition after his name the date of signing and his place of residence. In the case of a signer residing outside of a municipality he shall state the township and county in which he resides and in case of a resident of a municipality in addition to the name of such municipality he

nized that the legislature should have some leeway for quick action where the public welfare demands it, but legislatures are prone to abuse any constitutional privileges of this sort that are extended to them. The people have some protection, however, in their power to repeal even "emergency" acts through the Initiative.

[2] This section is an Ohio "joker" inserted because of the fear that the single taxers would immediately make use of the legislative Initiative to bring their characteristic program to a vote of the people. The section is foolish, as it attempts to prohibit not only the single tax, but also any effort to classify property for the purpose of levying different rates of taxes on different classes. This section, if fully effective, would embalm the general property tax, with all its unjust and fantastic results, in the constitutional law of Ohio indefinitely, except by grace of the General Assembly. The prohibition is not serious, however, as it does not forbid the use of the Initiative to make or authorize any desired changes in the tax system by constitutional amendment.

shall state the street and number, if any, of his residence and the ward and precinct in which the same is located. The names of all signers to such petitions shall be written in ink, each signer for himself. Each part of such petition shall have attached thereto the affidavit of the person soliciting the signatures to the same, which affidavit shall contain a statement of the number of the signers of such petition and shall state that each of the signatures attached to such part was made in the presence of the affiant, that to the best of his knowledge and belief each signature to such part is the genuine signature of the person whose name it purports to be, that he believes the persons who have signed it to be electors, that they so signed said petition with knowledge of the contents thereof, that each signer signed the same on the date stated opposite his name, and no other affidavit thereto shall be required.

The petition and signatures upon such petitions, so verified, shall be presumed to be in all respects sufficient, unless not later than forty days before election, it shall be otherwise proven and in such event ten additional days shall be allowed for the filing of additional signatures to such petition, and no law or amendment to the constitution submitted to the electors by initiative petition and receiving an affirmative majority of the votes cast thereon shall ever be held unconstitutional or void on account of the insufficiency of the petitions by which such submission of the same shall have been procured; nor shall the rejection of any law submitted by referendum petition be held invalid for such insufficiency.

Upon all initiative and referendum petitions provided for in any of the sections of this article, it shall be necessary to file from each of one-half of the counties of the state petitions bearing the signatures of not less than one-half of the designated percentage of the electors of such county.[1]

A true copy of all laws or proposed laws or proposed amend-

---

[1] This is one of the most important concessions made to the conservatives in the Ohio Convention. It will undoubtedly make the effective use of the Referendum within the short period allowed for filing the petitions considerably more difficult. It may also considerably increase the difficulty of initiating measures that are of primary interest to the large cities.

ments to the constitution, together with an argument or explanation, or both, for, and also an argument or explanation, or both, against the same, shall be prepared. The person or persons who prepare the argument or explanation, or both, against any law, section or item, submitted to the electors by referendum petition may be named in such petition and the persons who prepare the arguments or explanations, or both, for any proposed law or proposed amendment to the constitution may be named in the petition proposing the same. The person or persons who prepare the argument or explanation, or both, for the law, section or item, submitted to the electors by referendum petition, or for any competing law or competing amendment to the constitution or against any law submitted by initiative petition, shall be named by the General Assembly, if in session, and if not in session then by the governor.

The secretary of state shall have printed the law or proposed law or proposed amendment to the constitution together with the arguments and explanations, not exceeding a total of three hundred words for each of the same, and also the arguments and explanations not exceeding a total of three hundred words against each of the same, and shall mail or otherwise distribute a copy of such law or proposed law or proposed amendment to the constitution together with such arguments and explanations for and against the same to each of the electors of the state, as far as reasonably possible.

Unless otherwise provided by law, the secretary of state shall cause to be placed upon the official ballots the title of any such law or proposed law or proposed amendment to the constitution to be submitted. He shall also cause the ballots to be so printed as to permit an affirmative or negative vote upon each law, section of law or item appropriating money in a law or proposed law or proposed amendment to the constitution.

When competing laws or competing amendments to the constitution are submitted to the electors the ballots shall be so printed that the elector can express separately by making one crossmark (X) for each, two preferences, first, as between "either measure" and "neither measure," and secondly, as between one and the other. If the majority of the votes cast on the first issue is for "neither measure," both measures fail of adoption. If a majority of the votes cast on the first issue is in favor of "either measure," then the measure receiving a majority of the votes cast on the second issue shall be the law or the amendment to the constitution as the case may be.

The style of all laws submitted by initiative petition shall be: "Be it enacted by the people of the state of Ohio," and of all constitutional amendments: "Be it resolved by the people of the state of Ohio."

The basis upon which the required number of petitioners in any case shall be determined shall be the total number of votes cast for the office of governor at the last preceding election therefor.

The foregoing provisions of this section shall be self-executing, except as herein otherwise provided. Legislation may be enacted to facilitate their operation, but in no way limiting or restricting either such provisions or the powers herein reserved.

INDEX

ADVISORY Referendum, 137, 138
Alternative proposals: submitted by legislature, 26, 27
Amendment: of Initiative measures, 33; of measures in the legislature, 84, 85
Appointive officers: Recall of, 175, 176; chap. xxvi, 206–210
Appropriation bills: Referendum on, 146, 147
Arizona: emergency clause, 136; President Taft's discussion of Recall of Judges, 211–216
Athens: democracy in, 3 *et seq.*

BALLOT-BOX: a means of civic education, 278
Beard, Prof. Chas. A.: quoted, 232
Bryce, James: quoted as to town-meeting, 9
Burdens of the electorate: chap. xxxi, 247–255
Burgess, Prof. John W.: on difficulty of amending constitution, 43, 44–47

CALIFORNIA: emergency clause, 135, 136; Recall plan of, 173
Cities: Majority Rule in, chap. xxxix, 299–304
Civic bodies: a means of civic education, 276

Civics in the schools: a means of education in citizenship, 276, 277
Civil service: a means of civic education, 273, 274
Conservation: of public resources under the Referendum, chap. xvii, 154–159; of natural resources, 296, 297
Conservatism: a characteristic of the majority, 89–97; Majority Rule a bulwark of true conservatism, chap. xxxviii, 290–298
Constitutional amendments: Initiative for, 24 *et seq.;* prevented by promises, 39, 40; difficulty of securing, 42–50; independent of legislature, chap. xi, 115–119
Constitutional law: relation to statutory law, 23, 41–42; nature of a constitution, 39; power of judiciary to declare laws unconstitutional, 73–76, 165, 166
Constitutional stability: danger from the Initiative, chap. iii, 36–50
Cooley, Judge Thos. M.: on ease of amending constitution, 42
Corruption: removal of temptation under Referendum, chap. xvi, 149–153; of courts, 226, 227

Courage: of legislators, 139 *et seq.;* of public officials as affected by the Recall, chap. xxi, 177–184

DECLARATION of Independence: discussed, 256–258
De Tocqueville: on tyranny of majority in America, 52, 53, 60, 61; on the bar and the bench in America, 68–72, 220
Disfranchisement of the unfit: 31, 238–240

EDUCATION of citizenship: chap. xxxv, 272–279
Elections: general or special, 29; under Majority Rule, chap. xxx, 242–246
Electorate: limited to taxpayers, 30
Emergency legislation: exempted from the Referendum, 134–136; interfered with, chap. xv, 146–148
Equality: as the basis of Majority Rule, chap. xxxii, 256–259
Expense of frequent elections: chap. xxx, 242–246

FEDERAL government: relation of Majority Rule to, chap. xl, 305–312
Franchises: Initiative on, 25, 98–103; Referendum on, 132, 133

GOODNOW, Prof. Frank J.: on difficulty of amending the constitution, 43

Grote, George: quoted as to Grecian democracy, 9

HADLEY, Dr. Arthur Twining: on constitutional position of property, 224
Holmes, Oliver Wendell: quoted, 221

INDEPENDENCE: of officials as affected by the Recall, chap. xxi, 177–184
Indifference of people to public affairs: discussed, 249–252
Individual initiative in politics: utilized by the Initiative, chap. ix, 104–111.
Intelligence of the people: discussed, 253–255; in great cities, 301–303
Issues: simplification of, chap. xxxiv, 266–271

JUDICIARY: its relation to Initiative measures, 32; chap. v, 68–76; referendum on decisions, chap. xix, 164–166; Recall of Judges, chap. xxvii, 211–227
Jury system: a means of civic education, 273

LAWYERS: their attitude toward democracy, 68–72
Leadership: of representatives, 34; new type of, 288
Legislation drafted by its friends: chap. x, 112–114
Legislative bodies: not constituted to produce scientific legislation, 78, 79, 81–83; their temptations to corruption, chap. xvi, 149–153

Legislative interference: checked by Referendum, 162
Leisure of the people for public affairs: discussed, 252, 253
Liquor question: relation to Initiative and Referendum, 55-59
Long ballot: disadvantages of, 201-203, 208

MAJORITY: votes required to carry Initiative measures, 30, 283
Measures versus men: effect upon character of elections, 244, 245; intelligence of voters, 253-255; simplification of issues, chap. xxxiv, 266-271
Mill, John Stuart: on tyranny of the majority, 51, 52, 54, 55
Minority rule: alleged to be the outcome of Majority Rule, chap. xxix, 235-241
Mistakes: right to correct, secured by the Recall, chap. xxiv, 196-199
Municipal home rule: relation to Majority Rule in great cities, 303, 304

NATIONAL affairs: Initiative, Referendum, and Recall in, chap. xl, 305-312
Negroes: denied the suffrage, 61, 62, 124, 125
Newspapers: government by, chap. xxxiii, 260-265
New York *Times:* on majority rule, 53, 54, 63, 64

OBLIGATORY Referendum, 132, 133
Ohio: Initiative and Referendum

constitutional amendment, *appendix*, 313
Ontario: majority required on saloon question, 30
Optional Referendum, 133 *et seq.*
Organization, political: uses of, chap. xxxvi, 280-284

PARLIAMENTARY procedure: manipulation of, to defeat the will of the majority, 13 *et seq.*
Participation in public affairs: chap. xxxv, 272-279
People: burdens of, under Majority Rule, chap. xxxi, 247-255
Petitions: number of signatures required, 16 *et seq.*, 136, 137, 240, 241; verification of, 19 *et seq.*, 137; advantage of special interests in securing, 99; to be signed at designated places, 240; other safeguards, 240, 241
Political parties: a means of civic education, 277; made adaptable to needs of the time, chap. xxxvi, 280-284
Prerogatives of government: conservation of, 154, 155, 157, 158
Property, protection of: under the Initiative, 63-67, 90-94
Public credit: conservation of, 158, 159
Public office: attractiveness of, as affected by the Recall, chap. xxii, 185-191; tenure of, chap. xxiii, 192-195
Public property: conservation of, 154-157
Public sentiment: control over legislation, chap. xvii, 160-163

Publicity: in regard to Initiative measures, 27 et seq.; 264, 265
Pure democracy: in Athens, 3; in New England town-meeting, 5; under present conditions, 6 et seq.

RACE prejudice: effect of, under the Initiative, 63, 124, 125
Radical legislation: dangers of, from the Initiative, chap. vii, 89–97
Recall of Judges: chap. xxvii, 211–227
Repeal of Initiative measures, 33
Representative government: perfected by Majority Rule, chap. xxxvii, 285–289
Republican form of government: chap. xxviii, 230–234
Responsibility: effect of Referendum on, chap. xiv, 139–145; effect of Recall on, chap. xxv, 200–205
Roosevelt, Theodore: on woman suffrage, 123; referendum on judicial decisions, 165, 166
Rotation in office: relation to democracy, 200, 201; a means of civic education, 274–276

SHORT Ballot: relation of the Recall to, 203–205
Simplification of political issues: chap. xxxiv, 266–271

Special interests: their interference in politics, 80–83; their use of the Initiative, chap. viii, 98–103; influence on legislators, 140–142
Suffrage: in cities, 79, 304; extension or restriction of, chap. xii, 120–128

TAFT, President Wm. H.: message on Arizona Recall of Judges, 211–217; on reform of judicial procedure, 225, 226
Tenure of office: right to hold for full term, as affected by the Recall, chap. xxiii, 192–195; 201–205
Town-meeting, 5 et seq.
Tyranny of the majority: under the Initiative, chap. iv, 51–67

UNSCIENTIFIC legislation: causes of, chap, vi, 77–88; chap. x, 112–114

VETO: on Initiative measures, 31

WEALTH: concentration of, affected by the Initiative, 65–67
Weyl, Walter E.: quoted, 182
Woman suffrage: effect of, on difficulty of getting up petitions, 17, 18, 241; reasons for denial of, 122–124